Cross-Curricular Teaching in the Primary School

How can teaching across the curriculum improve children's learning?

How can you plan meaningful, imaginative topic work?

Cross-Curricular Teaching in the Primary School helps teachers plan a more imaginative, integrated curriculum by presenting in accessible language a rationale and framework for teaching across the subjects. Illustrated throughout with examples of effective topic work in successful schools, this book provides guidance on the underpinning theory and strategies to facilitate cross-curricular work with young children. Issues covered include:

- How children learn
- Developing the curriculum and lesson planning
- Teaching and learning in an integrated way at KS1 and KS2
- Whole school approaches and team teaching for cross-curricular teaching
- The role of support staff in cross-curricular teaching
- Improving children's thinking skills
- Supporting children with special needs
- Using new media and drama to facilitate cross-curricular learning
- Assessing cross-curricular learning.

Cross-Curricular Teaching in the Primary School provides much needed support for busy student and practising teachers. Packed with practical ideas, it offers an accessible guide to all aspects of introducing an integrated curriculum.

Trevor Kerry is Emeritus Professor at the University of Lincoln and Visiting Professor at Bishop Grosseteste University College, UK.

'Creative teachers, heads and teacher-educators seeking to offer children the best opportunities for quality, relevant learning, where problem-solving and purposeful thinking are more important than the acquisition of subject-related facts, will welcome this thought-provoking book. The authors use sound historical, theoretical and practical examples to propose an interdisciplinary holistic approach to a pedagogy – underpinned by a professional philosophy – which will benefit all involved in the learning process.' – **Pam Dowson, University of Cambridge, UK, teacher and author of** *The Really Useful Creativity Book*

'At a time when cross-curricular teaching is being explored and encouraged in a way that has not happened for a generation, Trevor Kerry's book is not only welcome and timely but thought-provoking and helpful. We should welcome this excellent contribution to the field.' – **Professor Mark Brundrett, Liverpool John Moores University, Editor of** *Education 3–13: International Journal of Primary, Elementary and Early Years Education.*

'Brings together the essential principles of a cross-curricular approach and links theory to practice in an accessible format . . . A valuable reference tool for practitioners studying at degree level and beyond.' – **Liz Hunt, Principal, Norland College, Bath, UK**

Cross-Curricular Teaching in the Primary School

Planning and facilitating
imaginative lessons

Edited by Trevor Kerry

Routledge
Taylor & Francis Group

LONDON AND NEW YORK

First edition published 2011
by Routledge
2 Park Square, Milton Park, Abingdon, Oxon, OX14 4RN

Simultaneously published in the USA and Canada
by Routledge
711 Third Avenue, New York, NY 10017

Routledge is an imprint of the Taylor & Francis Group, an informa business

© 2011 Trevor Kerry for selection and editorial material; individual
contributors for their own contribution.

The right of Trevor Kerry to be identified as author of the editorial material, and of
the authors for their individual chapters, has been asserted in accordance with
sections 77 and 78 of the Copyright, Designs and Patents Act 1988.

Typeset in Galliard
by Keystroke, Tettenhall, Wolverhampton
Printed and bound in Great Britain
by TJI Digital, Padstow, Cornwall

British Library Cataloguing in Publication Data
A catalogue record for this book is available from the British Library

Library of Congress Cataloging-in-Publication Data
Cross-curricular teaching in the primary school : planning and facilitating imaginative
lessons / edited by Trevor Kerry. — 1st ed.
    p. cm.
    Includes index.
    1. Reading (Elementary) 2. Reading. 3. Literacy programs. 4. Literature—Study
and teaching (Elementary) I. Kerry, Trevor.
    LB1573.C69 2011
    372.1102—dc22   2010017868

ISBN13: 978-0-415-56555-4 (hbk)
ISBN13: 978-0-415-56556-1 (pbk)
ISBN13: 978-0-203-84027-6 (ebk)

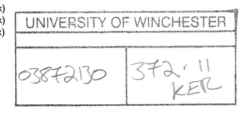

Contents

Figures

Tables

Case studies

Notes on contributors

Alex Bedford now leads on school improvement for the primary phase of Suffolk's re-organisation. From 2004 to 2009 he was headteacher of a new-build primary school in Suffolk. This innovative and highly successful school opened in 2005, with 150 places in the mainstream school and 12 places for those with moderate and complex learning difficulties. On opening 86 per cent of learners were hard pressed. The school was the only UK primary to win the 21st Century Learning Alliance 2008, for curriculum innovation. Alex is a director of the British Council for Schools Environments, learns alongside Tim Brighouse in the 21st Century Learning Alliance and speaks nationally about new build, curriculum development and learning spaces. He's the dad of two fantastic boys, husband to Becky, likes chopping wood and has a healthy respect for plants . . .

Christine Farmery holds a BEd (Hons) Primary Science; MSc Teaching Science 5 to 18; EdD. Christine is head of Anston Brook Primary School in South Yorkshire, a school for 3- to 11-year-olds. Christine has been a Visiting Lecturer in Primary Science and has delivered INSET to schools and groups of teachers in her local authority. Christine is also the author of articles and three books – *Teaching Science 3 to 11*; *Getting the Buggers into Science*; and *Successful Subject Coordination*. Christine and her staff have reviewed the curriculum and now hold a Leading Aspect Award for the creative and cognitive curriculum the school offers.

Pat Foulkes is a Principal Lecturer and Head of Division of Applied Education Studies at the University of Bedfordshire. She has been involved in the training of support staff in schools for many years, particularly in facilitating their progression into a career in teaching. She has carried out research into the training and development of support staff in schools and has evaluated induction materials for teaching assistants. She has a range of publications related to support staff development. She is currently a trainer and assessor for higher-level teaching assistants.

Peter Harrod taught in primary schools before being appointed as a Lecturer in Primary Education at Bishop Grosseteste University College, Lincoln. He gained an MPhil in Education from Nottingham University, and an MEd in Educational Psychology and Children's Language Development from Sheffield. His research interests have been in the fields of children's language and reading development, and more recently in the recruitment and retention of teachers in rural areas. He was an Open University part-time tutor for twenty-two years, and has been a primary school governor for fifteen years.

Jane Johnston is a Reader in Education at Bishop Grosseteste University College Lincoln, where she co-ordinates the MA in Education. She works extensively, both nationally and internationally, in three distinct areas: early childhood, primary science education, and practitioner research. Formerly she worked as a primary teacher, before moving into higher education and leading primary science education and early childhood studies. She is the author of many books, chapters and journal articles on early childhood, primary education, and science education, including *Early Explorations in Science, Enriching Early Scientific Learning, Teaching the Primary Curriculum*, and *Developing Teaching Skills in the Primary School*, all published by the Open University Press, and *Early Childhood Studies* published by Pearsons. She has also contributed to many other publications. In 2006, she was one of the first five teachers to be awarded Chartered Science Teacher status which recognised the important relationship between research and teaching.

Carolle Kerry is chair of governors at a Lincolnshire primary school. She has served in two schools as a governor, vice-chair, and chair over a period of more than ten years. Carolle gained her BSc in Social Science & Social Policy with the Open University, and a doctorate in Head Teacher Performance Management. She also holds a Fellowship of the College of Teachers for a collection of published works on the theme of governorship and able pupil performance. She has published on the latter topic over a number of years, and undertaken study visits to schools in Cyprus, Sweden, and Portugal. She was a co-author of the *Blackwell Handbook of Education*.

Trevor Kerry, contributing editor, is the University of Lincoln's first Emeritus Professor, Visiting Professor at Bishop Grosseteste University College, and the first person to hold professorial status in both of Lincoln's HE institutions. He has taught in primary and secondary schools, spent four periods as a teacher trainer, was a senior manager in FE, a Senior General Adviser for an LEA, and an Ofsted Inspector. He was formerly Professor of Education, Senior Vice-President and Dean of the College of Teachers. He is well known for his many authored and edited texts on teaching skills, and on aspects of education management. Trevor is a frequent contributor to education journals; he is a governor of two schools, and chair of governors of one of them.

Sue Lambert is currently the Head of Department for Postgraduate Primary ITT at Bishop Grosseteste University College. Prior to commencing her post in HE she taught in mainstream primary schools for nineteen years, teaching all ages in the primary phase. She was a SENCo for many years, which included responsibility for gifted and talented children. She was seconded for eighteen months as an advisory teacher for history and was a subject leader for a number of subjects. She completed an MA in Education, the NPQH qualification and recently completed a CPSE and gained fellowship to the HEA.

Judith Laurie taught in Lincolnshire and Humberside primary schools, including as an Advisory Teacher for English, before joining Bishop Grosseteste University College in 1996. She became deputy headteacher at a large urban primary school in Humberside and coordinated a reading initiative for schools in the Scunthorpe area. Following appointment to the University College, Judith completed an MA in Primary Education and eventually became Programme Leader for the four-year undergraduate ITT programme. More recently Judith was appointed Head of Department for PGCE and GTP Primary programmes at the University College, a post she held until her retirement in August 2009. She is now maintaining links with schools and ITE by working part time as a Link Tutor for Bishop Grosseteste GTP and PGCE trainees. She is also continuing in her role as External Examiner for the BEd degree at the University of Aberdeen and the PGCE course at Liverpool Hope University.

Karen Parsons has been teaching for the last six years in Suffolk. For the last four she has worked alongside Alex Bedford at the innovative Abbots Green Primary School. Karen has been leading Key Stage 2 and more recently has taken up the post of Acting Assistant Head Teacher supporting and leading teaching in the school and for other Suffolk colleagues. When Karen has spare time she likes to spend it with her husband and friends.

John Richardson is Headteacher at South Hykeham Community Primary School. He graduated in Psychology and has a PGCE and NPQH. He was deputy head in an urban primary school for seven years before taking up his current post in a rural primary school just outside Lincoln. His educational philosophy is driven by the need for first-hand learning experiences and creating an ethos where all are valued.

Kathleen Taylor began her career in education as an Early Years teacher in primary schools in York then, on completion of her MEd research into young children's narrative, joined Bishop Grosseteste University College Lincoln in 1995 as Senior Lecturer for Primary Education and English. In 2001 she became Programme Leader for the BA Hons in Primary Education with QTS and more recently Head of Department for undergraduate Primary Initial Teacher Training until her retirement in August 2009. Her work in education and particularly curriculum design led to her involvement in overseas teacher training projects in Macedonia and Bosnia Herzegovina as well as establishing a teacher training college for women in northern Pakistan. She continues to work in ITT as a Link Tutor for Bishop Grosseteste University College and is continuing her role as External Examiner for QTS programmes at the University of Wolverhampton and Birmingham City University.

Jill Wallis is currently a Senior Lecturer in Education Studies at the University of Bedfordshire where she manages an Honours degree programme for support staff in schools which provides professional development and offers the opportunity to progress to a career in teaching. Prior to that she was a teacher for twenty years and she specialises in teaching English. She is carrying out research into the experiences of mature students, mainly teaching assistants, studying for a degree in Education. She was, for a number of years, a trainer and assessor for higher-level teaching assistants.

Elizabeth Wood is Professor of Education at the University of Exeter, specialising in early childhood. She teaches on Primary PGCE, Masters and Doctoral programmes, and is involved with school-based research partnerships in the south-west of England and Wales. She convenes the Special Interest Group on Early Childhood for the British Educational Research Association, and has worked with the Department for Children, Schools and Families on developing guidance on play. Her research interests include play within and beyond early childhood; teachers' professional knowledge and practice; curriculum, pedagogy and assessment in early childhood education, and the policy/practice interface. She has published widely in these areas, both nationally and internationally, including the following books: Wood, E. (2008) *The RoutledgeFalmer Reader in Early Childhood Education*, London, RoutledgeFalmer; Broadhead, P., Howard, J., and Wood, E. (2010) *Play and Learning in Early Childhood Settings: Theory and Practice*, London, Sage; Wood, E. and Attfield, J. (2010) *Play, Learning and the Early Childhood Curriculum*, London, Paul Chapman Press (3rd edition).

Foreword

Having the opportunity to publish this text on cross-curricular working in primary schools has been a particular joy for three reasons: one related to pupils, one related to the past, and one to do with policy. Each of them will be rehearsed here.

With respect to the pupils, while my wife was talking to youngsters in the local primary school as part of her research for this text, she had a conversation with a ten-year-old boy. She asked him why he liked cross-curricular lessons. His reply stopped her in her tracks: 'Well, they're like life; life is cross-curricular.' Out of the mouths . . . as they say.

My second joy relates to a book which I co-wrote twenty-five years ago with a former colleague, Professor Jim Eggleston. Jim and I were engaged at that time with the Schools Council. The Schools Council was government-funded, and what we might now call a quango; but it financed school-based research with a strong emphasis on improving teaching and on using professional wisdom to do this. The Council was disbanded soon after our book came to fruition, to be replaced by more agenda-driven organisations that were concerned with implementing predetermined policy rather than genuinely open-ended research.

But the book – *Topic Work in the Primary School*, also published by Routledge – took what I still believe to be an innovative and entirely correct stance. As well as presenting the reality – good and bad – about cross-curricular topic work in schools across the East Midlands at that time, it looked in detail at lesson sequences. It deconstructed those lessons to look, in depth, a step at a time, at class management, at teachers' skills as explainers, as questioners, as task setters. It looked at children's cognitive skills and how to grow them. The book went on to draw out the lessons that could be learned about the management of curriculum, about objectives, about assessing and recording outcomes, about professional development to support this way of working.

In addition to writing *Topic Work*, Jim and I disseminated the findings around the country in person; and, with others, we compiled a written and audio-visual resource bank for teachers which was put into production as one of the Schools Council's final acts.

The Schools Council did a particular job very well: it gave teachers, with the help of training professionals, the opportunity to apply action research principles to their work and share their practice. For any sceptics out there, the only evidence needed to confirm this view is to look on the one hand at the impressive list of Schools Council publications and projects (which were very influential in schools at the time), and compare these with the trivialised 'case studies' that crop up in government reports over the last decade under the guise of 'research'.

Twenty-five years on from *Topic Work* I suggested to Routledge that a new book about cross-curricular approaches and the integration of knowledge in primary schools might be opportune, and the company had the foresight to agree. The book would not be a retrospective, I suggested, but a new vision of what integrated learning means in the twenty-first century and why it is even more important now than it was then. I said that I believed we stood at the gate of a new dawn of insight about the nature of learning in primary schools, after several decades straitjacketed by the National Curriculum. I made the point that almost all major advances in thinking over modern times had been made by cross-disciplinary teams. That view is both expanded and tempered in Chapter 1 of this text.

So to revisit cross-curricular themes after twenty-five years was both a challenge and an excitement, plunging me once more into the world of children's thinking and insight, and taking the journey back to some previous roots. To do this I gathered my own cross-curricular team of authors from the UK; with contributions from pupils, teachers, governors, headteachers, and teacher educators and researchers. My hope is that what has resulted is a rounded book, and one which absorbs a variety of perspectives into a coherent whole. In the process, though, a critical aim has been to encourage teachers to develop themselves professionally through these pages: by means of the text, the cases that rehearse real practice in today's schools, and the moments of reflection about one's own practice. In this, the new book will be true to the worthy spirit of the old Schools Council.

So, there was joy in the pupils and joy in the past. My third joy in writing for, and editing, this text relates to a point made a little earlier. There is a wind of change abroad in primary practice. The advent of the Rose Report in May 2009 put a whole new spin on curriculum in primary schools. The quotations that follow are short extracts from the summary provided by the following website: http://www.usethekey.org.uk/popular-articles/independent-review-of-the-primary-curriculum-an-overview.

Subjects will remain but will be complemented by cross-curricular studies.

Subjects remain vital in their own right – cross-curricular teaching works to strengthen them.

The current National Curriculum subjects will sit within six areas of learning. The knowledge, skills and understanding that all primary-aged children need are at the heart of these areas.

The proposed names for the six areas are:

- Understanding English, communication and languages
- Mathematical understanding
- Scientific and technological understanding
- Historical, geographical and social understanding
- Understanding physical development, health and wellbeing
- Understanding the arts

'Essentials for learning and life' skills run through the curriculum.

There is full scope for teachers to shape how the programmes of learning will be taught. The plan is to give: schools much more flexibility to plan a curriculum that meets the national entitlement and greater discretion to select curriculum content according to their local circumstances and resources.

For the first time since 1988 (the year of the National Curriculum) teachers will feel encouraged and empowered, both to teach in an integrated manner and also to loosen the boundaries even of the subject-based work that they do ('areas of learning' having replaced 'subjects'). The view was strengthened by the Cambridge Review, written by Robin Alexander (2009). This is a short extract from the summary of this Report:

> The report also rejects the claim that schools can deliver standards in the 'basics', or a broad curriculum, but not both, and argues that in any case the notion of 'basics' should reflect 21st century realities and needs. The report proposes a curriculum which is realised through eight clearly-specified domains of knowledge, skill and enquiry, central to which are language, oracy and literacy. It also guarantees entitlement to breadth, balance and quality; combines a national framework with an innovative and locally-responsive 'community curriculum'; encourages greater professional flexibility and creativity; demands a more sophisticated debate about subjects and knowledge than currently obtains; and requires a re-think of primary school teaching roles, expertise and training.

Areas of knowledge (Rose) or domains of knowledge (Alexander) – both imply integration and cross-curricular approaches. Both reports seek greater teacher autonomy. Both emphasise the need for schools – not merely governments – to have a steer on the tiller of curriculum.

So why is this book such a joy? Because, at last, there is a public admission that – in primary education at least – subject disciplines are not exclusive and should not be wholly dominant as a way of learning, important though they may be in some respects. We need other layers of understanding, too, to make sense of our rapidly changing world. We always did, of course; which is why schools have often struggled over the last twenty years. But now we can import them openly. This Foreword tells us something else significant regarding this emerging world of cross-curricular approaches: the pupils recognise its importance; the academics and trainers recognise it; and even the government recognises it.

For the first time for a long time it is possible to be optimistic about the shape of primary education.

Trevor Kerry
Lincoln

References

Alexander, R. (2009) *Children, Their World, Their Education* London: Routledge
Kerry, T. and Eggleston, J. (1988) *Topic Work in the Primary School* London: Routledge
Rose, Sir Jim (2009) *Independent Review of the Primary Curriculum: final report* London: DCSF

Acknowledgements

Versions of the paper that underpins Chapter 1 were read and commented upon by Peter Harrod and Dr Carolle Kerry. The author is grateful for their comments and suggestions, but is entirely responsible for any shortcomings. The copyright for the article is vested in the author, but he is grateful that the item is freely available to reproduce (with some amendments) here. The item originally appeared in *FORUM for 3–19 Education* Volumes 49 (1, 2) Special double issue, 2007.

For parts of Chapter 5 the authors would like to thank Mike Russell, the coxswain and crew of the Whitby Lifeboat Station. Readers may like to see the web-page at http://homepage.ntlworld.com/dave.brining/welcome.htm.

With respect to Chapter 9, the author would like to express sincere thanks to Kevin Flint, headteacher, Alison Navas, deputy headteacher and Rachel Belk, Key Stage 1 teacher, at Dunsville Primary School, Doncaster, for spending time to discuss and share their philosophy and examples of planning.

For Case Study 11.2 the author of the chapter would like to thank Steph Neale, headteacher of Beatrix Potter School, London. Readers may like to follow up the references to Beatrix Potter School at: http://www.beatrixpotterschool.com. For Case Study 11.3 thanks go to Rowena Hill of South Hykeham Primary School, Lincoln.

In Chapter 12 the authors wish to thank the headteacher and staff of the Priory Witham Academy Foundation and Infant Stage, Lincoln.

A number of items emanated from the children, staff, and headteacher of South Hykeham Primary School, Lincolnshire, whose contributions are gratefully acknowledged. In particular, the authors of Chapter 8 acknowledge the help and assistance of Sally Hillier, Deputy Head and art and RE subject leader at South Hykeham.

If any contributor has been inadvertently omitted from this list, please accept apologies; the mistake will be rectified in any future editions.

The editor would like to put on record thanks to all the authors for their part in seeing this book to fruition in the midst of extremely busy professional lives.

The greatest vote of thanks goes, as always, to Dr Carolle Kerry for a lifetime of support, affection and hard work.

Introduction

Cross-curricular teaching in the primary school: planning and facilitating imaginative lessons

Trevor Kerry

We have seen already that this book could hardly be more opportune, coming as it does at the moment when two major reviews have been carried out on the primary school curriculum. Both of those reviews recommended handing back to teachers some of the professional decision-making, and both suggested that the straitjacket of the National Curriculum was due to have its traces loosened. The result is that the profession needs to revisit some old skills, some new skills, and some lost skills. That is the intention of this text as set out in the Foreword. But the book is more than just a text about a specific teaching approach: cross-curricular working. Embedded within it is an integrated approach to education, not just an integrated approach to curriculum content. The conceptual underpinning of the book consists of attitudes and philosophies; it is not a 'tips for teachers' volume providing a 'painting by numbers' formula with no basis in real skills or grounded theory.

The book falls into four parts. In Part 1 we examine some of the theoretical issues that underpin working in a cross-curricular way. Part 2 shifts the perspective to the ages and stages of the primary curriculum. Exceptional children form the focus of Part 3. Part 4 then examines some skills of learning and teaching that teachers need in cross-curricular contexts.

Part 1: Some theoretical issues

Chapter 1 examines the notion of integrated studies as a way of organising curriculum in schools. Trevor Kerry draws on the insights of educational philosophy, curriculum theory, and learning theory to establish the soundness of a theoretical case for integration. The same author moves, in Chapter 2, to examine the ways in which theorists view children's thinking. He looks at systems put forward by Bloom, Wallace, Bowring-Carr and West-Burnham, Fisher, Gardner, and Wilding to track and build effectively on children's thinking. These two chapters, taken together, provide the qualified teacher and the trainee with a carefully argued but not over-technical statement of the theoretical underpinning for cross-curricular approaches in the context of effective primary school learning.

Part 2: Across the age-range

The opening chapter of this section (Chapter 3) begins with Elizabeth Wood focusing on the ways in which teachers can support child-initiated learning, by developing integrated pedagogical approaches in the Early Years Foundation Stage (EYFS) and Key Stage 1. She argues that developing integrated approaches involves challenging traditional notions of 'child-centred' education and rethinking adults' roles and responsibilities; and she proposes that teachers need a deep and sophisticated understanding of learning.

Chapters 4 and 5 examine examples of cross-curricular work at Key Stages 1 and 2. In Chapter 4 Jane Johnston argues that learning should be child-centred and practical, and exploratory. She suggests that children learn best through motivating experiences; that effective peer interaction is an important factor; and that there should be effective adult support and interaction. Christine Farmery in Chapter 5 provides an informative case study of the changing curriculum at Key Stage 2, with an eye both on learning and on leading learning. Overall, the section advances a practical but carefully argued and clear-sighted case for cross-curricular teaching throughout the primary years.

Part 3: Supporting all learners

From overarching concerns with curriculum and its implementation, the debate now moves in Chapter 6 to how best to help exceptional pupils. Alex Bedford and Karen Parsons tell the story of Abbots Green Primary where inclusion is integral to the school's mission and operation. In particular, the chapter draws a distinction between inclusion on the one hand, and meeting special educational needs on the other. The agenda of inclusion is progressively being worked into government policy for special education, and so the theme is timely. The chapter looks at some strategies that schools can adopt to make inclusion more of a reality. The relevance of working across the curriculum is considered as an integral part of this approach.

Chapter 7 then examines the role of the Teaching Assistant, which is so integral to special needs provision. Pat Foulkes and Jill Wallis identify that support staff have a range of areas of strength in a cross-curricular approach and some exemplar case studies serve to illustrate these strengths. However, key issues recurring in the management and deployment of support staff must be addressed if their contribution is to be fully effective.

But gifted and talented children also have special needs. Carolle Kerry, John Richardson, and Sue Lambert attempt in Chapter 8 to bring four distinct approaches to the issue of teaching gifted and talented pupils in primary schools, and to do this in the context of an actual school setting. First, they argue for an approach to analysing learning that depends on assessing cognitive demand. Second, they promote the cross-curricular theme by looking at South Hykeham School's 'themed weeks', which bring learning together across subject areas. Third, they discuss the teacher/headteacher/governor partnership which reviews work with gifted and talented pupils across the curriculum. Fourth, they pursue their normal policy in the school of listening to pupils' voices, and how the young people themselves view the cross-curricular approach. In the process they look at the rigour of how to audit the progress of the gifted or talented pupil and link the processes to debates about identification, lifelong learning, and the nature of knowledge. This chapter deals with the now more widely received view that pupils are individuals with individual strengths that need to be developed.

Overall, Part 3 sets out to tackle the contentious issues that attach to meeting the needs of all pupils within a cross-curricular context. The authors provide working examples of this happening to counter common objections that such approaches are impractical.

Part 4: Issues, skills, and approaches

The final part of the book deals with a range of issues, and with the skills that teachers will need to be successful in cross-curricular settings. These are not different skills from the conventional, but they are differently applied. This quickly becomes clear in Judith Laurie's Chapter 9, which considers why planning is at the heart of successful teaching. By analysing feedback from educationalists, Her Majesty's Inspectorate (HMI) and Ofsted on past cross-curricular approaches, the chapter suggests principles for more successful topic planning, especially at medium and short term.

In Chapter 10, Kathleen Taylor argues that assessment works best when children adopt it as part of the integrated classroom experience. This chapter recognises that learning in primary schools is changing, and that assessment for learning techniques has to change in order to match these movements in educational thinking.

One aspect of assessment involves deciding how children can present work and display the outcomes of classroom tasks. Chapter 11 contains a survey by Trevor Kerry of some potential methods. It covers such topics as ICT, video presentation, photography, video-conferencing, role play and dramatic productions, and media reporting. Examples are drawn from the real world of schools and classrooms and analysed for their practicality and effectiveness as learning tools. Prominence is given to a case study of a Second World War Evacuation project at Beatrix Potter School in London.

In Chapter 12 Peter Harrod and Trevor Kerry then go on to examine a specific set of teaching skills: team teaching. They suggest that team teaching may be used for all or part of a child's learning experience, but that it is especially suited to periods where learning is presented as cross-curricular. The chapter examines some definitions of team teaching; various models which can be applied to it; its advantages as a means of organisation; and its limitations. The chapter also emphasises that team teaching is an advanced skill which demands proper preparation and appropriate staff training.

Finally, in the Postscript to the book, the editor puts out a plea and a challenge to return to a time when the teacher was one of the intellectual elite of the community.

How to use this book

Trevor Kerry

This is a book about the knowledge, understanding, and skills required of a teacher in a primary school in order to use cross-curricular approaches to best advantage. The book uses a variety of means through which to set out, examine, and exemplify these skills:

- Text: to provide information, discussion, and continuity
- Tables and figures: to convey data quickly or in graphic form
- Lists: to set out key issues or skills
- Reflections: to encourage the reader to apply the text to their own situations
- Case studies: to provide real examples of teaching situations.

The book can be used in a variety of ways:

- It can be read as a textbook.
- It can be used as a source book – you can consult the relevant sections (such as those on assessment or inclusion) as the need arises.
- It can be used as a self-training manual by an individual; in which case you will work through it systematically, pausing to carry out each Reflection as you come to it.

The book is based on the philosophy that teachers need specific skills for the job. These skills can be identified, analysed, refined, broken down into sub-skills, taught, learned, and even assessed. We hope that the book will be seen by busy teachers as a kind of *vade mecum* – a source of comfort and inspiration. It would be useful, too, as the basis of a systematic dialogue between a teacher and a mentor.

We trust that this manual of skills, based as it is upon grounded theory and experience, will bridge the gap that often exists for teachers who want to improve their effectiveness.

Part I

Some theoretical issues

Chapter 1

Introducing cross-curricular teaching

Why an integrated curriculum?

Trevor Kerry

This chapter examines the notion of integrated or cross-curricular studies as a way of organising curriculum in schools. Drawing on the insights of educational philosophy, curriculum theory, and learning theory, it establishes the soundness of a theoretical case for this approach. It examines what this view means for the art and science of teaching, and notes examples of successful cross-curricular approaches in schools. The chapter identifies the roots of this philosophy in the thinking of the Plowden Report (1967) and suggests that the approach is equally valid today.

Purpose

Forty years ago, Plowden (1967) made an important assertion which was later blamed (erroneously, if theorists like Eisner (1996) and practitioners like Campbell and Kerry (2004) are right) for a diminution in children's knowledge. It was this: 'Throughout our discussion of curriculum we stress that children's learning does not fit into subject categories' (para. 555).

Throughout a long career in education I have been convinced not only that this assertion is correct but that it applies equally to effective learning in any context; and Clyde (1995: 115) talks of children's learning as 'An interpretive network which spreads across domains'. This chapter intends to provide a rationale and some conceptual underpinning for this belief in order that like-minded educators in any context (and indeed, in any phase) may be able to justify their approach on the basis of the best elements in educational thought. It then goes on to explore the implications of cross-curricular content in education.

Introduction

At the heart of the problem lies what is learned and how it is learned – I shall talk mainly about learning in schools, especially primary schools, but the context is easily widened by the reader, and is widened here from time to time to establish the point of the argument. The root question is: should learning be divided into segments known as 'subjects', or would it be better and more effectively acquired in some more homogeneous form?

Answering this question is difficult not because the answer is obscure but simply because a complete answer has many strands. Within the compass of this I will attempt to deal, albeit cursorily, with just four of them. If the answer is difficult it is because it defies convention (and people, even teachers, fear change) and because that convention itself supports a structure of vested interests.

The four strands that I will deal with, in turn, are these:

- The supposed reality of 'subject disciplines'
- Theories and models of curriculum
- Theories and models of learning
- Models of teaching that underpin integrated studies.

For teachers and those in training it is important to note that part of one's professionalism is to be able to justify the way in which one works; understanding the rationale that underpins cross-curricular teaching is essential to putting it into action effectively in the classroom.

The supposed reality of 'subject disciplines'

Why do some educators oppose the use of integrated or cross-curricular approaches to learning in schools? Generally, the answer rests with convictions about how knowledge is constructed. The conventional argument goes something like this:

> *Knowledge falls naturally into 'domains' called subjects which are bounded by specific kinds of conceptual thinking, specific ways of constructing knowledge that fit the content of the subject, and by procedures that are specific to that content.*

This view, or something approximating to it, has become embedded into educational practice and to depart from it requires a kind of intellectual conversion. But how accurate is it?

The problem is best explored through an example. To avoid becoming mired in controversy and emotional attachment to a subject on the primary timetable, let us take a neutral stance and talk about the subject area physics; the principles can then be applied to other areas of learning. Physics is a 'subject discipline' in conventional thought. So what makes a physicist distinctive compared with a chemist or a theologian? First he (or, of course throughout, she) will have a content knowledge that is bounded by 'how the world works', the laws of the universe – at a simple level, the characteristics that define how electric current flows. Our physicist will have a scientific or positivist approach to problem-solving: hypothesising, testing and observation, drawing conclusions, constructing a theory or law – and a multiplicity of these will provide a conceptual view of the universe. Then he will use particular conventions to record and communicate his discoveries and other information (symbols, formulae and so on).

So far, so good; every pupil, even in primary school lessons on electric circuits, for example, has experienced this. So then our pupil moves on to a lesson whose focus is rooted more in chemistry. What changes? Well, not the scientific process and underpinning. Nor the use of particular conventions to record discoveries and information, even though the actual symbols and language may be slightly different – volts and forces may be replaced by valency and states of matter. What has changed fundamentally is not the approach to knowledge but the content of the lesson: the difference between physics and chemistry is in large measure down to content: what is learned, not how it is learned.

But (the reader may be thinking) this example is a poor one because we are comparing two closely allied 'subjects'. Fine; then select theology (and again, as noted above, to distance ourselves from personal attachment to the argument we will use this term rather than

RE here) instead of chemistry. Theologians have specific subject knowledge (systems, sacred books, rituals); but they too 'solve problems' such as ethical hypotheses, based on observations (of human and divine acts), collect evidence (of good and evil), draw conclusions (moral codes), and speak in symbols (Allah, sacraments). All that has really changed is the content of their studies, not the epistemology that underpins them.

Then, all three of our 'subject specialists' – the physicist, the chemist, the theologian – find themselves in higher education, teaching their subjects to undergraduates, and behold! Each is trying to offer a rationale for the universe, an explanation for human and material events, and ideas about how people should live within the contexts of the physical, chemical, or spiritual universe and even how their own subjects 'work'. So they all become philosophers!

Their answers and starting points may be different but they are bounded by the same concerns, the same need to establish conceptual structures, the same need to communicate knowledge, and the same requirements to invent symbols and laws to make sense of the universe. Their perspectives may be conditioned more or less by their content concerns, but their knowledge operates quite similarly and to quite similar ends. What distinguishes 'subjects' is not, at root, their 'distinctive disciplines' but rather their 'distinctive content' – and even then that content is directed to similar core purposes.

Furthermore, while the physicist, the chemist, and the theologian may each have a content-led distinctive contribution to make to human insight, each insight alone is partial, potentially blinkered, and ultimately unsatisfying. Only by drawing all the insights – and others – together can the jigsaw puzzle of human life and the universe ever be more than a relatively random and incomplete corner of the real puzzle.

Let us advance the argument one stage further and ask: what of the 'new' subjects so reviled by traditionalists but in which our primary children will, in a few years' time, be seeking university entry – media studies, film studies, American studies, sports studies, forensic or food sciences, and so on? Are these 'subject disciplines' in a traditional sense, or are they indeed intellectually undemanding hotch-potches as their detractors claim? In trying to answer this question I have taken arguments as they commonly emerge in the education press or in discussion.

If we take media studies (which probably started life in the primary school as some element of technology) as an example of a 'new' subject for our future undergraduate, then typically one suspects that it involves its own conceptual structures (e.g. understanding how various media influence the public, principles for judging the validity of information, etc.), its own ways to construct knowledge (drawing perhaps on areas like the psychology of perception or the sociology of communication), and its own languages and symbolism (such as headline writing or picture editing). In other words, these new subjects are really just like old subjects except that the content that underlies them is specific to their own area of knowledge and expertise. So we are back to content as the distinguishing feature. Our conclusion is that there are not, as it were, a limited number of pre-existent subject disciplines 'out there' that impose concepts, symbols, and procedural processes on their students; we impose those on the material studied. Subjects impose on students only the content that defines them: a piece of knowledge either is, or is not, psychology, or astrophysics, or music. Even that content is to some extent fluid: today's knowledge in media studies is tomorrow's history curriculum.

If this is a fair portrayal, then we have to ask why the 'subject discipline' approach has lingered so long in educational institutions. There are probably a number of reasons (which would each require a longer study than is possible here), so let us merely suggest some indicators. The first is historical: the 'old' subjects, often invented by 'traditional' universities, existed first and so claimed some form of 'precedence'; but actually, if subject disciplines are traced back far enough only three or four could trace their roots any distance. In the genuinely 'old' universities a would-be graduate had first to achieve his degree in arts (a generalism) before he could proceed to the higher (in the view of the time) 'subject disciplines' such as theology and medicine. But in this context 'disciplines' such as geography, history, Spanish, and so on would have been considered avant-garde.

Other reasons are just as illogical and even more pragmatic. School-promoted posts may be linked to subjects, and to be a generalist (at least in a post-primary context) is a career disadvantage. People feel more secure if they can label themselves: how often do you hear teachers, on first introduction, announce, for example, 'I'm a historian'? And, since school timetables are subject-based, so parallel pigeon-holing of people is convenient. Then there is the simple fear of change: we've always done it this way. And there is arrogance: to be a physicist provides more kudos than to be a geographer or an economist (the argument is circular: it must do, because the promoted post is worth more). In these ways, the vested interests of subject specialists are served, and to adopt another epistemological approach is to abandon one's advantage and launch into a sea of change that both demands thought and provokes insecurity about personal worth.

Those antagonistic towards cross-curricular or interdisciplinary approaches often call on educational philosophers to help them establish a case for discrete 'disciplines'; see especially the work of Hirst (1974). However, this approach is not entirely helpful. Hirst did not establish the discrete nature of 'subjects' in the traditional sense, but of 'forms of knowledge' which he listed as: pure mathematics and logic, empirical sciences, history and human sciences, aesthetics, morals, philosophy, and religion. This list is rather different from a conventional school timetable list consisting of areas like biology, French, IT, geography, and so on. To qualify as a 'form', the knowledge had to be subject to demonstration as to truth (itself a debatable proposition); but also had to contain key notions or concepts specific to that form of knowing. Thus, while Hirst's classification of forms of knowledge does attempt to define the limits of those forms, the forms are none the less far broader than traditional 'subjects'. Nor have we proponents of cross-curricular approaches ruled out the existence of concepts, rules, laws, or symbols peculiar to certain areas of knowledge; we have simply pointed out that all subjects share such (albeit different) codes and procedures, while what they don't share is the subject content. Once again, the key discriminator is content.

In this context, a productive approach was adopted by Lawton (1997), who proposed four principles of change away from content-led curriculum (including specifically the National Curriculum), which were:

- Replacing the thrust of content and objectives, with a concern for skills and processes
- Moving from subjects and attainment to cross-curricular themes and the affective domain
- Shifting the emphasis from didactic teaching to self-directed learning
- Moving from the academic/vocational divide to integration of both aspects.

Lawton, wisely it is suggested, concludes that 'subjects may be useful up to a point' but that 'more pressing [human] problems are not conveniently packaged within a single subject', so there is a need to move 'beyond subjects' (1997: 85). (For devotees of Plowden, let it be said that the Report allows for the co-existence of subjects within and alongside thematic approaches (chapter 17 passim).)

So it is important to say one more thing about this argument. It should not be construed as in any way devaluing the worth of any area of knowledge, its content, or forms of thinking. Insight, understanding, and problem-solving can be advanced either by sharing thinking and factual information across areas of knowledge or by pushing back boundaries in some more closely defined corner of learning. Each has its place and its validity. This approach promotes the worth of knowledge as a whole, rather than seeking competition between different forms of knowledge in some kind of possibly spurious hierarchy.

Reflection

Can you think of an instance in your own learning where a problem was solved by using data and skills from across a range of disciplines?

Theories and models of curriculum

But if subject disciplines are redefined as relating more to discrete areas of content than to separate and ring-fenced forms of knowing, then adopting cross-curricular approaches to learning becomes far more respectable and attainable. Indeed, this redefinition forces educational planners not to construct a syllabus based on areas of knowledge *per se* (the very trap into which National Curriculum fell, it is suggested) but to construct a curriculum on the basis of what pupils and society need: to begin not from content but from the learner: 'at the heart of the educational process lies the child' (Plowden 1967: para. 9).

I will not rehearse Plowden's arguments (see paras 508–55), but simply summarise a few modern views about curriculum that support and sustain the Report's position, and provide some examples of such curricula at work to establish their feasibility and effectiveness.

Eisner (1996), in conclusions not entirely removed from Hirst's, considers curriculum to consist of 'forms of representation': auditory, kinesthetic, tactile, olfactory, visual, and gustatory . . . which are manifested in art, music, speech, drama, text, mathematics, etc. These forms of representation require an affective context based in social learning and in society. He urges that knowledge ('content' is the label used above) can be understood and appreciated from a variety of perspectives; but that if pupils believe, say, that a 'text possesses a single correct meaning' they will seek only that meaning and will fail to look for other meanings. This attitude, he says, does 'little to promote intellectual values . . . multiple perspectives . . . judgement, risk-taking, speculation and interpretation' (1996: 71). The result of such a paucity of approach is that so-called learning becomes confined to factual material, to what is testable in simplistic ways, and to phenomena such as league tables of achievement that reflect only a fraction of potential intellectual activity – phenomena that resonate with today's educational practices.

In a related critique, Ross (2000: 81, 82) sets out a social transformative theory of curriculum in which 'each individual gets the opportunity to . . . come into a living contact with a broader environment' and to gain 'knowledge as something constructed by the learner as an active experimenter, provoked into enquiry by the teacher'. This theory takes us to a third Plowden principle: that of 'discovery' (para. 549), in contrast with subject-based and content-driven didactic approaches.

Ross also identifies other metaphors for studying curriculum, among which is his metaphor of the 'natural landscaped curriculum'. In this, 'subjects are . . . highly artificial, dividing forms of knowledge with contrived distinctions . . . of process, knowledge and procedure' (after Rousseau 1913). Plowden had predated this view with the assertion (para. 521) that 'learning takes place through a continuous process of interaction between the learner and the environment'. The Report's basic stance on the integration of curriculum is supported by modern writers such as Stenhouse (1975), Elliott (1998), and Kelly (1999). Indeed, this brief review leads one to ask whether learning would be subdivided at all, into subject disciplines or otherwise, if it were not for the bureaucratic straitjacket of schooling and timetabling.

Both Eisner and Kelly challenge the exam culture of modern education systems, identifying the failure of content-led teaching in even achieving the declared purpose of communicating the content itself (Kelly 2001), and pointing out the cultures of blame for pupils' failures that are generated among teachers by politicians. The Plowden Report warned against over-prescription (para. 539) of curriculum by individual schools; since that time we have seen prescription by government, championed by Ofsted, and measured by a variety of closed approaches – a far worse scenario than Plowden could have envisaged. Carr (2003: 146) challenges the governmental approach strongly: 'Any philosophy of education that models educational development on the pattern of uniform initiation into a pre-specified range of forms of knowledge and understanding may be dangerously procrustean.' Later, we shall see that it is not only curriculum theorists who find the Plowden vision liberating, feasible, and preferable, but also many influential learning theorists concur. But for the moment the point is made, and it is opportune to ask whether cross-curricular approaches can work even in the inimical context of today's education system. In a recent article, Campbell and Kerry (2004) described the construction and implementation of a form of integrated curriculum at Key Stage 3 (KS3). Not only was the KS3 curriculum remodelled on these lines, but pupils were accelerated through it, taking the appropriate (subject-based) Standard Attainment Tests (SATs) a year early. In the first year of operation, therefore, two cohorts of pupils were tested simultaneously, one having moved through to KS3 SATs following conventional studies over three years and one having studied the more integrated curriculum in just two. The results were outstanding, the outcomes of the two cohorts almost identical, and that in one of the country's highest-performing schools.

In another account (Kerry 2005) a further example was outlined, of a comprehensive school which was planning to revert from heavily subject-orientated teaching back to integrated approaches. Cryer School's problem related to providing adequate post-16 opportunities for its academic and less academic pupils; and the solution was seen in a re-examination of both curriculum and learning and teaching methods. Rather less surprisingly, perhaps, the same article describes a similar reversion to integrated approaches in a primary school, Quinnan School; the views of a number of heads are reported to the effect that 'Curriculum has to be more pupil-centred, more integrated, and more demanding [i.e. than the National Curriculum]' (Kerry 2005: 17). However, the article also notes a headteacher's view that, of a cohort of teachers trained post-NC:

Most . . . know how to access lesson notes from the Internet, but they can't devise material for themselves, from the ground up. They don't understand how to lead pupils into high levels of thought because they're fixated on the content. They need some basic help in structuring learning cognitively, and they need teaching skills to draw pupils' thinking out.

This, apparently, is the professional legacy of a generation of educational planners who poured scorn on the Plowden Report. However, Carr (2003: 15) would urge us to define our terms, drawing a distinction between the narrow purposes of schooling (which might include content acquisition for its own sake) and education (which implies that pupils acquire 'an understanding of themselves, the world and their relations with others that enables autonomous recognition and pursuit for their own sake of interests and projects of intrinsic satisfaction').

So how can one sum up the argument of this chapter so far?

First, an attempt has been made to establish that the notion of subject disciplines, if not actually spurious, has at least been overplayed and too restrictively applied in the English education system. Motivation for adhering to this epistemology has been related more to self-interest or convenience, with strong underlying issues of pragmatism, rather than to reality. Second, curriculum theorists in a respectable line from Rousseau to Ross have espoused the cause of cross-curricular approaches. Third, it has been demonstrated that integrated curricula work in practice in both secondary and primary schools. Finally, it is suggested that these cross-curricular approaches avoid the worst pitfalls of the National Curriculum (NC) and testing system: limited tests of content-learning reduced to league tables which are decontextualised to make judgements about schools. But, to do justice to the cause of integration one has to move on two more steps in analysing how best it can be implemented; and first to examine the place of cross-curricular learning in learning theory.

Theories and models of learning

It would be wrong to assume that Plowden represents a merely dated view of the nature of learning; it makes a genuine effort to review the (then) contemporary and progressive theories. The Report also anticipates one of the latest and most popular learning theories among modern teachers: Gardner's multiple intelligences (Gardner 1999). Gardner's list of intelligences will rapidly be seen to relate to Eisner's theories about how to classify curriculum. Gardner's learning categories (see also Chapter 2 of this volume) include: linguistic/verbal, logical/mathematical, visual/spatial, kinesthetic, musical, naturalist, interpersonal, and intra-personal. First, let it be said that this contiguity between curriculum and learning theories is important if one is to construct a sound approach to pupils' educational experiences, and it is exemplified in the Brooke Weston KS3 curriculum innovation outlined above. There, Campbell and Kerry describe the new curriculum as underpinned by CELTIC approaches and socially valuable themes (see Campbell and Kerry 2004: 392–6 for a definition of CELTIC). Jarvis, while posing some critical reservations about multiple intelligences, quotes Kornhaber:

> The theory validates educators' everyday experience: students think and learn in many different ways. It also provides educators with a conceptual framework for organising and reflecting on curriculum, assessment and pedagogical practices.
>
> (Jarvis 2005: 53, 54)

This link between learning theory and curriculum design is an important one: indeed it was one drawn to teachers' attention in Kerry and Eggleston (1988), where reflections on learning effectiveness led to the design of a tentative integrated curriculum for able children in schools based on themes rather than subjects (these included scientific studies, literature, aesthetics, thinking skills, technology and computer studies, cultural studies, life skills, and languages). By contrast, the traditional approach – and that of NC – began from subject disciplines and projected them on to the learner. Plowden adopted an opposite view and began from the learner. Seen from this end of the telescope the learning picture looks different.

This last was a conclusion born out of my own empirical research in the 1980s which has been, I believe, under-exploited. Research which was carried out between 1976 and 1981 (for the Department of Education and Science's Teacher Education Project, directed by the late Professor Ted Wragg and managed by the author) explored classroom learning from the perspective of cognitive demand. My work took the Bloomian (1956) categories of cognition (slightly redefined for fieldwork purposes) and explored how much cognitive demand was made by teachers on pupils during lessons through verbal interactions and in the tasks they set in class and for homework. These studies were carried out initially in what are now Year 7 (Y7) classes; the idea was later extended to compare the findings with those in primary schools, and with similar research among older students. The findings were published in a range of journals, but the broad picture is captured in my chapters in Wragg (1984), since reprinted many times. Here only the bare bones of the argument need to be rehearsed.

In the original research teachers' talk, teachers' questions, and classroom tasks set in Y7 classes were assessed for cognitive demand using an adapted Bloomian scale which allowed an overall measure of how many teacher inputs, questions, or tasks in a lesson were at a higher level of cognitive demand and how many at a low level (and also, the nature of the higher level demands, but these need not detain us for the present purpose). A very broad conclusion from the wealth of analysis was that fewer than 5 per cent of all verbal transactions and fewer than 15 per cent of tasks were at a higher level. In fact, verbal transactions related to class control occupied between 14.5 per cent and 29.4 per cent of all transactions in the studied schools – much more frequent than higher-order learning activity. This does not bode well for learning.

Within the data it was possible to compare results across subjects, and one of the most surprising and interesting outcomes related to the tasks set in lessons across the schools in the initial study (Table 1.1). Here it can be seen that English and science perform relatively well, but other subjects tail off, with even mathematics performing rather poorly. But, as luck would have it, the organisation of these Y7 classes meant that in some schools there was an element of the timetable taught as integrated studies. In integrated studies lessons, which used cross-curricular approaches, the higher-order task demand rose on average to 41 per cent. In other words, learning was deeper and more effective in lessons where subject content was cross-curricular than in lessons where it was organised simply by subject discipline. So, one might hypothesise, not only is it logically preferable according to the principles of curriculum and learning theory to integrate lesson content, it is actually more effective in producing cognitive outcomes.

Two other findings reinforced the stated conclusion. The first was that in an accelerated examination group (current Y10) cognitive demand actually fell, because the lesson transactions were related only to the acquisition of content in order to address examination

Table 1.1 The levels of higher-order cognitive demand in classroom tasks, by subject, in Teacher Education Project research (%)

English	33.3
Science	23.0
History	11.5
French	11.3
Maths	8.9
Music	6.7
Religious education	5.0
Geography	4.2

questions. The other was that, when the measures were applied to primary classrooms where work was, without exception, cross-curricular, these lessons scored consistently higher in cognitive demand on pupils than did subject-discipline lessons overall in secondary schools. The clear message from all this research appeared to be: if you want pupils to think, integrate.

These findings might have been the subject of more research and might have resulted in a more widespread adoption of integrated learning but for an unfortunate confluence of factors. The project came to the end of its funded life and so the original team split up (though both Wragg and I continued to make similar informal small-scale measurements, with similar outcomes). No other researchers took up and exploited these indicative findings. The DES itself was in a period of change. Not long afterwards the National Curriculum was initiated with its bias towards subject disciplines. Interestingly, this had a negative effect in another, unintentional, way. An early version of the assessment of NC by teachers required them to record pupil achievement using a kind of Bloomian system. But the system was bastardised, poorly explained, with teachers untrained in its use, and recording was cumbersome. So this potentially useful approach was quickly abandoned in favour of easier solutions that were administratively less hassle – even if somewhat lacking in meaning.

What, however, is clear is that not only are narrow subject-disciplines not a necessary part of how knowledge is constructed, but school curriculum can be built on a sound body of theory about curriculum and learning that supports an integrated approach. Furthermore, in pedagogical terms, there is research evidence that integration 'works', that it produces good learning and perhaps superior learning. So what are the implications for teachers and teaching?

Reflection

How, and to what extent, do the research findings reported above resonate with your own classroom experiences?

Models of teaching that underpin cross-curricular studies

If we are to move beyond functionality (how much revenue is required to teach ring-fenced content to a given level of acquisition) into a holistic view of curriculum as an approach to the self-development of the learner, then we place not less but more onus on effective teaching. In turn, that teaching has to be redefined. Teaching in a cross-curricular context makes the place of the learner central, rather than the place of content, and requires a different kind of approach to teaching in order to be effective. Overall didactic approaches won't do, though at times they may have a place.

Though Ofsted has always denied that it favoured didactic teaching, a former Chief Inspector has made it clear that such was his own position (Woodhead 1995), more recently calling papers like this chapter 'pernicious' (Woodhead 2002). Indeed, alternatives to didactic teaching are illogical within a subject-restricted, content-led curriculum; and it was Woodhead who helped establish that curriculum, even though in his 2002 speech he rejected it as ineffectual! For, if NC is espoused, it ought to be admitted at the same time that schooling has ceased to be education and has become training. (A parallel process took place in teacher education during the same period.)

The Plowden Report (para. 503) identified a series of 'danger signs' to indicate when effective teaching had collapsed, a list which reads today almost like an indictment of NC. In a study of the learning of able pupils after NC implementation, Kerry and Kerry (2000: 38) were given a very similar list of NC failures by teachers. Table 1.2 puts these lists side by side in what is a very telling juxtaposition.

Plowden, however, is aware that to be effective the teaching required by cross-curricular approaches cannot be less well executed than that of didactic approaches. Paras 549–52 assert that words like 'discovery' cannot be used lightly, that teachers must bring to their teaching 'a stringent intellectual scrutiny', that the progress of pupils must be assessed and monitored (in appropriate manners), and that the quality of individual schools must kept under review. None of this smacks of the 'nambyism' and woolly thinking attributed to the Plowden Report by its detractors, for example Grossen (1998).

So, given that the Plowden vision of curriculum and of learning is accepted, what are the actual implications for teachers and models of teaching? I would suggest that teaching, while not an easy process, is essentially a simple one. By that is meant that the agenda for teaching skills is clear, even if the skills themselves require to be learned, constantly reflected upon, honed, and improved. The complexities of this process of teaching, and of understanding it, are summarised by Bennett (1997: 139–40). To teach an integrated curriculum effectively (in fact, to teach anything effectively) there are some basic essentials in the teacher's armoury, and these can be seen as areas of teaching skill:

- Skills in class management
- Skills in explaining
- Skills in questioning
- Skills in task setting and differentiation and, increasingly,
- Skills in assessment.

Within the scope of a short chapter such as this, it is impossible even to outline these skills, but they can be accessed readily in other published work (Kerry 2002a, 2002b; Kerry and Wilding 2004). These skills represent the agenda for teaching competence, and should be high on the priority list of all teacher education establishments. This is not to say that other skills do not exist or are unimportant, but simply to state that these are fundamental – the building blocks of all other classroom teaching and learning. At present, not enough time is spent on them, and too few teachers have genuine command of them. This list evolved from the Teacher Education Project, mentioned above, but is slightly extended over the original

Table 1.2 Comparison of Plowden's indicators of failing lessons with teachers' views of National Curriculum

Plowden's 'danger signs'	Teachers' views of NC
Fragmented knowledge	Prescriptive content
Limited creative work	Lack of creativity
Much time spent on teaching (as opposed to learning)	Restricted teacher initiative in curriculum and teaching
Few questions from the children	Compartmented thinking
Too many exercises	Failures of pace and level
Straitjacketed learning	Narrowed expectations
Concentration on tests	

version; they are not plucked out of the air but based on research and grounded theory. However, many teachers will warm to the version of these events recounted inimitably by Wragg (1984: 8):

> The areas on which we chose to focus, class-management, mixed ability teaching, questioning and explaining, seemed ... to represent activities which required skill, intelligence and sensitivity from teachers. They were not so vague as to defy analysis, nor so minute and piddling as to be silly.

It is heartening to discover, as reported earlier, that many schools are now reconsidering curriculum approaches and are tending to move closer to an integrated approach with a renewed interest in pupil learning. But it is important to stress the need to move in parallel to make teachers' activities and teaching appropriate to the new curriculum and learning intentions. Indeed, where this does not happen, any experimentation may prove at best ineffectual and at worst disastrous; Kerry and Wilding (2000: 259–71) reported just such a case.

The problem with government-led curriculum reform, along with related views about pedagogy and assessment, has been that Britain has been overly prescriptive, as noted by Power, in order to 'Position subjects in ways that hark back to some imagined past, rather than forwards into more globalised times' (2002: 103).

Reflection

What do you think will be the skills needed of learners when your pupils are at the peak of their working lives, in twenty or thirty years' time? How will they differ from the ways in which you learned?

In other words, rather than accepting that in an information world knowledge itself will be beyond the capacity of the human brain, and that the important skills will be in evaluating and applying knowledge, successive governments from 1988 sought to narrow views of class and social position through a kind of constrained 'received wisdom' imposed through compulsory curricula and teaching methods. Aldrich *et al.* (2000: 164) call this 'the renewed dominance of the old humanists and of a traditional academic culture'. Yet this position is proving as unsustainable as it is illogical and there are, just, the glimmerings of hope of a fresh approach, however grudging, even by officialdom. Thus Docking (2000: 81) notes that 'under subject headings [i.e. in the National Curriculum revisions] there are suggested links with other subjects and with ICT'. Even the government's own literature is, in guarded ways, suggesting that a more creative and less restrictive approach must be adopted, and is being adopted by the 'best primary schools':

> Ofsted's new inspection framework . . . requires inspectors to evaluate the extent to which curriculum provides a broad range of worthwhile curricular opportunities that caters for the interests, aptitudes and particular needs of all pupils. In *The Curriculum in Successful Primary Schools*, Ofsted explains this change in the context of encouraging schools to use their own professional judgements, and make full use of curriculum flexibilities, in order to take ownership of the curriculum . . . Ofsted is actively encouraging a new culture of innovation.
>
> (DfES 2003: 25)

The same document takes the argument on a step further (DfES 2003: 30): 'The focus will be on building teachers' capacity to manage really effective learning and teaching across the curriculum, rather than on presenting identikit blueprints for teaching.' The Rose Report (DCSF 2008) is the most recent attempt (discussed later in this volume) to fill a gap in curriculum provision that was created by the very government bodies that are now trying to patch up the hole in the ship. Successive governments removed curriculum autonomy and flexible teaching; but let us be grateful for the small mercy that they are now beginning, belatedly, to hand some elements of these things back to the profession.

Summary

This chapter has tried to establish: first, that the Plowden ideals of a cross-curricular approach are relevant in the modern world; and second, that they are soundly based in both the groundwork of research and theory, and in the pragmatism of teachers' experience and classroom understandings. But the essential nature of cross-curricular working is best illustrated by a real example in the real world, and it is to this that I would now like to turn.

Some years ago the C4 Television Equinox team made a programme about the Ten Plagues of Egypt (Platt 1998). The plagues are recorded in the Book of Exodus (see Table 1.3).

The research featured in this programme was instigated by Dr John Marr, who wanted to seek a rational and historical explanation. His questions were whether each of these plagues could have happened and was the sequence of them a clue to their true nature. As a study in cross-curricular approaches and integration of knowledge from across disciplines, this story was a masterpiece. My summary of it does it less than justice, but gives something of the bare bones.

While the original study of the Old Testament stories implied a theological interest and a skill in ancient Hebrew to translate the text, the river of blood was a mystery. It took work by the marine microbiologist Dr JoAnn Burkholder to establish the presence of algae that can and do cause this effect. To discover how the increase in frog numbers might have

Table 1.3 The Ten Plagues of Egypt

1	Water to blood
2	Frogs
3	Lice
4	Flies
5	Murrain of cattle
6	Boils and blains
7	Hail
8	Locusts
9	Darkness
10	Death of the first-born

worked following the red bloom event, they turned to Professor Richard Wasserug of the University of Halifax, Nova Scotia, who identified the creatures as toads, not frogs, which in the right conditions can reach plague proportions. The plague of lice needed the curator of the Mississippi Entomological Museum to supply an explanation; and the flies, probably stable flies, were identified by a professor at the Harvard School of Public Health. When the cattle died it was Dr Breeze at the US Department of Agricultural Animal Research who named the diseases involved. Marr and his collaborator found the plague of boils and blains less surprising under the circumstances and identified a culprit in the disease known as glanders. Locust swarms are well recorded in the literature of natural history. The plague of darkness was identified by a Dutch physician as most likely explained by a phenomenon known as *khamsin* – a fierce wind that produces sandstorms, thus blotting out vision and light. But the death of the first-born, despite this chapter of accidents, was baffling. The explanation lay, they thought, in myco-toxins, chemicals produced by fungi growing on organic substances such as corn – these could have been borne from the faeces of the locust hordes and their occurrence tallied with an event in Ohio described by Eduardo Montana of the US Centers for Disease Control and Prevention.

So a journey around the Ten Biblical Plagues involved Egypt, Canada, the USA, Europe, theologians, linguists, physicians, and the disciplines of marine biology, epidemiology, epizootiology, entomology, microbiology, and toxicology: a classic study to illustrate how complex problems in the modern world need not specialists alone but specialists in context. It is, too, a great detective story. What is clear, in personal conversation, is the increasing goodwill of a new generation of teachers to rediscover these interdisciplinary ideas and ideals at the school level too. They are disillusioned with today's prescriptions and yearn for the kind of autonomy that will convert their work back from that of hoop-jumping government technicians to independent-minded professionals. In fact, in this they mirror that other great insight about children's learning (Plowden 1967: para. 1233): 'Finding out has proved better . . . than being told.'

References

Aldrich, R., Crook, D., and Watson, D. (2000) *Education and Employment: the DfEE and its place in history* London Institute of Education: Bedford Way Papers

Bennett, N. (1997) 'Voyages of discovery: changing perspectives in research on primary school practice' in C. Cullingford (ed.) *The Politics of Primary Education* Buckingham: Open University Press

Bloom, B. (1956) *Taxonomy of Educational Objectives* New York: McKay

Campbell, A. and Kerry, T. (2004) 'Constructing a new KS3 curriculum at Brooke Weston CTC: a review and commentary' *Educational Studies* 30 (4): 391–408

Carr, D. (2003) *Making Sense of Education* London: Routledge and Kegan Paul

Clyde, M. (1995) 'Concluding the debate' in M. Fleer (ed.) *DAP Centrism: challenging developmentally appropriate practice* Watson, Australia: Australian Early Childhood Association

DCSF (Department for Children, Schools and Families) (2008) *Independent Review of the Primary Curriculum Interim Report (The Rose Report)* Nottingham: DCSF

Department for Education and Skills (2003) *Excellence and Enjoyment: a strategy for primary schools* Nottingham: DfES

Docking, J. (2000) *New Labour's Policies for Schools: raising the standard?* London: David Fulton

Eisner, E. (1996) *Cognition and Curriculum Re-considered* (2nd edn) London: PCP

Elliott, J. (1998) *The Curriculum Experiment: meeting the challenge of social change* Buckingham: Open University Press

Gardner, H. (1999) *Intelligences Re-framed: multiple intelligences for the 21st century* New York: Basic Books

Grossen, B. (1998) *Child-directed Teaching Methods: a discriminatory practice of Western education* Occasional Paper 1.12.98 Oregon: University of Oregon

Hirst, P. (1974) *Knowledge and the Curriculum* London: Routledge and Kegan Paul

Jarvis, M. (2005) *The Psychology of Effective Learning and Teaching* Cheltenham: Nelson-Thornes

Kelly, A.V. (1999) *The Curriculum – theory and practice* (4th edn) London: PCP

Kelly, A.V. (2001) 'What did Hitler do in the war, Miss?' *Times Educational Supplement* 19 January 2001: 12

Kerry, C. and Kerry, T. (2000) 'The effective use of school time in the education of the most able' *Australasian Journal of Gifted Education* 9 (1): 33–40

Kerry, T. (2002a) *Explaining and Questioning* Cheltenham: Nelson-Thornes

Kerry, T. (2002b) *Learning Objectives, Task Setting and Differentiation* Cheltenham: Nelson-Thornes

Kerry, T. (2005) 'Forthcoming success: back to the future?' *Education Today* 55 (1): 14–19

Kerry, T. and Eggleston, J. (1988) *Topic Work in the Primary School* London: Routledge

Kerry, T. and Wilding, M. (2000) 'Managing a new teaching space' *Education Today* 50 (2): 8–20

Kerry, T. and Wilding, M. (2004) *Effective Classroom Teacher: developing the skills you need in today's classroom* London: Pearson

Lawton, D. (1997) 'Curriculum theory and a curriculum for the 21st century' in P. Mortimore and V. Little (eds) *Living Education: essays in honour of John Tomlinson* London: PCP

Mortimore, P. and Little, V. (1997) *Living Education: essays in honour of John Tomlinson* London: PCP

Platt, S. (1998) *Equinox: the Ten Plagues of Egypt* London: Channel 4 Television

Plowden, Lady Bridget (1967) *Children and Their Primary Schools: a report of the Central Advisory Council for Education volume 1* London: HMSO

Power, S. (2002) 'The overt and hidden curricula of quasi-markets' in G. Whitty (ed.) *Making Sense of Education Policy* London: PCP

Ross, A. (2000) *Curriculum: construction and critique* London: Falmer Press

Rousseau, J.-J. (1913) *Émile* London: Dent, Everyman Library

Stenhouse, L. (1975) *An Introduction to Curriculum Research and Development* London: Heinemann

Woodhead, C. (1995) 'Teaching quality: the issues and the evidence' in *Teaching Quality: The Primary Debate* London: Office for Standards in Education

Woodhead, C. (2002) 'The standards of today: and how to raise them to the standards of tomorrow' Paper to the Adam Smith Institute

Wragg, E.C. (ed.) (1984) *Classroom Teaching Skills* London: Croom Helm

Chapter 2

How children learn

Improving cognition through cross-curricular teaching

Trevor Kerry

Introduction

This chapter takes a straightforward look at the ways in which theorists view children's thinking. It looks at systems put forward by Bloom, Wallace, Bowring-Carr and West-Burnham, Fisher, Gardner, and Wilding to track and build effectively on children's thinking. The practical application of these ideas to a section of the curriculum is explored. It is suggested that there is a need for thinking and higher-order cognition to be made central to curriculum planning and to classroom learning and teaching.

Background: a Bloomian view

The information age has increased rather than diminished the need for individuals to think. In a world of what seems like infinitely expanding information, the need to process and evaluate all these data becomes not only essential for all of us but the cutting-edge skill of the movers and shakers. Fisher and Scriven (1997: 20) define critical thinking as 'skilled, active, interpretation and evaluation of observations, communications, information, and argumentation'. The more information is directed at us, the more discerning we have to be in processing it. Yet the sad fact is, if you want to find thinking at work, the classroom – whether in primary school or even a university course – is often the last place you might discover it.

This last statement seems like a fairly trenchant judgement, and one that many (teachers and others) might take exception to or require evidence for. But there is evidence: and while things might be changing and it is unfair to tar all institutions with the same brush, you can come to your own judgement by carrying out a fairly simple test using the tools described below.

The guru of thinking was Benjamin Bloom (1956). He established a system for judging what kind of thinking occurs in classrooms. In previous research beginning as long ago as the 1980s (Kerry, in Wragg 1984) I adapted and simplified his system so that it could be applied easily to classrooms. In effect, much of the cognitive life of classrooms can be allocated to one of these categories of thinking (see Table 2.1).

Table 2.2 provides some examples of how the system works for classroom questions. Management questions (category 0) would be things like: 'Jane, will you take this register to the office, please?' or 'Can someone close the door, please?' They may 'oil the wheels' of classroom living but they do not add to its cognitive level. Other categories are exemplified in the table. A simple way of conceptualising the difference between low and higher-order operation is that low-order questions or tasks require a passive reception or parrot-like

Table 2.1 Categories of thinking adapted from Bloom (1956)

Category	Activity	Low-order (L) or higher-order thinking (H)
0	Management statement, request, task	L
1	Recall	L
2	Simple comprehension	L
3	Application	H
4	Analysis	H
5	Synthesis	H
6	Evaluation	H

Table 2.2 Examples of higher-order questions using the system adapted from Bloom (1956)

Type of task	Examples
1 Recall	• In your homework reading what did you find out about King Harold?
2 Simple comprehension	• Teacher: instead of 'goodbye' a French person might say 'Au Revoir'. What would he or she say?
3 Application	• How did Icarus and his father come up with the idea of using wings? • How could we try out different kinds of wings to see which shape flies best?
4 Analysis	• Why did Jesus concern himself so often with the lives of the poor and the down-and-out? • Looking at the map, why do you think Hadrian built his wall in that location?
5 Synthesis	• In the first story Tracey behaves meanly to her friend; in the second one she acts differently. What things bring about this change?
6 Evaluation	• Looking at this painting, what do think is going through the heads of the people the artist has drawn? • In *Wind in the Willows*, how do you assess the characters of Ratty and Toad?

repetition of data, whereas higher-order skill requires pupils to manipulate the data in some way.

In previous publications I have outlined how teachers' questions and explanations or talk can be enhanced to improve cognitive demand on pupils of all abilities (Kerry 2002a), and how the same principles can be applied to task-setting in classrooms (Kerry 2002b). These skills' manuals coach teachers through the processes of translating research outcomes into effective classroom practice. In this chapter, where the emphasis is more on the principles than on skills' acquisition, it is important to make a further point about outcomes from this work.

One of the most telling points from my own researches on thinking in mixed ability classrooms using this adapted Bloomian system, and one which was in no way related to mere chance, was concerned with integrating subject matter (see also Chapter 1). In lessons where the subject matter was integrated, as opposed to taught discipline by discipline, the cognitive life in the classroom rose by a factor of at least four (Kerry in Wragg 1984: 177). Several strands of causation probably contributed to this result. First, teaching in an integrated way inevitably involves a lot of synthesis of material across disciplines and sources – and synthesis is, of itself, a higher-order skill. Second, much of this work was rooted more closely to problem-solving, so the nature of the tasks set was more cognitively demanding. Third, children of all levels of ability probably become more discerning as a result of the first two factors, and thus begin to make more intellectual responses to material offered and to ask more demanding questions of the teacher. Thus, fourth, learning ceased to be a didactically delivered stream of passively received knowledge data, and became an actively collaborative enterprise between teacher and pupil in investigating issues. Something of this process is described in this book, in Chapters 8 and 12 for example.

Various educationists have championed particular approaches to thinking and to training children to think. What follows is a review of some of these systems, with some assessment of their strengths and weaknesses. It is not the intention to promulgate any particular system but to urge teacher-readers to select among them those facets that hold promise in their own classrooms. What is important to understand are two things: first, that generally these 'thinking skills' are not for able pupils only but for all pupils; second, that they run counter to the view that puts learning facts (usually through single-subject lessons) at the centre of the education process. This stands at the heart of this book: education does not operate on the Skinnerian hoover-bag principle – it is not about children sponging up decontextualised information merely to regurgitate it later with little appreciation of its significance or application. Facts are important; but they are important as the building blocks upon which thinking and insight can be based. Though systems to improve thinking are often developed as a relatively crude response to improving the progression of the most able, their value in motivating and stimulating all children, without exception, quickly becomes apparent.

TASC – Thinking Actively in a Social Context

Thinking Actively in a Social Context is a system developed and used by Belle Wallace (www.nace.co.uk/tasc/tasc_home/htm). Though often used to stimulate able pupils in primary schools, TASC is by no means confined to that context. The broader perspective is reflected in a comment posted on a government website: 'We have used the TASC Framework to lift our school out of "Special Measures". TASC gave us a framework for developing pupils' ownership of their learning. Their motivation and interest soared' (http://www.teachernet.gov.uk/schoolinfocus/ramridgeprimary/). Wallace claims that her work encourages self-confidence in pupils by allowing them to work independently, discovering research skills. Through their problem-solving they gain increased self-confidence and become active learners capable of working across the curriculum and engaging in self-assessment. These are bold claims but Wallace has a track-record of achieving these aims in schools nationally.

TASC works in a series of stages, often depicted as a wheel. Pupils work around the segments of the wheel:

- To gather and organise information
- To define the task required, using the information available
- To define more ideas around the task
- To select the best of the ideas

- To operationalise the best idea(s)
- To evaluate what they have done
- To tell others what they have done
- To make a final assessment of the experience and learning.

TASC is a form of structured learning where the structure is based, not on a series of pieces of information, but on learning to think – creatively, logically, laterally. Part of its success rests on this sequencing process: even when they are at the early, less secure stages, of the process, pupils have a structure to fall back on.

   That TASC can work in a wide range of contexts is demonstrated by comments from the school quoted earlier:

> there's been a real improvement in children's thinking skills and greater confidence about tackling problems, verbalising views and finding possible solutions . . . these aren't quantifiable outcomes that you can test, but the children have learned to be more in control of their learning which is highly important as . . . many children [have] complex needs. The school is in an area of high social deprivation and those identified as having learning difficulties and disabilities are well above the national average, as is mobility.

In following TASC principles teachers have to stand back and surrender some responsibility for learning to pupils – something that many find difficult initially. However, in so doing, they are exercising true professionalism. Users report improved behaviour through increased interest and engagement, the opportunity for pupils to adopt their preferred learning styles, and even that dreaded word – outlawed in the Woodhead era – fun!

Reflection

How might you apply the ideas of Bloom, Kerry and Wallace to your classroom?

An approach through philosophy

Another highly effective primary educator, Robert Fisher, prefers to approach thinking through philosophy (Fisher 2003). Teachers might find this a harder system to learn initially as it involves what is often called 'socratic' questioning, but in fact the process is not very different from teaching using questions in the way which is outlined in Kerry (2002a), referred to earlier. Jarvis (2005: 107) sums the method up well: '"Philosophy" is used less in the sense of teaching philosophy as a discipline than in the sense of teaching children to *philosophise*. The aim of this is to develop creative and critical modes of thinking.' The system requires that everyday modes of thinking (guessing, assuming, judging, and inferring) are replaced by critical modes (estimating, justifying, analysing, and reasoning). Like TASC, the method requires social learning, the establishment of a 'community of enquiry' where freedom of expression and speculation are welcome. In place of the Bloom–Kerry question types, Fisher proposes that thinking can begin from stories about which seven types of question can be asked:

- *Contextual*: geographical, historical, cultural, etc.
- *Establishing the temporal order*: what happened before, after, and its significance
- *Particularity*: challenging pupils to say what else might have been done or said in the circumstances
- *Intentions*: requiring the analysis of e.g. emotions, motivation
- *Choices*: uncovering the moral analysis
- *Meanings*: hidden messages behind the overt events
- *Telling*: how the telling influences the understanding.

This form of thinking can be applied successfully to current news stories every bit as easily as to ancient myths or novelistic productions. A strong feature of Fisher's approach is the centrality it gives to questioning as a learning and teaching tool.

Shallow and deep learning

By now, the reader will have picked up the message that raising the cognitive stakes in lessons is about trying to find effective systems for analysing the thinking that happens in classrooms and to establish better ways to harness its power for all pupils. It is a very different process from simply scoring the number of facts learned or the conformity of pupils to reiterating received mantras of information, things these writers maintain impinge on us 'not one whit' (Bowring-Carr and West-Burnham 1997: 77). Bowring-Carr and West-Burnham are less concerned with the 'how' and more concerned with the 'what' of thinking – with trying to establish what is, and what is not, useful learning. As a result they develop a theory of shallow and deep learning, which is important and persuasive. In doing so they quote Willis (1993): 'Quality learning is about conceptual change – seeing the world differently is an essential outcome.' Once again, they are forced back into identifying those verbs that epitomise the kind of learning they see as achieving the desired ends: explaining, giving examples, applying, justifying, comparing, contrasting, contextualising, generalising, selecting the appropriate medium for communication of the idea. They advocate the use of mind-maps to track the changes in pupils' understandings – a kind of metacognitive process (see below).

   Thus it is possible to progress from surface to deep, or profound, learning. This learning has certain essential characteristics. Beginning from the pupil's initial mind-map the teacher and pupil proceed with the learning in a context where the learning process is itself the subject of discussion. The assessment procedures, too, will reflect the profound learning required. Pupil and teacher explore and agree the ways in which learning is best demonstrated. Over time the kinds of intelligences required (these are discussed in the next section) will all be involved. The approach to learner and learning will be holistic, and the intention will be to explore material in depth rather than cover a syllabus superficially. Curiosity will trigger and promote the learning, and is not confined to the school context or day. The purpose of the learning is to 'enable the individual to change, grow and become autonomous' (Bowring-Carr and West-Burnham 1997: 83).

   So what are these 'intelligences' that need to be explored and educated? The classic answer to this question has been provided over many years by the work of Howard Gardner in an evolving theory. It is to this that we now turn.

Multiple intelligences: the work of Gardner

The most recent exposition of Gardner's theory at this moment of writing is to be found in Chau and Kerry (2008). Here Gardner extends his theory of multiple intelligences from his previous seven or eight intelligences theory into a theory of nine intelligences. So we should begin by establishing what these are, and in so doing I have used a shortened version of his own words from the text cited above:

1   *Linguistic intelligence*: the intelligence of a writer, orator, journalist.
2   *Logical mathematical intelligence*: the intelligence of a logician, mathematician, scientist.
3   *Musical intelligence*: the capacity to create, perform and appreciate music.
4   *Spatial intelligence*: the capacity to form mental imagery of the world – the large world of the aviator or navigator, or the more local world of the chess player or the surgeon – and to manipulate those mental images.
5   *Bodily-kinesthetic intelligence*: the capacity to solve problems or fashion products using your whole body, or parts of your body, like your hands or mouth. This intelligence is exhibited by athletes, dancers, actors, craft people, and, again, surgeons.
6   *Interpersonal intelligence involves the understanding of other persons*: how to interact with them, how to motivate them, how to understand their personalities, etc.
7   *Intrapersonal intelligence*: is the capacity to understand oneself – one's strengths, weaknesses, desires, fears.
8   *Naturalist intelligence*: involves the capacity to make consequential distinctions in nature – between one plant and another, among animals, clouds, mountains, and the like. The scientist Charles Darwin had naturalist intelligence in abundance.
9   *The 'intelligence of big questions'*: When children ask about the size of the universe, when adults ponder death, love, conflict, the future of the planet, they are engaging in existential issues.

These intelligences are largely self-explanatory, and they are an attempt to define more closely the areas of understanding that teachers need to encourage their pupils to develop. Once more, they do not challenge the necessity for factual information, but they do transcend data to look at the thinking processes from a number of perspectives. Gardner is constantly moving on this theory, and he emphasises that – allied with his theory of intelligences – there is need to recognise what he calls 'kinds of mind'.

The minds that teachers need to develop include the cognitive: the disciplined mind that is concerned with knowledge and skill, the synthesising mind that orders knowledge in useful ways, and the creative mind that moves beyond the current boundaries. But, he suggests, our success as human beings depends on more than even these: on the respectful mind that is about tolerance and working together, and the ethical mind that weighs the effects and motivations for our actions.

What Gardner has done – and it is an insight born out of a current socio-political worldview – is to extend his theory into the realm of behaviour and the rationales that govern it. This is an extension of the Bowring-Carr and West-Burnham position and represents an important insight. But we need to return to the classroom, and to ask how all this learning can be tracked by the teacher within the realities of the busy social relationships that are current class sizes. To this end we turn to the concept of metacognition which, until this point, has been mentioned only in passing.

Reflection

Gardner's work is well respected and received around the world. To what extent and in what ways does it influence your own thinking about your work?

Metacognition

A clumsy word for a useful concept, metacognition is the process of reflecting on one's own learning, and it is a process as applicable to pupils as to learning adults. In the drive to listen to pupils' voices, one of the areas of hearing must be about how pupils learn. Stoll *et al.* have a useful definition:

> Human beings can reflect on their own thinking processes. Experts describe their thinking as an internal conversation – monitoring their own understanding, predicting their performance, deciding what else they need to know, organising and re-organising ideas, checking for consistency between different pieces of information and drawing analogies that help them advance their understanding.
>
> (2003: 26)

While Stoll *et al.* (2003: 70) note that using metacognitive processes in the classroom is an advanced teaching skill, Wilding (1997) suggests that pupils will learn more effectively if they understand their own learning processes. In an interesting article describing work with younger primary children she argues that almost every pupil can be helped to learn by using this process. She introduced 'learning diaries' into her primary school with children as young as six, to great effect. Her conclusion about using this method is optimistic. So let us consider metacognition as a tool for teachers in helping children to learn and reflect on their own thinking processes and their efficacy.

Having experimented with various approaches to children recording what they had learned, including one-to-one discussions with the teacher, Wilding (1997: 20) concluded that a number of problems beset these approaches:

- The reviews were extremely time-consuming.
- Children generally only remembered and referred to very recent activities. Also they used very general labels and imprecise language, such as, 'My maths was best 'cause it was good'.
- I found myself constantly drawn towards 'putting words in their mouths' as they struggled with the language.
- There was a wide spectrum in the level of sophistication in the responses of different children.

The issue of language is picked up by Loughran (2002), who describes a metacognitive approach to teaching in an Australian setting, where learning the 'language of learning' was an important prerequisite in order to enable students and teachers to communicate about the processes of learning. Wilding decided that a solution to achieving metacognitive practice was to put aside some timetabled time on a regular and fairly frequent basis for the compilation of learning logs:

I anticipated that, once the children were familiar with the task, it would only take up about 30–40 minutes . . . I felt there was time available during Friday morning . . . It could be justified in terms of the English National Curriculum as providing a meaningful purpose for Speaking and Listening, and Writing . . . the majority of the children had the necessary writing skills (Y2/3 class) . . . in the case of the four children who might struggle my ancillary or myself should be able to give extra support.

(Wilding 1997: 20)

Each child was issued with an exercise book in which to write the log, and some prompt questions were added to the front page:

- What have I enjoyed most during this week? Why?
- What have I done best during this week? Why?
- What have I found difficult during this week? Why?
- What am I going to try harder at next week? Why?

The sophistication of the children's learning diaries increased rapidly – the rather bald statements of the kind quoted earlier soon turned into:

I have enjoyed writing on the computer. Why – because it is good but I did make some mistakes. I have been best at my stamp ready reckoner. Why – because it is a bit hard but I got used to it. I have found it difficult doing my Ancient Greece research. Why – because it is hard to get information. I am going to try harder not to shout. Why – because it is hard to keep it under control.

It is important to remember here that metacognition is not only about supporting the learning of the less able (Lovey 2002), useful though this is; it is a tool for all pupils including the very able. Wilding, in fact, went on to give a number of other examples of how the learning diary had not only helped the pupils understand their own learning processes – their strengths, weaknesses, and distractions – but also had helped the teacher.

Example 1. 'I have done my best at pot drawing this week because it is the only time you have said "Well done".' (This shows how important the teacher's response can be to children, and reminds us of the importance of being positive.)

Example 2. 'I have found reading difficult because I am guessing the words.' (The teacher followed this up with the child and found that he was feeling very unsuccessful with his reading book; the book was changed to one he understood and enjoyed. It was also possible to explain that careful 'guessing' can be a very useful and appropriate strategy in reading.)

Wilding goes on to conclude that the aim of this process is to raise the pupil's stake in the learning process – to put the pupil at the centre of learning (see Chapter 4). To do this it is important to show that what pupils say has an effect on what happens in the classroom: they need to 'see the point' of the activity, and to see it expressed in action. The learning diary – the metacognitive process – was subsequently introduced throughout the school: in an oral version with the youngest pupils.

Reflection

How might metacognition help your work and the pupils in your classes?

This survey of ways of thinking about thinking in classrooms is not exhaustive. No mention has been made, for example, of De Bono's work (2000) or of the Activating Children's Thinking Skills (ACTS) project in Northern Ireland (which was more orientated towards the secondary sector) (McGuiness 2000). Nor have I included the work of Fuerstein which, though interesting, may seem somewhat impenetrable at times. None the less, the survey has demonstrated several insights.

Though differing in detail, each system has attempted to explore what might be called 'learning beyond the facts'. All are agreed that this kind of learning is of a higher order of cognition. All imply that, to achieve these ends, teachers need to operate at an advanced skill level, and also by implication, that teachers need training in these skills. All the systems identify improved learning performance, and some improved behaviour, in pupils as a result of the provision of more meaningful learning tasks. The systems are more important for their similarities than for their differences. Individually, each system has strengths and drawbacks. TASC has a proven track-record, but may appear a touch mechanistic. Fisher's philosophical approach is very logical but may be off-putting to some teachers at first encounter. Bowring-Carr and West-Burnham's work is more theoretical than practical but involves good insights. By contrast, most educators are familiar with Gardner's approach; if it has a weakness it is that it is sometimes employed too simplistically by those who do not delve adequately into it, and serves only to justify a range of curriculum knowledge and skills rather than to reach into the more obscure 'minds' that are so essential. Metacognition is valuable, and features as a part of most of the systems, but can be time-consuming and requires some effort to train pupils to use it. The Bloomian-based approach can work very successfully, making teachers very self-aware of the performance, but it is demanding on teachers' willingness to be self-analytical.

Thinking and the National Curriculum

I have remarked elsewhere that, when the National Curriculum was delivered in its init form in 1988, what most of us had expected and hoped for was a national minimu entitlement for children, but what we got was a series of subject syllabuses. Education I been marching down that cul-de-sac ever since.

The NC did not, and was never intended to, deliver children's ability to think, only know. In the very earliest versions of the assessment processes attached to the NC do ments, there was a brief attempt to encourage teachers to make judgements of pu progress on the basis of a Bloomian model. However, since teachers were untrained in operation, and the instructions about it were so poorly (even erroneously) set out in documentation, the experiment became the first of a long line of need-driven changes make NC workable. Should the reader be tempted to suggest that my judgement on t issue is too harsh let him or her consult the words of David Blunkett, Secretary of State Education – in the year 2000, twelve years after the NC was introduced – when he said:

I have been very impressed by the *growing evidence* in this country and abroad of the impact on standards of systematic and disciplined approaches to the teaching of higher-order thinking skills. For these reasons, from this autumn, we shall pilot a professional development programme designed to ensure secondary teachers know how to teach higher-order thinking skills through their subjects.

(6 January 2000; http://www.thinkingcorner.com/msg7.htm; my italics)

To redress some of this balance the Qualifications and Curriculum Authority (QCA) has recently attempted to overlay the NC with some intentions about teaching thinking. They are couched in the now-familiar platitudes of government-driven initiatives, and they contain the inevitable agendas about citizens as economic units which are often traced back as far as Callaghan's Ruskin College speech in 1976 (Docking 2000: 4, 158). The following short extract is typical:

Creativity and critical thinking develop young people's capacity for original ideas and purposeful action. Experiencing the wonder and inspiration of human ingenuity and achievement, whether artistic, scientific or technological, can spark individual enthusiasms that contribute to personal fulfilment.

Creativity can be an individual or collaborative activity. By engaging in creative activities, young people can develop the capacity to influence and shape their own lives and wider society. Everyone has the potential for creative activity and it can have a positive impact on self-esteem, emotional wellbeing and overall achievement.

Creative activity is essential for the future wellbeing of society and the economy.

(http://curriculum.qca.org.uk/key-stages-3-and-4/cross-curriculum-dimensions/creativitycriticalthinking/index.aspx)

The QCA also expresses a keenness to add on (the 'after-thought' semantics of its statement are significant) critical thinking to its knowledge content. To encourage imagination, the generation of ideas and connections between them, to explore the links between subjects, to give pupils' ideas audience and for them to pursue their individual interests are not rocket-science and they are belated – but they are steps in the right direction. But thinking is not an add-on. Its omission as an integral part of the original NC is an indictment. So how ˙ ˙ etter than this, where it matters – in our schools?

ng lesson

ɔn I want to move from the theory of higher-order thinking and learning to a beit far too short, exposition of its nature: an example in miniature. So what n attempt to give a flavour of a piece of primary curriculum seen from the of a teacher who wants to achieve both higher-order thinking and, through it, ement. Table 2.3, then, is an outline of a cross-curricular lesson series on the ld War, giving something of the process and outcomes of the work. It is based ɔns in real classrooms, and the principles are easily adaptable.

characterises this process? It is, of course, a voyage of discovery. It involves what e to call 'research' – though I prefer the concept of investigation, which is similar ɔt imply originality. The structure of the series of lessons is not far from the

Table 2.3 Cross-curricular lesson series on the Second World War

Lesson series	Activities	Outcomes
Find out what the pupils know	**Question and answer session** Establish key facts – dates, names, local events of the period One or two have memorabilia at home Some have watched TV programmes One has read a story about the evacuation Most have seen *Dad's Army* – discuss role of fiction – what's real what's not Fashion, rather different, why? Shortages – why? Why didn't the Germans roll in and invade us like they did Poland? Look at a map – 'island race'	Enough basic knowledge established to get everyone thinking, and to ensure that all the pupils have at least a grain of empathy with the topic even if their real knowledge is minimal
What do they want to know and explore?	**Collect a fairly random list of ideas or interests** Rations, ration cards, what could you buy to eat? Could we try some? What was the real Dad's Army like? Luke's family has some medals Jane likes the maps, chronology – Where? When? Why? Life as an evacuee Tanks War planes – Spitfire What was it like to be bombed? What makes people do terrible things to other people? What was it like to walk or drive around in the dark with no signposts? Churchill What happened to schools in the war? Who else was involved besides us and the Germans?	Several pupils think they have old ration books and similar artefacts available from grandparents Luke says his dad would lend the medals Resource collection available from Library service Jake has a book about planes Teacher has had the foresight to collect resources on DVD and in pictures Pupils want to send off for copies of newspapers of the time Tracey says she'll ask her great-gran about how she went to school in the war

Table 2.3 continued

Lesson series	Activities	Outcomes
Finding out	**How could we get to know more?** Books Films (probably now on DVD?) Old newspapers People – who was there? ('Were you, Miss?' 'No, I'm not *that* old.') Look around – any buildings that might have been destroyed or rebuilt? Family photos? Local army base?	The early lessons are devoted to some 'research' using the collected materials in the classroom and from the sources identified above
Deciding what to do	The pupils decide among themselves what their interests are Planning session, vetted by the teacher, to see what each group has decided and its overall direction and value Decision is for groups to work on agreed topics, and for some whole-class activities	**The outcome of this are several pieces of group-research:** Luke's group is going to begin from the medals and look at some of the famous battles – one of the medals has a bar which says 'Eighth Army' Jane's group is going to draw maps of the countries involved and how the battles moved to and fro Donna's group wants to get the mums together to put on a wartime austerity meal using things like spam and powdered egg Will and Samantha have seen pictures of the day the war ended, with people dancing in the streets; they want to gather some of the others to produce a VE Day newspaper, with stories about wartime experience and plans for a new and happy life [And so on] **Also, there will be several whole-class activities spread over the study period, led by the teacher:** Tracey's great-gran and several other relatives are coming to spend an hour reminiscing The groups are going to take it in turns to sit in the sport store with the light off and play DVDs of the sirens, the bombing, and the all-clear

		The teacher is going to give everyone a token for a piece of cake (a rare treat for which mum would have queued for hours) – but if you lose the token you don't get the cake! All the pupils have a 'WW2 art afternoon' where they convey their impressions in paint, collage, and other media
Relaying what is done:		The work has taken in literacy (reading, writing); historical knowledge and understanding; some geography to support the historical data; time-management, to produce the newspaper on time; aesthetics through artistic expression; emotional intelligence; communication skills; science of flight, etc.
To each other	**The project draws to a close with each group presenting their findings, including their drawings, maps, newspaper, etc, to the rest**	
To others	**The teacher arranges for them to visit the school in the next village to share their new-found knowledge at a special assembly**	Pupils have dealt in concepts such as fear, uncertainty, pride, aerodynamics, editorial truth, resilience, team-work – and so on

TASC principles rehearsed earlier. The teacher's questions and tasks move into the higher-order realms as measured by the Kerry–Bloom categories. The work is high on involvement. It rests within the community. It generates knowledge, but knowledge contextualised. And it ends by making the knowledge each child's, not the teacher's – indeed, they are the teachers. So it is deep or profound knowledge. In the process, it addresses Gardner's ethical mind; and the teacher can now ask the children to reflect on what and how they have learned – metacognition.

Alternatively . . .

Alternatively, I could sit you down in rows and, with voice well modulated and interesting, I could entrance you with the data that you need to know about the Second World War. I could explain how the German empire under its somewhat unlikely leader began a series of annexations (look, here on the map, this is Austria; and this is Czechoslovakia, which does not exist as such any more); and I could show you a picture of a grey-haired man waving a piece of paper, and tell you how empty the promise on it had been. I could tell you about the precautions that were taken for the population: gas masks, shelters, 'digging for victory', and eventually evacuation of the children. I could enliven this bit by showing you a picture of kids, labelled and suitcased, bidding a tearful farewell. . .

. . . and I could feel you slipping away already, entranced by Wayne's five-legged spider in a matchbox under the desk. Only another three weeks to go but distraction is setting in. So you could be told to read about it instead so you didn't get fidgety. And if I was very lucky you'd remember enough to write something sensible in the assessment, and all the world would be happy.

Except you. For you would have been reinforced in your belief that school was boring, that learning was of little relevance, and that only the score counted. And you would be able to remember the dates but have absolutely no idea about the fear, the desolation, the destruction, the legacy of poverty, the joy, the hope, the anticipation of a brave new world, or the big questions about humanity, mortality, and morality.

References

Bloom, B. (1956) *Taxonomy of Educational Objectives* London: Longman
Bowring-Carr, C. and West-Burnham, J. (1997) *Effective Learning in Schools* London: Pearson
Chau, M.H. and Kerry, T. (eds) (2008) *International Perspectives on Education* London: Continuum
De Bono, E. (2000) *Six Thinking Hats* Harmondsworth: Penguin
Docking, J. (2000) *New Labour's Policies for Schools: raising the standard?* London: David Fulton
Fisher, A. and Scriven, M. (1997) 'Critical thinking: its definition and assessment' *Argumentation* 16 (2): 247–51
Fisher, R. (2003) *Teaching Thinking* London: Continuum
Jarvis, M. (2005) *The Psychology of Effective Learning and Teaching* Cheltenham: Nelson-Thornes
Kerry, T. (1984) 'Analysing the cognitive demand made by classroom tasks in mixed ability classes' in E.C. Wragg (ed.) *Classroom Teaching Skills* London: Croom Helm
Kerry, T. (2002a) *Explaining and Questioning* Cheltenham: Nelson-Thornes
Kerry, T. (2002b) *Learning Objectives, Task Setting and Differentiation* Cheltenham: Nelson-Thornes
Loughran, J. (2002) 'Understanding and articulating teacher knowledge' in C. Sugrue and C. Day (eds) *Developing Teachers and Teaching Practice* London: Routledge Falmer
Lovey, J. (2002) *Supporting Special Educational Needs in Secondary Classrooms* 2nd edn London: David Fulton

McGuiness, C. (2000) 'ACTS: a methodology for enhancing children's thinking skills' Paper presented at the ESRC TLRP First Programme Conference, Leicester University, November

Stoll, L., Fink, D., and Earl, L. (2003) *It's about Learning (and it's about Time)* London: Routledge Falmer

Wallace, B. (2001) *Teaching Thinking Skills across the Primary Curriculum* London: NACE Fulton

Wilding, M. (1997) 'Taking control: from theory into practice' *Education Today* 47 (3): 17–23

Willis, D. (1993) 'Learning and assessment: exposing the inconsistencies of theory and practice' *Oxford Review of Education* 19 (3): 383–402

Wragg, E.C. (1984) *Classroom Teaching Skills* London: Croom Helm

Part 2

Across the age-range

Chapter 3

Cross-curricular teaching to support child-initiated learning in EYFS and Key Stage 1

Elizabeth Wood

Introduction

This chapter focuses on the ways in which teachers can support child-initiated learning, by developing integrated pedagogical approaches in the Early Years Foundation Stage (EYFS) and Key Stage 1. The outcomes of the Independent Review of the Primary Curriculum (DCSF 2009) and the Cambridge Primary Review (Alexander 2009) proposed a number of challenges for teachers in England in how they reconceptualise learning, curriculum, and pedagogy. Though these were not adopted as policy following the 2010 election, a change of climate in primary education remains. The chapter intends to help teachers meet these challenges and looks at contemporary socio-cultural theories that align with these directions: integrating child-initiated and adult-initiated learning activities is central to high-quality education. However, developing cross-curricular approaches involves the teacher in challenging traditional notions of 'child-centred' education and rethinking adults' roles and responsibilities. To meet the challenges, I will argue that teachers need a deep and sophisticated understanding of learning, and a wide pedagogical repertoire, in order to develop the curriculum in ways that combine structure and flexibility, and support play and playfulness. Examples are used to link theory and practice, and illustrate integrated pedagogical approaches.

Background

The Independent Review of the Primary Curriculum (Rose Review) (DCSF 2009) recommends an upward extension of the pedagogical approaches in the Early Years Foundation Stage (EYFS) (DCSF 2009) into Key Stage 1. The six areas of learning in the EYFS will be aligned with the new Primary Curriculum in order to improve progression and continuity in curriculum organisation. In addition, key recommendations include reduced curriculum content, more flexibility than has been possible under the National Curriculum and National Strategies, and more opportunities for teachers to develop cross-curricular approaches, and to integrate key skills with the subject content in the six areas of learning. The Independent Review also recommends extending and building on active, play-based learning across the transition from the EYFS to Key Stage 1, in order to improve continuity of pedagogical approaches. However, the review is less clear about how teachers can develop challenge and extension in play in order to sustain progression.

As a result of the Cambridge Review, Alexander (2009) has argued that teachers need to move towards 'repertoires rather than recipes', with greater emphasis on professional knowledge and decision-making than has been possible under the National Strategies. The content and recommendations of both these reviews require teachers to undertake a reconceptualisation of traditional notions of child-centred education. Teachers will need to develop a more critical focus on cross-curricular work, and on their own roles. I argue that by developing their repertoires of teaching, teachers can extend children's repertoires of participation and learning, and that this can be achieved via cross-curricular pedagogical approaches.

Whilst the recommendations of the Independent Review are to be welcomed (and are long overdue) there are a number of challenges for teachers in supporting the upward extension of integrated pedagogical approaches. In the first section of this chapter, therefore, I examine the case for a reconceptualisation of established theories that have underpinned child-centred education in the light of current directions towards cross-curricular pedagogical approaches, and contemporary socio-cultural theories. In the second section the intention is to develop the concept of child-initiated learning in the light of changes in policy directions and theoretical perspectives. To do this it is important for teachers to take into account the complexity and diversity of children's socio-cultural life-worlds and experiences. Examples from actual classroom practice and empirical research provide illustrations of cross-curricular pedagogical approaches, and the ways in which teachers might anticipate and implement curriculum change. In the final section of the chapter I look at how these trends for improving pedagogical and curriculum continuity from the Foundation Stage to Key Stages 1 and 2 can be implemented in practice.

Child-centred education – change and challenge

Early childhood education (defined here as birth to seven) has been based on a strong ideological commitment to child-centred approaches, which embrace child-initiated learning through free play and free choice, discovery and exploration, and 'hands-on' experiential activities. Child-initiated learning, it is argued, provides the foundations for building meaning and understanding from experience.

In order to support these approaches to learning, teachers are expected to provide richly resourced learning environments (both indoors and outdoors), and to support children's choices, which lead to autonomy and ownership and control of their learning. By observing and interacting with children, it is claimed that teachers can build the curriculum around children's emerging developmental needs and interests, and stimulate further learning through adult-initiated as well as child-initiated activities. The concept of child-initiated learning is grounded in the assumption that children intuitively know what they want and need to do, and can follow their own interests through free choice and free play (Wood 2009).

Moreover, many teachers of this age-range would see children as being developmentally 'primed' to learn from their self-initiated activities because they are intrinsically motivated, and have natural inclinations for curiosity, investigation, discovery, and playfulness. Play has always enjoyed a high status within this ideology, again on the assumption that, when children are playing, they are more engaged, more motivated, and more likely to learn than in adult-initiated activities. These claims are central to the 'play ethos', in which play has been given a privileged position in early learning and development (Smith 2009). There is, though, a danger here: play is often used as an umbrella term to include all child-initiated activities. However, an uncritical devotion to the play ethos masks the reality that children-initiated learning is not always play-based, and that play does not consistently offer the best or most effective ways of learning (Wood 2010).

The commitment to child-initiated learning has been incorrectly interpreted as a 'laissez-faire' approach, in which adults did not take proactive roles in supporting children's learning and development. Because of this, teachers have come under fire from the press and politicians – and, sometimes, even from parents who are anxious to accelerate their children's progress. Thus, there have been long-standing debates about play versus work, processes versus outcomes, freedom versus structure, child-initiated versus teacher-directed learning, which have tended to polarise rather than synthesise pedagogical approaches. This lack of consensus about the values of child-initiated learning made early childhood education vulnerable to the downward pressures of the National Curriculum and National Strategies.

So, whilst the principles of child-initiated learning are ideologically seductive, they have not provided a universally agreed underpinning for educational practice. This is because these principles are based on a range of theories about the different ways in which young children learn and develop, and have produced contrasting views about pedagogy, and the content and organisation of the early childhood curriculum.

There have always been varied, and sometimes contradictory, views about the pedagogical models that adults should use with young children, from predominantly non-interventionist (laissez-faire), to mixed child-initiated and adult-initiated activities, and to highly interventionist, in which adult-planned activities are prioritised, with little time for children's free choice (other than in dedicated 'choosing time' on a Friday afternoon). Where teachers do mix child-initiated and adult-initiated activities it is not always the case that these are actually integrated.

Child-initiated activities are sometimes planned as preparatory curriculum-based skills training (Fassler and Levin 2008), or to keep children occupied whilst adults are engaged in more formal activities which are related to curriculum goals (Rogers and Evans 2008), for example where a teacher allows some pupils to 'choose' an activity while she deals with the more formal process of listening to other children read. It follows that if teachers have little involvement in child-initiated activities (through observation and interaction) then they are not able to plan in ways that are responsive to children's interests, or that extend children's play. Another assumption is that beyond the pre-school years, children can tolerate more sedentary and formal activities that are predominantly teacher-directed, and focus on specific learning outcomes. This means that, beyond the pre-school phase, children typically experience reduced opportunities for child-initiated activities and play, even though they have developed considerable expertise as players and learners, and are more able to benefit from such activities (Wood and Attfield 2005).

Diversity and complexity

Some of the principles stated above carry implicit assumptions that all children benefit from self-initiated activities, and that all children can direct their own learning through free play and free choice. Teachers will be aware that there are always dangers in making blanket assumptions about children's learning and needs. We need to be aware, too, that our assumptions may be based on ethnocentric assertions of predominantly Western child development theories, which are not universally applicable in diverse and complex societies (Genishi and Goodwin 2008).

In contrast, contemporary theories of child-initiated learning acknowledge the role of culture as a dynamic and complex process that both influences and is influenced by people's everyday lives and experiences in different communities. Culture is not expressed merely in everyday artefacts and images (such as having chopsticks and saris in the role-play area), but is expressed as ways of living and being which reflect traditions, values, beliefs, customs, and child-rearing practices. These in turn profoundly influence children's ways of learning, perceiving, thinking, and experiencing the world. So the interests that children express, and the ways in which they are able to learn through self-initiated activities, vary widely according to social and cultural diversity, which take into account the dimensions of diversity identified by Genishi and Goodwin (2008): gender, race, ethnicity, religious affiliation, ability or disability, sexuality, social class, and language.

Teachers may have very different perceptions of this issue of culture according to their school contexts: for example, a school where more than forty languages are spoken by pupils will inevitably be different from a small, isolated school where there is perhaps one pupil whose origin is not within the local community. Thus, when rethinking 'child-centred' education, it is important to consider what is at the centre of the child in terms of identity and cultural diversity, what personal meanings the children hold, and the ways in which these shape children's interests and orientations to schooling.

The influences of identity and cultural diversity are exemplified in research by Levinson (2005, 2008) and Brooker (2002, 2010). This research is important to teachers because it highlights the tensions that can arise for a child as a result of two different sets of expectations and experiences. Levinson has carried out ethnographic studies of children and their families in Gypsy and traveller communities, and has provided some striking contrasts between the range of child-initiated activities that children experience in their home settings and their experiences in schools. He argues that children's orientations to learning in school and home contexts are divergent, for a number of reasons:

Apart from the skills that are acquired at home, less tangible learning is also occurring – the acquisition of wider social skills, the ability to adapt quickly between tasks, the growth of self-confidence, independence and group identity. To some degree, such learning might be expected to complement that acquired in formal schooling, but there are certain tensions that make this less likely. In both content and style, learning is divergent from that encountered at school; of still greater significance, from an early age, children are part of an adult world. Already socialized into such a world, the hierarchical divisions at school are likely to strike the Gypsy child as being neither natural nor logical.

(Levinson 2008: 74)

Levinson also juxtaposes the concept of learner autonomy in home and school contexts:

At home, they were often expected to work on their own initiative, and this brought status. J.R. (aged 20s) was proud that his 7 year old son, Billy, could be left to change spark-plugs on a car, a skill acquired through observation then encouragement. In contrast, it is argued that school education does not permit children to 'learn at their own speed' or 'to pick things up on their own'. Such remarks are revealing in their implication of: (a) undue pressure on the learner at school, and (b) a substantial degree of autonomy granted to the learner at home. This entails both the (spatial) freedom to move around during learning, and the (temporal) freedom to decide when to stop, start and take breaks in learning.

(Levinson 2008: 75)

This is an interesting juxtaposition, because it alerts teachers to the fact that concepts such as choice, freedom, and autonomy have contrasting meanings in home and school contexts. The interests that children develop at home may not be easily expressed or accommodated in school contexts, especially if teachers have little knowledge or understanding of children's home cultures and experiences. Therefore it may be difficult for children to initiate learning if they cannot make meaningful connections.

Similarly, research by Brooker (2002) on young children's transition to a reception class highlights cultural differences between the participants (working-class Anglo and Bangladeshi families) that influenced children's orientations to school and their expectations of appropriate behaviours and activities in the classroom. The established pedagogic discourse of free play and free choice made it difficult for the children from Bangladeshi homes to adjust to the culture of the classroom. In their home environments, they had not been prepared for these approaches to learning, and the concept of children being independent and autonomous was unfamiliar to parents. Brooker's research also highlights some of the tensions in the traditional child-centred pedagogic discourse: children are required to show compliance with the rules of the setting, but at the same time are expected to direct their own learning through choosing their own activities (both individually and with others). The studies by Levinson and Brooker ask teachers to raise some challenging questions about an uncritical commitment to child-centred education, and to child-initiated learning, particularly in relation to the skills and interests children develop at home, whether these can be transferred into school contexts, and even whether they are recognised by teachers as valued forms of learning.

Teachers themselves, or schools, may be sources of tension for children's self-initiation. For example, certain types of interests and activities may be banned if they do not meet with the teacher's approval, or if there are health and safety implications. Such activities include rough and tumble play, superhero play and war or weapons play (Holland 2003; Jarvis 2010). In addition, children's interests that are based on popular culture may be sidelined in favour of interests that are approved by teachers.

It follows that if certain interests are banned, then certain areas of learning may also be denied to children. For example, in her research on young children's self-initiated activities during playtimes, Jarvis (2010) identifies many complex skills and routines that children develop to initiate and maintain play. These included older children mentoring the younger ones into the complex rule construction that framed their games of football, modelling the negotiation of rules, communicating playground rituals and customs, and developing social networks. The research by Jarvis reveals that child-initiated learning activities may incorporate levels of complexity that are not accessible to teachers unless they take the time to understand the ways in which children's interests are the driving force for forms of learning that are intrinsically meaningful for them. Therefore a key pedagogical challenge is to consider how the levels of motivation and engagement that children demonstrate in their self-initiated activities could be harnessed during teacher-initiated activities.

Reflection

How would you analyse and define the culture of your school? How does that culture affect your planning in terms of the curriculum you teach and the learning/teaching methods you use?

Child-initiated learning – new directions

One of the key principles of the Independent Review is that planning the curriculum around 'a carefully constructed amalgam of areas of learning and subjects' deepens children's interests and understanding as they use and apply the knowledge and skills gained in one subject, or area of learning, in another (DCSF 2008: 34). The Independent Review has opened the door to more cross-curricular approaches, but has none the less explicitly rejected the more open-ended kind of 'laissez-faire' approaches:

> Good primary teaching involves far more than waiting for children to develop by following their every whim. It deliberately deepens and widens children's understanding by firing their imagination and interest and paving the way to higher achievement through 'scaffolding' learning in a community of learners. As envisaged by Vygotsky and other well-respected cognitive researchers, good teaching means that 'what children can do with adult support today they can do unaided tomorrow'.
>
> (DCSF 2009: 56 para. 3.6)

The rejection of laissez-faire approaches reflects the long-standing tensions in teachers' pedagogical roles, particularly regarding the extent to which teachers should respond to or provoke children's interests as a means of supporting child-initiated learning. Imagine a line, or continuum, with teacher-controlled learning at one end of it and laissez-faire approaches at the other. Most of us would feature at a point along the line rather than at one extreme or the other. We take a pragmatic view that this is not an 'either/or' choice, because cross-curricular pedagogical approaches should enable teachers to do both.

As De Vries (1997) argues, providing activities that appeal to children's interests shows respect for the child's point of view, and for how they learn and develop. She also distinguishes between general interests and specific purposes: general interest in an activity gives the teacher an opportunity to challenge children to pursue a specific purpose, and to find their own purposes in an activity. But it should also be remembered that children's interests can be content-rich, in that those interests typically form the springboard for developing their knowledge, skills understanding, and areas of specialist expertise, as demonstrated by Jarvis (2010) and Levinson (2008). In addition, shared or group interests (especially in play activities) support social affiliation, friendship skills, empathy, and collaborative learning.

Responding to children's interests therefore implies reciprocal engagement between adults and children, in ways that challenge and extend children's knowledge. In addition, children should develop 'mastery orientations' to learning, which involves taking risks, making mistakes, using enquiry and problem-solving capabilities and developing meta-cognitive awareness of their own learning capabilities. The concept of reciprocal engagement is fundamental to cross-curricular pedagogical approaches. Teachers inevitably tune in to the many different ways in which children learn, in order to understand their interests and motivations, and how these can be supported through responsive curriculum planning. This concept is illustrated in an example (Case Study 3.1) from a Year 1 class.

This vignette demonstrates what experienced teachers already know: that children's interests by themselves do not constitute the basis for successful learning. Rather it is the ability of the teacher to help children to make connections across areas of learning and experience, by integrating subject content knowledge as well as real-life experiences, and making creative use of indoor and outdoor learning environments. Children's interests are

Case Study 3.1 Integrated pedagogical approaches – learning outdoors

A primary school had recently invested in developing the outdoor learning environment, which included a vegetable garden, spaces for play and den-building, a fire circle, and a wild area with a pond. A group of four boys developed an interest in 'bugs' which was provoked by finding a large colony of woodlice under some rotting logs. This was developed by the teacher as a group interest, to include learning about respect for the environment, and finding ways of investigating insects and other creatures without harming them or their natural habitats. As the children's interests developed, their purposes became more refined: they used a range of equipment to investigate living things in the environment, including binoculars, digital cameras (still and video images), and magnifying glasses. They recorded their investigations in different ways, including drawings, classification charts, and ICT equipment. Their interest in classification was supported by the teacher through guided use of books, websites and understanding how entomologists study and classify insects. As a result of their observations, the children were highly motivated to learn how to use the electronic microscope, and to upload and record the images on the computer. Some children pursued related activities at home such as visiting museums and creating small wild areas in their own gardens. Artistic responses included making large sculptures and models of some of the creatures from natural materials, which were placed in the outdoor area, and doing detailed observational drawings based on the enlarged computer images.

The initial interests of the four boys became shared interests across the whole class as new investigations were planned. The teacher continued to challenge their thinking, add new areas of knowledge and understanding, and suggest further areas for investigation. This combined responsive planning (building on what emerged from the children's activities and interests) with her own planning (making decisions about what areas of knowledge and understanding to add, or what investigations to provoke with the children). She responded to their affective as well as cognitive engagement in the project, and made sure that the indoor and outdoor learning environments were well equipped to support the development of the topic. In these ways, the children's interests became the focus for shared and purposeful modes of enquiry, where they were engaged in creating and solving problems, and gaining new knowledge and skills. Moreover, the teacher and children co-constructed contexts for using and applying cross-curricular knowledge and skills, which is a key recommendation in the Independent Review of the Primary Curriculum (DCSF 2009). The integrated pedagogical model used here is based on theories of guided participation and co-construction, where differently knowledgeable people support each other's learning, drawing on the tools, knowledges and resources of the community (Plowman and Stephen 2007).

often driven by their fascination with the world, and their motivation to become more knowledgeable, more competent, and more confident in using and applying their skills in different contexts. In other words, their interests are dynamic and not static. Children's interests are also linked to the diverse ways in which they develop and express personal identities, and the extent to which they feel included, respected, and valued in a learning community. If children are surrounded by discrimination and conflict, they will learn that their interests are not valued, which may lead to feelings of exclusion and disaffection. Therefore, contemporary versions of child-centred education must see learning as a multi-dimensional process whereby children's interests arise and can be extended in diverse home and school contexts.

Developing cross-curricular pedagogical approaches

There is clear theoretical justification for supporting teachers and headteachers in developing cross-curricular pedagogical approaches in schools in order to incorporate new approaches to learning through information and communication technologies (ICT), to integrate formal and informal approaches to learning, and to build on children's interests in ways that provoke further challenge and extension. From a theoretical perspective, latest theories suggest that children's learning, development, and identity formation are socially and culturally situated – that is, they cannot be divorced from their social contexts. Children are an integral part of, not separate from, complex cultural belief systems and practices. They are bound up in complex relationships between the home and community, educational institutions and wider society (Hedeggard and Fleer 2008). As teachers we need not simply to appreciate this theoretical standpoint but to apply that knowledge to our understanding of our own pupils' learning and learning experiences.

New interpretations of child-initiated learning rest on a number of theoretical assumptions. Important among these are the following:

- Children are not just 'active learners' but are active agents in their own learning and development and active participants in cultural communities.
- Children's repertoires of activity and participation are culturally shaped with adults and peers, and with cultural tools, resources, and symbol systems.
- Thus different social practices provoke qualitatively different changes in children's learning and development, as documented by Levinson (2008) and Brooker (2002).
- It follows that children's repertoires of participation provoke different forms of activities, based on their motivation and interests.
- Participation also provokes situated agency – children actively engage in the social construction of their own identities and subjectivities (how they see themselves as individuals, and how they see themselves in relation to others).

Children's interests derive from many different sources, including shared childhood cultures and popular culture. Childhood cultures involve shared meanings and experiences, and opportunities for building peer relationships, all of which contribute to shared interests and identities. Children are also fascinated by the world of adults, but their interests are driven not merely by wanting to be adults, but by wanting to experience what they perceive as adult control, autonomy, and decision-making. These processes are often visible in children's imaginative play activities when they act out adults' roles, particularly when they exaggerate power and control, or create roles that disrupt adults' power, such as being wild animals, destructive monsters, and naughty pets, or taking on magical powers as fairies, witches, and wizards (Wood and Cook 2009).

From children's perspectives, play is also about subversion and inversion, order and disorder, chaos and stability, inclusion and marginalisation, which is where issues of power, agency, and control are played out. Therefore the interests that children pursue in their play tend to have personal relevance for their social, affective, and cognitive development. Anyone who has watched children at play can see these processes at work, for example in the child who knocks over the brick tower he and others have been building with great care; in the comings and goings of friendships and alliances; and in attachment to some traditional (if not politically correct) entertainments such as Punch and Judy.

A key to successful learning lies in the teacher's awareness of children's play activities and the learning which is associated with it. In order for teachers to achieve a successful upward extension of the EYFS pedagogies into Key Stage 1, much greater attention needs to be paid to how children's play changes and develops, and the ways in which school provision can support challenge and extension.

Learning takes place in many different contexts – in homes, schools, communities, and in virtual and online worlds. Traditional boundaries between these different learning contexts are dissolving, and the increasing use of electronic media is merging the personal, the local, and the global in terms of the knowledge that can be accessed, and the ways in which it can be used. Therefore child-initiated learning is increasingly taking place not just in new technological spaces but in much wider spheres. In developing cross-curricular pedagogical approaches, teachers need to utilise ICT and new media technologies in creative ways, because they are helping to break down hierarchical barriers between 'teachers' and 'learners', and to create contexts for collaborative learning where risk-taking, creative problem-solving, and creativity are encouraged (Yelland et al. 2008).

But a key issue for education – that is, for teachers and heads – is whether policy frameworks are keeping pace with these changes, and whether school-based practices are reflecting the complexities and diversities of children's everyday interests, knowledge, and experiences. Children's opportunities for successful self-initiated learning depend on flexible learning environments in which they can draw on their own funds of knowledge and experience and incorporate them into school experiences, in traditional face-to-face and virtual contexts.

Cross-curricular pedagogical approaches create opportunities for co-construction and engagement between adults and children, and between peers, which contribute not just to achieving defined learning outcomes but also to children's identities, self-image, and self-esteem. In pursuing their own interests, children generate and test out their own ideas, build personal (and sometimes idiosyncratic) theories about their social and cultural worlds, and often build identity markers, such as developing expertise in using computers, being an expert footballer, or being a good co-player. Contemporary research (especially in the field of ICT) indicates that peer learning can be productively co-constructive within integrated approaches (Plowman and Stephen 2007; Yelland et al. 2008).

In summary, as teachers explore their new curriculum freedoms in a changing climate of increased teacher autonomy, the concept of 'repertoires not recipes' is central to the kinds of changes that need to come about in terms of repertoires of teaching, and in the repertoires of learning activities that are available to children. By using cross-curricular pedagogical approaches, teachers can plan in proactive and responsive ways. Proactive planning involves identifying intentional learning outcomes, and designing activities that will lead to those outcomes. Responsive planning includes observing and responding to the ways in which children develop the teacher's planned activities, as well as initiating their own activities.

An integrated model of planning (see Chapter 9) is likely to be quite demanding of teachers' time, skills, and expertise. In addition, it may mean that schools review their adherence to fixed planning cycles centred on specific themes or topics (if it's autumn term in Year 1 then it's 'People Who Help Us'). Letting go of the recipes may prove to be a challenging and potentially difficult process, which does not mean 'going back' to outdated models of planning themes and topics. Developing cross-curricular pedagogical approaches is challenging but much more rewarding than the command and control models of the last twenty years. Teachers will be able to use their pedagogical repertoires in creative and innovative ways, but will need to develop a much more critical understanding of child-initiated learning.

Reflection

How can you find out about the diversity and complexity of children's knowledge and interests, based on their home and community cultures?

In what ways can ICT be used to support children's choices, and to enhance their learning?

To what extent does your provision enable children to choose how they communicate in multi-modal ways?

What resources would enable you to create multi-literate and multi-modal means of enhancing children's learning, thinking, and communicating?

Analysing learning in a classroom setting

It is usually the case that the youngest learners in educational settings have the most freedom to choose and initiate their own activities. But how do we come to understand the value of those activities in terms of what the children choose to do, how the activity developed, what actually happened, and how we plan further activities? Read the observation in Case Study 3.2. You should reflect on your own responses to the observation, in terms of how you read and interpret what is happening before you read the accompanying notes that follow. This Case Study indicates the importance of adult observations of children's activities, and how these can inform integrated pedagogical approaches.

Reflection

How do you think the children are interpreting what is happening in Case Study 3.2? How would you plan responsively to support the children's learning and development? What does this episode reveal about child-initiated learning?

Case Study 3.2 Learning in progress

Foundation Stage setting (children are all age 3–4), Listening corner, 15.7.09, 9.45am (CD player with six headphones which the children are able to manage themselves).

Leanne, Jed, Joseph, and Alfie are wearing headphones and using the leads as microphones. They are singing and dancing along to the music. Jed, Joseph, and Alfie are wearing capes. Gail and Owen try to join.

Leanne (to Gail and Owen): You two aren't allowed in here. Go away, you haven't got these on (points to headphones) so you aren't allowed.

Gail: I'm allowed cos I'm the policeman. (She is wearing the police tabard and cap.)

Owen leaves the area and returns wearing headphones. He plugs them in and starts dancing along with the others, with obvious enjoyment.

Leanne: Look, Owen's allowed cos he's got these on, same as me (points to headphones).

Jed: You can't come in here if you're not a bat cos we're all bats.

Jed, Joseph, and Alfie are trying to negotiate some rules about imaginative play involving bats. They leave the area. Gail has tried to take the earphones from Leanne, who immediately goes into high-pitched crying and sobbing. The teacher persuades her to give her headphones to another child, and Leanne leaves the area. Close by two younger girls are absorbed in playing with a large doll's house. Leanne stands close by, absolutely still. She drops her head and looks sad, but at the same time glances sideways at the doll's house activity. I ask her what she wants to do.

Leanne: There's two girls and they don't want another girl to play with them.

I suggest that Leanne asks the girls if she can join, which she does. Henry has already joined without asking permission, and takes a place in front of the doll's house. The two girls walk away without saying anything.

Leanne: Henry, Henry, Henry, Henry, Henry.

Henry ignores her.

Leanne: Henry can I play? Can I play with you?

EW: Henry, Leanne is asking you a question. I think she would like to play with you.

Henry looks at Leanne.

Leanne: Can I play, Henry?

Henry nods. They play in parallel, with some self-speech and some interaction. Faye joins in, but is not interacting with Henry and Leanne.

Leanne: Here's the baby, Henry. Look at the baby.

Henry looks in her direction but offers no response. Leanne places her pony and play people very precisely in two rooms. There is some brief interaction between Henry and Faye but mostly about which rooms they can play in. They are each sticking to their own spaces, even though there has been no negotiation of which space 'belongs' to each child. Parallel play continues to 10.35 (snack time), with little engagement between the children.

Some reflections on Case Study 3.2

Once you have read Case Study 3.2 and carried out the Reflection associated with it, read on to compare your views with my own as I analyse this sequence. In the paragraphs that follow I reflect on this episode and suggest some ways in which it may have contributed to children's learning.

The six children at the listening corner were clearly enjoying the experience, so it could be claimed that they were learning to use the technology and to enjoy shared participation in a very lively activity (dancing, singing along, laughing). However, negotiating access and inclusion was, for these young children, more problematic, which makes me think more carefully about the ways in which children might be interpreting these events. They had some understanding of how the 'rules' of access sometimes work in child-initiated activities – having the right props, being a member of an established friendship group, or being seen as a play leader. Jed, Joseph, and Alfie left the activity because they seemed to be more engaged in their ongoing 'bat' play. Leanne left because she knew the rules about taking turns, but seemed unable to cope with this at an emotional level.

It could be argued that Leanne needs further support with her social skills in terms of accessing an activity and taking turns, both of which require some degree of empathy and altruism – seeing another person's perspective and giving up one's own place willingly to someone else. In the house play the children have chosen the same activity, but their actions and perspectives are not aligned, and there is little interaction between them. As there is little language or social interaction, it is difficult to determine the content or focus of their individual activities, or what they might be learning. From a pedagogical perspective, it might be useful to consider what other experiences could be planned to develop the children's social skills and play skills, and to enhance the learning potential of their self-initiated activities. However, at a deeper level, I am left pondering the personal meaning of these activities to the children, and the social and relational complexities involved in self-initiated activities.

Conclusion

The trends at work within the Primary Curriculum offer considerable scope for change and development in early years and primary education, particularly regarding a 'ground-up' extension of cross-curricular pedagogies from the Foundation Stage into Key Stages 1 and 2. However, as is always the case, teachers need to be proactive (rather than merely reactive) in how these policies are implemented in practice. In order to develop cross-curricular pedagogical approaches, teachers need detailed understanding of children's funds of knowledge, and the ways in which these can be connected and extended across adult-initiated and child-initiated activities. It is also important for teachers to take into account children's diverse backgrounds, and the ways in which they can use their interests as the springboard for further learning, so that children can develop as master players and master learners.

References

Alexander, R. (2009) *Children, Their World, Their Education* London: Routledge

Brooker, L. (2002) *Starting School – young children learning cultures* Buckingham: Open University Press

Brooker, L. (2010) 'Learning to play in cultural context' in P. Broadhead, J. Howard, and E. Wood (eds) *Play and Learning in Early Childhood Settings* London: Sage

Department for Children, Schools and Families (2008) *The Interim Report of the Independent Review of the Primary Curriculum* http://publications.teachernet.gov.uk (accessed June 2009)

Department for Children, Schools and Families (2009) *Independent Review of the Primary Curriculum* http://publications.teachernet.gov.uk (accessed October 2009)

Department for Education and Skills (2008) *The Early Years Foundation Stage* http://www.standards.dfes.gov.uk/primary/foundation_stage/eyfs/

DeVries, R. (1997) 'Piaget's social theory' *Educational Researcher* 26 (2): 4–17

Fassler, R. and Levin, D. (2008) 'Envisioning and supporting the play of preschoolers' in C. Genishi and A.L. Goodwin (eds) *Diversities in Early Childhood Education – rethinking and doing* New York: Routledge

Genishi, C. and Goodwin, A.L. (2008) *Diversities in Early Childhood Education – rethinking and doing* New York: Routledge

Hedeggard, M. and Fleer, M. (2008) *Studying Children: a cultural-historical approach* Maidenhead: McGraw Hill

Holland, P. (2003) *We Don't Play With Guns Here: war, weapon and superhero play in the early years* Maidenhead: Open University Press

Jarvis, P. (2010) '"Born to play": the biocultural roots of "rough and tumble" play, and its impact upon young children's learning and development' in P. Broadhead, J. Howard, and E. Wood (eds) *Play and Learning in Education Settings* London: Sage

Levinson, M.P. (2005) 'The role of play in the formation and maintenance of cultural identity: gypsy children in home and school contexts' *Journal of Contemporary Ethnography* 34 (5): 499–532

Levinson, M.P. (2008) 'Issues of empowerment and disempowerment: gypsy children at home and school' *International Journal of Citizenship Education* 4 (2): 70–7

Plowman, L. and Stephen, C. (2007) 'Guided interaction in pre-school settings' *Journal of Computer Assisted Learning* 23: 14–26

Rogers, S. and Evans, J. (2008) *Inside Role Play in Early Childhood Education: researching young children's perspectives* London: Routledge

Smith, P. (2009) *Children and Play* Oxford: Wiley-Blackwell

Wood, E. (2009) 'Conceptualising a pedagogy of play: international perspectives from theory, policy and practice' in D. Kuschner (ed.) *From Children to Red Hatters®: diverse images and issues of play. Play and Culture Studies, Vol. 8,* Lanham, Maryland: University Press of America

Wood, E. (2010) 'Challenging play' in S. Edwards and L. Brooker (eds) *Engaging Play* Maidenhead: Open University Press

Wood, E. and Attfield, J. (2005) *Play, Learning and the Early Childhood Curriculum* (2nd edn) London: Paul Chapman Press

Wood, E. and Cook, J. (2009) 'Gendered discourses and practices in role play activities: a case study of young children in the English Foundation Stage' *Journal of Educational and Child Psychology* 26 (2): 19–30

Yelland, N., Lee, L., O'Rourke, M., and Harrison, C. (2008) *Rethinking Learning in Early Childhood Education* Maidenhead: Open University Press

Chapter 4

The cross-curricular approach in Key Stage 1

Jane Johnston

Introduction

This chapter is based on a case study example of good practice at Key Stage 1 (KS1) which illustrates the following principles of effective KS1 practice:

- Learning should be child-centred.
- Learning should be practical and exploratory.
- Learning is best acquired through motivating experiences.
- Learning is enhanced through effective peer interaction.
- Learning requires effective adult support and interaction.
- Learning is most effective in cross-curricular contexts.

It also considers how children move from the early Early Year Foundation Stage (EYFS) to KS1 and into Key Stage 2 (KS2). Thus the chapter links Chapters 3 and 5.

Thematic teaching at Key Stage 1

Childhood today is significantly different from other generations. For example, children are rich in electronic stimuli, but poor in the quality of relationships (Bowlby 2006). Children have more pressures on them to grow up and yet they have less freedom in which to develop (Palmer 2006). Education is more formalised than in the 1960s and 1970s and yet educational performance is considered to be less good. Whilst teaching, particularly at KS1, we have to accommodate not only social changes but also the conflicting pedagogical advice and changes to the curriculum. We have to navigate our way through the expectations and demands placed upon us and still provide motivating and relevant experiences for children, which are manageable in the school context and have clear learning outcomes. An integrated approach to learning popular in the 1960s was weakened by the introduction of a National Curriculum with discrete subjects, discredited by the Alexander *et al.* (1992) discussion paper and further weakened by national strategies (DfEE 1998, 1999a). When most primary teachers had adapted their practice or left the classroom and new teachers had no real experience of integrated, thematic approaches, it was realised that the curriculum lacked relevance and pedagogical approaches stifled creativity. The introduction of a skills-based and more thematic early years curriculum (QCA 2000; DCSF 2008a) has had a positive impact on learning and teaching at KS1. For example, some primary schools are using the six key areas of the Early Years Foundation Stage (DCSF 2008a) as a basis for planning, teaching, and learning at KS1; and the introduction of the primary strategy (DfES

2003a) and advice on improving creativity (QCA 2003; Wilson 2009) have also been supportive of changes towards more integrated and child-centred approaches and away from the more formal curriculum-focused approaches which were common in KS1 in the late 1990s. The Rose Review (Rose 2009) advocates a cross-curricular approach to learning and teaching, identifying that it strengthens subjects and supports understandings.

Planning for cross-curricular or topic work

Cross-curricular topic work has some distinct advantages over teaching discrete subjects or concepts. It makes learning relevant and motivating for children and enables children to see the relationships between different subjects. It also enables larger areas of the curriculum to be covered, as one activity can address objectives in a number of areas. For example, when baking (see example below) children can be developing aspects of speaking and listening (English), measurements (mathematics), how materials change (science) and evaluation skills (design technology). The groupings of subjects proposed in the Rose Review (2009) are these:

* Understanding English, communication, and languages
* Mathematical understanding
* Scientific and technological understanding
* Historical, geographical, and social understanding
* Understanding physical development, health, and wellbeing
* Understanding the arts.

This suggested grouping goes some way to support more thematic approaches to development and learning. It is still disappointing that there remain differences between the curriculum approaches of the Early Years Foundation Stage (DCSF 2008a) and the new review of primary education (Rose 2009): effective planning is essential in any teaching, but is particularly important in a topic approach (see also Chapter 3 in this volume). This is because, when planning for topic work, we need to be familiar with the concepts inherent in the National Curriculum (DfEE 1999b) to ensure that we are aware of the learning outcomes we desire for the children we teach. We also need confidence in the pedagogical approaches that are the most effective for this type of teaching. Planning needs to ensure that learning approaches are well matched to the needs and abilities of each child in the class. Whilst this sounds daunting in reality, well-planned topics that take into account individual needs:

* Have clear learning outcomes in a number of National Curriculum areas (even crossing the groupings of the new primary curriculum (Rose 2009)
* Are open-ended enough to allow individual children to develop at their own rate (see Kerry 2002a; Johnston et al. 2007)
* Use assessment for learning (Black and Wiliam 2004) to inform on individual children – this last is different from the Assessing Pupils' Progress initiative (DCFS 2009), which conflicts with the principles of personalised learning and assessment for learning.

Planning should also consider the learning environment, as this supports development in a whole range of ways. The classroom environment should be such as to encourage and motivate children, through interactive displays and motivating resources that encourage children to be curious, to want to learn and to feel safe to learn. A questioning environment is one that encourages curiosity and interest and enquiry.

Planning for the learning environment should also consider the opportunities for using the outside environment. Even urban schools set in concrete and brick playgrounds provide a multitude of learning opportunities. Exploration of the school grounds and pavements in the surrounding area will identify evidence of life, such as plants growing in cracks in the paving (science). Patterns can be seen in grates, brickwork, and roof tiles (art). Local shops can be visited so that children can map the variety of community services (geography), customers interviewed to see how they rate the services (English and geography), and a tally of the number of customers can be made and later plotted on a graph (mathematics). A local general store can lead to consideration of the origin of different products (geography), how goods are packaged (design and technology), and value for money (mathematics). Observing the buildings in the street can produce evidence of the ages of the buildings through different brickwork, windows, front doors, and general construction (history; design and technology). Visiting the local church, mosque, temple can lead to under-standing of the local community and different religions (religious education; citizenship) and their musical traditions (music). Some local industries will be happy to allow the children to visit them and set some community or personal tasks for the children. For example, rubbish collectors could set 'green' targets for children to recycle or compost waste; the local park can give children seeds to grow, which can later be planted in the park or window boxes, giving children pride and ownership over their local community; a community dentist may encourage children to improve their dental hygiene.

Reflection

Look at your classroom environment and local community and consider opportunities for topic work.

- How could you change the classroom environment to make it more encouraging for cross-curricular topic work?
- How could you make better use of the local environment to develop opportunities for topic work?

Recent visits to Key Stage 1 classes have identified a variety of different practices in planning. Some schools and teachers advocate detailed weekly plans which have clear learning outcomes and map out ideas for activities and resources. Others provide more detailed daily plans, which identify specifically what children and adults will do throughout the session, differentiated tasks and outcomes, and questions to focus on the learning outcomes. In many ways it does not matter which type of planning is used, but what is important is that planning is effective and focused on the identified learning outcomes, and that the teacher is well prepared for any eventuality. The worst scenario is where teachers spend lengths of time planning but it is wasted time; in reality the teachers are not well prepared, with the result that the activities do not match the learning outcomes, they are not well differentiated for individual learners, they do not challenge, question, or support individual children, and the pace of the activity is too fast or too slow, leading to frustration or boredom.

Case Study 4.1 Mr Bembleman's Bakery

Our case study involves a topic stimulated by the story of Mr Bembleman's Bakery (Green 1978), which is a rich opportunity for looking at a range of curriculum areas in a holistic way, through:

- Reading and deconstructing the story (En2 Reading)
- Understanding the need for standard measures (Ma3 Shape, Space and Measures)
- Exploring materials and how they change when mixed and baked (Sc3 Materials and their Properties; En1 Speaking and Listening)
- Writing recipes for bread (En3 Writing)
- Making bread using different recipes and evaluating the product (D&T)
- Understanding of different family and community traditions (Citizenship).

Specific learning outcomes should be tailored to your own context and children

The topic starts with the story of Mr Bembleman's Bakery (Green 1978). Activities focus on the book, its structure, vocabulary, grammar, tense, and sentence construction. This was planned as a whole-class activity with follow-up activities carried out in small groups of about six children throughout a week. These included:

- The setting up, with the children, of a bakery play area with a range of resources such as balances, oven, tables, playdough, trays, cutters, bowls, spoons, aprons, and baker's hats. If this can be set up near a sink, the children can also be responsible for ensuring their hands are clean when they make and play with dough and for washing up tools used at the end of a session. The children can suggest and collect the resources to go into the bakery. This can also include a range of different breads (fahita, pita, chapatti, sourdough, brioche, ciabatta, etc.).
- Semi-structured play where children can play in and explore the bakery with support, where needed. Children decide what to do and how to do it and usually will start from their own level of learning and decide where they should go next. This approach provides an element of self-differentiation, which is motivating and supports both learning and behaviour.
- Adult-led making of playdough for bakery play area and bread for baking.

Differentiation by support, questioning, and outcome can all be planned for. Support is needed while making playdough and bread to ensure safety and to achieve learning outcomes by challenging the more able and supporting the less able children. Likewise planned questions will be varied to support, challenge, and extend. For example when looking at the use of measures (Ma3), questions include: *Why do we not measure the ingredients with our hands? Why should we not use handfuls and spoonfuls when measuring?* When focusing on the way materials change when mixed or baked (Sc3), questions include: *What does this feel like? What do you think will happen if we cook this?* Questions that focus on vocabulary and speaking and listening (En1) include: *Can you think of another way to describe this? How did you make the bread?*

Differentiation by outcome involves clearly planned expectations for children at different levels. During and after the activity, these can aid assessment (of children) and evaluation (of teaching). For example in this case study differentiated expectations are:

High achievers

- Be able to describe the similarities and differences between materials in their own words and using some scientific vocabulary.
- Be able to predict what will happen when materials are mixed, heated, and cooled.

Middle achievers

- Be able to describe the similarities and differences between materials in own words.
- Be able to suggest what will happen when materials are mixed, heated, or cooled.

Low achievers

- Will require support to describe materials in their own words.
- Can make a simple suggestion as to what will happen to the materials with some support from an adult.

Using differentiated expected outcomes allows us to identify whether the expected learning is at the correct level for the children; if most children achieve the expectations for higher-ability children, then the expectations were too low and if most children needed support to achieve the outcomes, then the expected outcomes were too high. Individual children can be assessed using the expected outcomes and their next step of learning can be planned for.

Reflection

Consider your current planning format and reflect on its effectiveness for:

- Motivating children
- Meeting individual needs through challenge, support and appropriate questioning
- Achieving the learning outcomes in a number of curriculum areas
- Incorporating assessment for learning.

How can you develop your planning in the future?

Individualising cross-curricular topic work

Research tells us, rightly, that learning at Key Stage 1 should be child-centred and personalised as identified and advocated through many policy documents and initiatives, such as the primary strategy (DfES 2003a), *Every Child Matters* (DfES 2003b), *2020 Vision* (DfES 2006) and *Personalised Learning – a practical approach* (DCFS 2008b).

A major aim in education should be to encourage children to take ownership of and responsibility for their own learning; a feature of the High/Scope Cognitively Orientated Curriculum (Hohmann and Weikart 2002). Although the curriculum was designed for children in the Early Years Foundation Stage (DCSF 2008a), some aspects appear relevant for older children. For example, encouraging child autonomy and independence should be a universal goal; yet we structure our curriculum in such a way that whole-class interactive formats initiated by the introduction of the national strategies (DfEE 1998, 1999a), which advocate whole-class teaching approaches, with minimal personalisation and very little real engagement, are too often paramount.

From observations of KS1 lessons it seems that most tend to have the whole-class introduction, individual written tasks (maybe grouped through ability), and a whole-class plenary, even when this format is inappropriate for the task. For example, if the learning objectives involve the development of individual skills, whole-class approaches are less likely to be effective. Children are often passive: sitting and listening for long periods of time. My own analysis of the actual learning or time on task by children in an hour's literacy or numeracy lesson can be very depressing, with individual children learning for less than 25 per cent of the lesson. The High/Scope approach (Hohmann and Weikart 2002) involves children planning their activities before carrying them out and then reviewing them afterwards, in a child-centred, reflective cycle of plan–do–review.

Involving children in their topic has advantages in motivating children, which in turn maximises learning and supports good behaviour. Children are the best resource for identifying their own current abilities and can be involved in identifying what their next learning needs are. As teachers, we can elicit knowledge, understanding, and skills in a variety of ways, such as group concept maps, a simple interactive activity, use of a puppet in a discussion, and use of a concept cartoon. Effective teacher questioning (see Kerry 2002b; Johnston *et al.* 2007) can lead to developed questioning skills for both children and teachers and lead to improved understanding of learning needs as well as raising new questions for exploration, which is the next step of learning. For children to be fully involved in their own learning, it is important that they have clear understandings of their learning expectations and that these are not changed. All too often one sees a child who had been undertaking enthusiastically the work set for him or her; but, when he or she has completed the work early, the teacher sets more work to do. This not only demotivates the child, but creates behavioural problems which can lead even to disruption.

Case Study 4.2 A class discussion

In our topic on Mr Bembleman's Bakery (Green 1978), the adult-led baking provides an opportunity to focus on volume and measurement. Whilst making some bread rolls, the adult asked the children why they thought they needed to measure out the ingredients and why they could not just use their hands (as in the book). This led to an interesting dialogue:

Kelly: My hands are smaller than yours, Miss.
Adult: Do you think that will make a difference when we make our bread?
Joe: We could all put a handful in like in the story.
Kyle: But, but . . . if we did that . . .
Kelly: It would not work right.
Adult: Why?
Kyle: Our hands are different.
Kelly: . . . and the bread would not work properly.
Siobhain: Should we use a spoon?
Joe: The weights!
Adult: Yes, that is right, we should measure the flour and make sure we have the right amount.
Adult (a little later): What should we use to measure the water?
Joe: A cup?
Adult: A good idea. Which cup would be best?
Simon (picking up a measuring beaker): This one with numbers on it.
Adult (asking the other children): What do you think?
All: Yes, Yes.

Later, in the role-play bakery area, Kyle spent a long time pouring water from one short and fat measuring beaker into another taller and thinner (but which held the same volume) and then pouring it back again. He repeated the action over and over again, muttering to himself, '*But that one's bigger*' before he announced to the teacher, '*They are BOTH the same!*'

Reflection

Consider the interactions above:

- How did the two different interactions help Kyle to understand the conservation of volume?
- How could Kyle's understanding be further supported?
- How was Kyle taking ownership over his own learning?

Consider your own teaching:

- How do you provide opportunities for children to take ownership over their own learning?
- What steps can you take to provide more opportunities for children to make their own learning decisions?

Creative topic work

Creativity is a complex concept that has numerous and seemingly diverse definitions, from making or creating in both the arts and science (Prentice 2000), making connections (Duffy 1998), thinking and problem-solving (De Bono 1992; Beetlestone 1998), and risk-taking as well as discovery (Johnston 2004) and innovation. The importance of creative teaching and learning is now well recognised (e.g. DfES 2003a; QCA 2003) and creative topic work is endorsed through recent curricular changes (Rose 2009). Creative topic work is likely to:

- Be planned by teachers who are creative risk-takers and will not just follow imposed pedagogical approaches and who are knowledgeable about the subjects and pedagogical approaches
- Make the links between the different areas of the curriculum in a meaningful and relevant way (Duffy 1998; Rose 2009)
- Allow children to make decisions for themselves, plan their own learning with support and discover things for themselves (DfES 2003a; DCSF 2008a)
- Include learning which is practical and exploratory, with motivating experiences, so that they develop understandings, skills and important attitudes (Johnston and Nahmad-Williams 2008; Bruce 2009).

There are different ways in which creative cross-curricular topic work can be included in the curriculum. Some schools are using the six key areas of the Early Years Foundation Stage (DCSF 2008a) to plan thematic work throughout the primary school (up to Year 6), which incorporates social, emotional, and cognitive development in a seamless way. Some schools provide relevant play areas in all classrooms, so that a history topic on the Second World War may have an air raid shelter, or a geography topic comparing the local environment with a more tropical environment may have half the classroom set up as a school room in a tropical area and the computer corner as the 'School of the Air' schoolroom. Some schools have topics that bridge the transition from one key stage to another and link different aspects of the curriculum and the key stage. Some schools abandon the normal curriculum for a week when the whole school focuses on some thematic topic.

In one school, a teacher had planned a topic week (see also Chapter 10) involving the children in exploring other countries and learning about their geography, history, and nature. The topic started with the children making passports (English, ICT) so that they could travel by air to their chosen destinations. The first destination was Brazil and the children visited a travel agent (geography), decided on their exact destination within Brazil, looked up Brazil on the internet (ICT) and packed their bags ready to go (geography, science). The chairs in the classroom were set out in front of an interactive whiteboard in rows to represent the inside of an aircraft. The teacher acted the role of the air steward and gave them the safety notices and told them to fasten their seat belts. She then put on the screen pictures of Brazil and played some Brazilian music. Finally the pictures change to aerial views of Brazilian landscapes as though they were looking out of an aeroplane window. The final part of the lesson concerned where Brazil was on the map (and colouring it in) and copying the Brazilian flag (geography) and unfortunately did not follow the creative lead of the first part.

An alternative and more creative follow-up would have been to analyse the Brazilian flag, which is full of symbolism: the green background represents the forests, the yellow rhombus the mineral wealth of Brazil, the blue circle shows the sky over Rio de Janeiro on the day Brazil was declared a republic (15 November 1889) and each star group represents the Brazilian states and the number changes when new states are created (originally it was 21 stars and now it is 27). The band represents the equator which crosses Brazil and the motto *Ordem e Progresso* ('Order and Progress') is inspired by a motto by Auguste Comte, *L'amour pour principe et l'ordre pour base; le progrès pour but*: 'Love as a principle and order as the basis; progress as the goal' (Wikipedia 2009).

Analysis of the flag could lead to children designing their own flag to go on their passports with symbols that represent their lives (design technology). Visits to other countries could also look at their flags and the symbolism of each (geography). There are, of course, plenty of other creative ways to follow up such a lesson, such as focusing on the animals of the Amazon (science) and looking at weird or amazing facts about the animals. They could then apply them to themselves (if I had the strength of a soldier ant I could

Figure 4.1 The flag of Brazil

lift . . .; or if I could move as slowly as a sloth, it would take me . . . long to get to school). They could also create a fictional animal using a number of the weird and amazing facts about different animals. Another follow-up could include using some of the songs from *Yanamamo*, a musical written by Peter Rose and Anne Conlon (2006) which is very suitable for young children (music).

Case Study 4.3 Creativity

In our case study exemplar of Mr Bembleman's Bakery (Green 1978), the role-play area provides opportunities for children to be creative. The children decide whether to make pizzas, bread, cakes, and for what purpose. They create new pizza toppings, design advertising leaflets or sales lists or packaging for the products they make. They design and change the layout of the bakery so that it runs efficiently and decide the roles and responsibilities of the different people working there.

Rajat and Hafiza decided to turn the bakery into a cake shop making sweets for the festival of Diwali. They found a recipe for Sohan papdi (a square sweet made with sugar, gram flour, flour, ghee, milk, and cardamom) on the internet and printed it out.

Ingredients
1¼ cup gram flour
1¼ cup plain flour (maida)
250 g ghee (clarified butter)
2½ cups sugar
1 cup water
2½ tbsp milk
½ tsp cardamom seeds

Instructions
1 Sift both flours together. Then heat ghee (clarified butter) in a pan.
2 Add flour mixture and roast on low heat till light golden. Keep aside to cool a little, stirring occasionally.
3 Now make syrup out of sugar. Bring syrup to 2½ thread consistency. Pour at once into the flour mixture.
4 Beat well with a large fork till the mixture forms thread-like flakes. Pour on to a greased surface or thali and roll to 1 inch thickness lightly.
5 Sprinkle the elaichi (cardamom) seeds and gently press down with palm.
6 Cool, cut into squares, store in airtight container.

The teacher purchased the ingredients and the children in the class all made some sweets for their Diwali celebrations. Whilst they were doing this, Omar and Hafiza decorated the bakery role-play area and dressed themselves in their best clothes. They explained the festival of Diwali to the rest of the children and then all the class joined in the Diwali celebrations using the role-play area.

Reflection

- How do your plans for cross-curricular work provide opportunities for creativity?
- How can you develop your plans to increase opportunities for children to be creative?

Try out some of your ideas and reflect on the learning outcomes.

- How did the creative aspects aid the learning outcomes for the children?

Interactive learning through cross-curricular approaches

A key feature of topic work involves children in learning with others in an interactive way. In learning at Key Stage 1, children should not only be independent learners, who develop through solitary play and activities, but should also learn through peer interaction. Rogoff (1995: 139) has identified three 'inseparable, mutually constituting (sociocultural) planes': the personal, interpersonal, and community/contextual, which together aid learning. Children learn as much, if not more, from the social interaction they have with their peers and so topics that take this into account and maximise the opportunities for interaction are likely to be the most effective. However, the importance of effective adult support and interaction (Vygotsky 1962) cannot be overestimated. This interaction should challenge all children, advancing them cognitively (see Shayer and Adey 2002), and supports individuals appropriately by scaffolding learning and modelling learning and behaviours as appropriate.

Case Study 4.4 Increasing vocabulary

In our case study exemplar of Mr Bembleman's Bakery (Green 1978), the adult-led activity of baking encourages children to describe the material ingredients in their own words and introduce new words as appropriate to develop scientific vocabulary. Children are encouraged to predict what will happen when the materials are mixed, heated, or cooled, and to describe changes in their own words, with the adult modelling predictions and making their own suggestions that the children can discuss.

In the bakery role-play area, the children weigh, measure, play with dough, using the words used in the adult-led area, thus internalising the words into their own vocabulary, and gaining a better understanding of them.

Reflection

Set up an interactive topic activity so that children can interact with each other during their learning. Observe their interaction; you could try videoing them and make notes of the interactions you observe.

- How does the interaction affect the children's learning?
- What parts of the interaction are the most effective? Why do you think this is?

Video your own interaction with a child or group of children. This could follow on from the peer interaction or precede the peer interaction. This can be a bit scary, but can be very helpful in improving your own practice.

- How does your interaction support the children's learning?
- What else could you do to facilitate the children's learning through your interaction?

References

Alexander, R., Rose, J., and Woodhead, C. (1992) *Curriculum Organisation and Classroom Practice in Primary Schools: a discussion paper* London: Department for Education and Science

Beetlestone, F. (1998) *Creative Children, Imaginative Teaching* Buckingham: Open University Press

Black, P. and Wiliam, D. (2004) *Working Inside the Black Box: assessment for learning in the classroom* London: Nelson.

Bowlby, R. (2006) *The Need for Secondary Attachment Figures in Childcare* www.telegraph.co.uk/opinion/main.jhtml?xml=/opinion/2006/10/21/nosplit/dt2101.xml#head5Childcareproblems

Bruce, T. (2009) *Early Childhood* (2nd edn) London: Sage

DCSF (2008a) *The Early Years Foundation Stage: setting the standard for learning, development and care for children from birth to five; practice guidance* London: DCSF

DCFS (2008b) *Personalised Learning – a practical approach* Nottingham: DCFS

DCFS (2009) *The National Strategy – assessing pupils' progress (APP)* accessed on http://nationalstrategies.standards.dcsf.gov.uk/primary/assessment/assessingpupilsprogressapp

De Bono, E. (1992) *Serious Creativity* London: Harper Collins

DfEE (1998) *The National Literacy Strategy* London: DFEE

DfEE (1999a) *The National Numeracy Strategy* London: DFEE

DfEE (1999b) *The National Curriculum: handbook for teachers in England* London: DfEE/QCA

DfES (2003a) *Excellence and Enjoyment: a strategy for primary schools* London: DfES

DfES (2003b) *Every Child Matters* London: DfES

DfES (2006) *2020 Vision: report of the Teaching and Learning in 2020 Review Group* London: DfES

Duffy, B. (1998) *Supporting Creativity and Imagination in the Early Years* Buckingham: Open University Press

Green, M. (1978) *Mr Bembleman's Bakery* New York: Parents Magazine Press

Hohmann, M. and Weikart, D.P. (2002) *Educating Young Children* (2nd edn) Ypsilanti, Michigan: High/Scope Press

Johnston, J. (2004) 'The value of exploration and discovery' *Primary Science Review* 85 (November/December): 21–3

Johnston, J. and Nahmad-Williams, L. (2008) *Early Childhood Studies* Harlow: Pearson

Johnston, J., Halocha, J., and Chater, M. (2007) *Developing Teaching Skills in the Primary School* Maidenhead: Open University Press

Kerry, T. (2002a) *Learning Objectives, Task Setting and Differentiation* Cheltenham: Nelson-Thornes

Kerry, T. (2002b) *Explaining and Questioning* Mastering Teaching Skills Series Cheltenham: Nelson-Thornes

McClure, L. (ed.) (2007) *The Primary Project Box. KS1* Sheffield: The Curriculum Partnership/GA

Palmer, S. (2006) *Toxic Childhood: how the modern world is damaging our children and what we can do about it* London: Orion

Prentice, R. (2000) 'Creativity: a reaffirmation of its place in early childhood education' *The Curriculum Journal* 11 (2): 145–58

QCA (2000) *Curriculum Guidance for the Foundation Stage* London: DFEE

QCA (2003) *Creativity: find it promote it* London: QCA/DFEE

Rogoff, B. (1995) 'Observing sociocultural activity on three planes: participatory appropriation, guided participation, and apprenticeship' in J.V. Wertsch, P. Del Rio, and A. Alvarex (eds) *Sociocultural Studies of Mind* Cambridge: Cambridge University Press: 139–64

Rose, J. (2009) *Independent Review of the Primary Curriculum: final report* Nottingham: DCFS

Rose, P. and Conlon, A. (2006) *Yanamamo: an ecological musical for soloists, chorus, narrator and stage band, commissioned by the Education Department, World Wide Fund for Nature* London: Josef Weinberger

Shayer, M. and Adey, P. (eds) (2002) *Learning Intelligence: cognitive acceleration across the curriculum from 5 to 15 years* Buckingham: Open University Press

Vygotsky, L. (1962) *Thought and Language* Cambridge, Massachusetts: MIT Press

Wikipedia (2009) Flag of Brazil http://en.wikipedia.org/wiki/Flag_of_Brazil#Symbolism

Wilson, A. (2009) *Creativity in Primary Education* (2nd edn) Exeter: Learning Matters

Chapter 5

The cross-curricular approach in Key Stage 2

Christine Farmery

Introduction

This chapter draws together much of the content presented in this book, illustrating the theory in practice within Key Stage 2. It mirrors the preceding chapter, which provided a living example of the integrated approach to the curriculum in Key Stage 1, and leads on to a consideration of the whole-school focus. The chapter thus builds on the theoretical framework set out in Chapter 1 and demonstrates the use of the teaching skills outlined in other chapters, specifically with regard to how effective planning is essential to the success of the approach. A current example of work in progress in Key Stage 2 is set out here in order to provide a critical and analytical commentary of the approach in practice.

Background

This chapter is a personal story. It is not intended as a polemic or even as a mission statement – i.e. follow me, it's the only good way. But it is the story of a conviction: of what works, of why it works, and how others may benefit from its advantages.

As a class teacher I was fortunate to work for many years with a headteacher who believed very strongly that an integrated curriculum was the most effective and successful teaching approach at the primary level. His view was that the introduction of the National Curriculum Orders in 1989 merely brought about a prescribed content to be included within the approach rather than imposing a need to change the approach and move to individual subject lessons. Although this view provided many challenges for the class teacher, time was given to matching the subject-specific content within the individual National Curriculum Orders to suggested topics, and so the school continued to deliver the curriculum using the cross-curricular approach. The later introduction of the National Strategies for Literacy and Numeracy – in 1998 and 1999 respectively – and revisions of the National Curriculum (introduced in 1995 and 2000) did not affect this way of working and were subsumed into the school's curriculum delivery. Consequently, as a new headteacher, I took this philosophy into my headship as I had seen for myself how effective it is for engaging children in their learning, and for providing both the links that enable them to make sense of new knowledge and a meaningful context for developing skills and understandings. My own view was then strengthened by the introduction of *Excellence and Enjoyment* (DfES 2003) and is validated by both the Cambridge Review (Alexander 2009) and the Rose Review (DCSF 2009).

Getting started

On taking up my headship I was presented with a curriculum delivery that was not grounded within the philosophy I was committed to, and therefore I started to introduce the ways of working I wished to see in the school. Previously, the curriculum was addressed through lessons that were mostly subject-exclusive and based firmly on the QCA (Qualifications and Curriculum Association) Schemes of Work. The teachers now needed to become familiar with the requirements of the current National Curriculum Orders (DfEE 2000) upon which the QCA Schemes of Work were based, and to recognise that the Orders set out *what* to teach but not *how* to teach it or at what age they are to be taught. This familiarisation started quite a journey towards the cross-curricular approach that is now embedded across the school.

The staff worked together during the initial move to the integrated approach to allocate the National Curriculum (NC) Programmes of Study to specific year groups, ready for the class teachers to identify a range of topics that would ensure coverage of the NC objectives. However, the knowledge content set out in the NC Orders forms only one part of the Key Stage 2 curriculum; the development of skills – through discovery, thought, interpretation, and discussion – are also extremely important; indeed the key to success for the integrated approach is for children to be able to apply learned skills in different contexts. My school is also committed to using the curriculum to deliver the five outcomes of the *Every Child Matters* agenda (DfES 2004) and the non-statutory elements of the Warwick University Enterprise Education Award (CEI 2007); the planning for each topic thus takes these further requirements into account.

Reflection

Think about your own personal story of how your teaching and your pupils' learning have developed or are developing. What are the key influences? How is this text beginning to guide or change your thinking?

The cross-curricular approach in practice

The integrated approach to the curriculum we use has evolved and changed since it was first outlined by Plowden (1967); it is continuing to evolve as new research provides further theoretical understanding of how the approach can be effective in bringing about deep learning. Although it remains child-centred, as in 1967, it is now much more rigorous at the planning stage (see also Chapter 3). Whereas previously it was acceptable that topics were identified by their title, with the teacher then engaged in considering what activities would 'fit' with the topic title, the teaching and learning are now objective-led and it is this that determines the activities to be undertaken. Using objective-led planning thus ensures that each activity within the topic has a specific purpose, that of a vehicle for the planned learning to take place. Assessment is ongoing and used to identify what the child needs to experience next, thus leading to the identification of the objectives for the next stage of learning and, in turn, to progression in learning. This is illustrated in Figure 5.1.

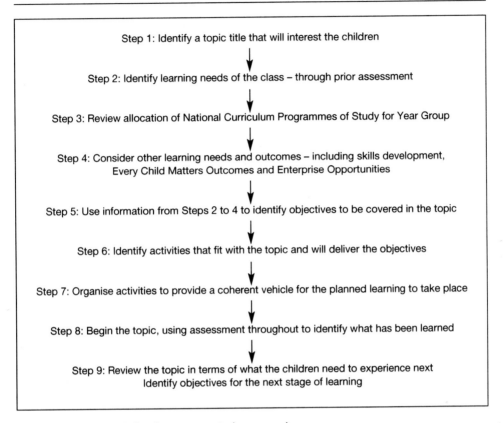

Step 1: Identify a topic title that will interest the children

Step 2: Identify learning needs of the class – through prior assessment

Step 3: Review allocation of National Curriculum Programmes of Study for Year Group

Step 4: Consider other learning needs and outcomes – including skills development, Every Child Matters Outcomes and Enterprise Opportunities

Step 5: Use information from Steps 2 to 4 to identify objectives to be covered in the topic

Step 6: Identify activities that fit with the topic and will deliver the objectives

Step 7: Organise activities to provide a coherent vehicle for the planned learning to take place

Step 8: Begin the topic, using assessment throughout to identify what has been learned

Step 9: Review the topic in terms of what the children need to experience next Identify objectives for the next stage of learning

Figure 5.1 Planning cycle for the cross-curricular approach

Planning cycle for the cross-curricular approach

Using the process outlined in Figure 5.1, the class teacher will begin by reviewing the prior learning of the children, initially through previous assessments and later through a simple activity to elicit the children's current knowledge of the topic, to determine the learning needs of the children. The assessments consulted will have been made the previous term; they may therefore have been made the previous academic year or the previous key stage – i.e. within Key Stage 1. The learning will therefore be identified in terms of the knowledge, skills, and understandings the children need at their next stage of learning. NC requirements will then be considered. As noted earlier, these have been allocated to year groups; the NC requirements are regarded as a minimum entitlement, which means that other areas may be covered but all the NC allocation must be planned for. The objectives to be covered during the full academic year are listed and so the teacher will identify which of the objectives fall naturally into each of the topics they have named for the coming year. However, where objectives to be covered do not naturally fit into a topic tenuous links are never made, and so some discrete lessons and/or mini-topics of a week or two may also be planned.

Other learning needs are then considered, including skills development, and the opportunities afforded by the topic to cover the *Every Child Matters* (DfES 2004) outcomes and the *Enterprise Education* (DCSF 2010) requirements. Through this process, the cross-curricular topic is ensured to be relevant, interesting, motivational, and meaningful to the children and will provide the learning opportunities needed to allow for the coverage of the learning identified thus far; the next stage is therefore to devise a range of activities within which each objective will be covered.

In order to further illustrate in practice the process outlined in Figure 5.1, an aspect of the current Year 5 spring term topic in my school will be outlined here. The full topic centres on a small fishing port and popular holiday resort in North Yorkshire that is a two-to three-hour journey from the school and so makes an ideal destination for a short residential visit. It is a traditional seaside resort that is compact and provides many opportunities for educational study, including the first-hand experience that is essential to the cross-curricular approach to curriculum delivery. Thus, when planning the topic, the learning opportunities to take place before, during, and after the residential visit are explored in order to ensure that the topic presents a coherent package of learning. It is this level of thought and planning that brings necessary rigour to the cross-curricular topic and ensures that learning is both meaningful and set in the context of the 'real world'. It is through this that the children are able to develop skills and understandings that are common to different subject areas and to have opportunities presented for making sense of their learning.

Reflection

Taking the topic title of a nearby coastal resort, what areas of learning can you identify that you could cover with a Key Stage 2 class during a half-term of six weeks?

Planning the cross-curricular topic

Using the process outlined in Figure 5.1, when Stages 1 to 7 have been completed, a topic plan is written but not yet finalised, as it is necessary to elicit the children's current knowledge of the topic to be studied. Thus each topic begins with a simple exercise to determine the children's knowledge and to enable them to initiate their own learning. The exercise requires the teacher to introduce the topic and an overview of the learning opportunities they have identified. The teacher will then ask the children to work in pairs or groups to record both the knowledge they already hold and what they would like to find out about the topic. This too is an essential aspect of the approach we have adopted as it ensures that the children's interests are built upon; previous assessments are brought up to date and the children are starting to take responsibility for their own learning. Therefore, it is following this exercise that the medium-term plan for the topic can be fully completed, although it is still subject to change if appropriate alterations are identified as the topic proceeds. However, it is at this stage that any learning that has been identified by the teacher but demonstrated by the children can be removed from the plan and the children's ideas for learning can be added.

The class teacher then provides an overview of the topic, setting out the activities to be carried out each week: this is known as the Curriculum Balance Matrix for the topic. The matrix is thus used to ensure there is a logical progression to the activities presented through which the learning needs will be addressed; the learning needs are identified as the learning objectives that appear on the medium-term plan. A brief extract from the matrix for the Whitby topic appears in Table 5.1, showing various activities that were identified within the topic; however, it is the study of a lifeboatman – Henry Freeman – that will be discussed in detail. The discussion of this one aspect only is for clarity as the learning taking place through the full topic is quite extensive; indeed, the discussion will illustrate the learning across a range of subject areas, where there are clear links and common skills to be used and developed. Also, for convenience here, the activities are listed under five headings only – those of the core subjects of English (literacy), maths (numeracy), and science; a foundation subjects heading and PSHE/RE heading (personal, social and health education/religious education).

The Curriculum Balance Matrix extract therefore sets out a number of learning opportunities presented through the study of Whitby, with the life of Henry Freeman as a main focus. However, there were other facets to the topic but, as noted earlier, where natural links between the topic and objectives to be covered are not identified, they do not

Table 5.1 Curriculum Balance Matrix: extract from the Year 5 Whitby topic

	Literacy	Numeracy	Science	Foundation subjects	PSHE/R.E.
Week 1	Introduction to topic Henry Freeman biography	Co-ordinates (link to atlas work / location of Whitby)	Investigation into floating and sinking	Location of Whitby (geography) History of RNLI Seascapes (art)	Parts of a church (RE)
Week 2	Write a newspaper article about Henry Freeman	Data handling – in preparation for shopper questionnaires	Coastal erosion	Water pollution (geography) Review water safety leaflet (D & T) Seascapes (art)	Feelings of Henry Freeman (PSHE)
Week 3 In Whitby	Talk by RNLI Visit local museum – includes a Henry Freeman display Visit Whitby Church Field sketches Shopper questionnaires Produce a film documentary and podcast Collate a Whitby fact file				
Week 4 Back in school	Recounting of Whitby visit	Data handling – of results of shopper questionnaires	Introduction to habitats and food chains	Comparison of local area to coastal area (geography) Review of museum exhibits (history) Development of field sketches (art)	Would you volunteer to be a lifeboatman? (PSHE)

feature in the full Curriculum Balance Matrix but are listed on the topic plan. For example, during the term that the topic of Whitby was being studied the focus for PE was coaching by the local rugby team, in preparation for an inter-school rugby tournament; it was accepted that this did not in any way link to the topic and so tenuous links were not made.

Henry Freeman

Henry Freeman is somewhat of a local hero in the resort: a brief biography is presented in the box. Although not born in Whitby he later became a resident of the town and is highly acclaimed for his achievements. Such is his standing that a bronze plaque of him hangs on the wall of the modern Whitby Lifeboat Station, having been chosen to represent the many lifeboatmen who have served locals and visitors to the area and their long history of saving lives at sea. In addition to this tribute at the lifeboat station, there is also a small display at the local museum, there is a written account of his life (Shill and Minter 1991), and various references to him are to be found on the internet. The story of Henry Freeman is therefore 'real' and readily accessible, both in the resort and using published material. It is of particular interest to boys, thus making his study an excellent motivator for them, with girls also enjoying the story of his heroism. It is this that makes the study of Henry Freeman a meaningful context for the children and leads to many learning opportunities, only some of which are explored here in order to enable the reader to understand how an integrated topic can be planned and effectively delivered. It is therefore the learning that it yields, and how such learning takes place across traditional subject boundaries, that are considered here.

Introducing the cross-curricular topic

As noted in Table 5.1, following the introduction of the topic and the exercise to elicit both the children's current knowledge and their desired learning, the life of Henry Freeman is used to provide a context for the learning to take place. It can already be appreciated from the brief biography in the box that the study of Henry Freeman readily lends itself to developing enquiry skills in history; for using and developing reading comprehension skills, and for considering a moral dilemma within PSHE. It also provides a real-life purpose for investigating floating and sinking in science.

Henry Freeman (1835–1904)

Henry Freeman was born in Bridlington, North Yorkshire. As a young man Henry was a brick maker; later in life he became a manager at the brick works where he worked.

Later, when the brick making trade declined, Henry turned to the sea and fishing. He moved to Whitby and became both a fisherman and a lifeboatman. In 1861 Henry was the sole survivor of a lifeboat disaster when a freak wave drowned all his companions. His survival was credited to the newly developed cork life jacket that only he was wearing.

The disaster occurred during Henry's first mission as a lifeboatman and made him a local hero. He went on to serve the RNLI for forty years, saving many lives at sea. He remains a hero to many and is remembered in Whitby to this day.

In literacy teaching the features of a biography are considered: comprehension skills are needed to look beyond the literal retelling of his life; this leads on naturally to a discussion about the character of this important man. Such questions as why he became a fisherman and why he decided to join the lifeboat service are thus explored. This yields many theories which further research may answer and lends itself to drama and role-play to investigate these and other questions raised by the children, thereby developing their speaking, listening, and reasoning skills. It is particularly interesting to consider his feelings at being asked to try out the experimental cork life jacket and his subsequent feelings when he knew he was the only survivor of the 1861 disaster, and that this survival was attributed to the jacket. Was he worried about the jacket? Did he feel guilt and/or relief to have survived? These are questions that require the children to empathise with Henry Freeman, to explore how they might feel if presented with the dilemma he had been presented with and their feelings following the disaster. The children are required to articulate their thoughts and to justify them; these are high-order skills for children aged nine but they are able to demonstrate them because they are discussing a real-life issue.

Already subject boundaries are being crossed as the above topic relates to the subjects of English through the use of a biography to introduce the story of Henry Freeman; history through the use of a story of a tragedy and how this impacted on the local area; and PSHE through the discussion of moral dilemmas. In addition, an understanding of floating and sinking is needed to appreciate how the life jacket that is integral to the story worked, and so the subject area of science is added to the list, followed by design and technology. The children are therefore provided with a meaningful context for investigating the properties of materials that float and sink and for researching the developments in buoyancy aids, leading naturally on to designing 'a life jacket of the future'. The learning is already being presented as a coherent package and children are using and developing knowledge, skills, and understandings that are necessary for the topic being studied but not in isolation within subject areas. The approach also ensures that there are opportunities for the children to apply newly acquired skills where they are needed, for example enquiry skills in both history and science.

The children are asked to use their knowledge and understanding thus gained to write a newspaper article about Henry. To do this they need to know the features of a newspaper article and understand the audience and purpose for which they are writing. They may also use ICT skills both to carry out further research into the life of Henry, the RNLI (Royal National Lifeboat Institution), and Whitby itself, and also to present their work. All ability levels are catered for here as the focus of the article is chosen by the individual child. The focus may be a simple retelling of the disaster; an investigative piece about the development of the experimental life jacket; or an in-depth interview with Henry Freeman – survivor of an incident at sea. It can be appreciated that each focus identified here requires understandings and skills at different levels to be used by the children.

The residential visit is then carried out: this is an essential part of the integrated learning as it provides the first-hand experience that really brings the topic *alive*. After being introduced to the story of Henry Freeman and carrying out the activities already noted, the children are able to find out further information for themselves and understand the context of his life. This first-hand exploration is therefore motivating and makes the learning relevant for the children. It also provides a vehicle for them to practise their speaking and listening skills, through a talk at the RNLI station and talking to adults in various situations. The visit requires the use of a range of observational skills, in order to identify the many references to Henry Freeman around Whitby and the legacy he has left the town. The visit thus enables the children to deepen their understanding of an influential character in history and his effect on his surroundings, specifically within the local lifeboat service and the area as a tourist destination.

The focus of the residential visit thus easily leads on to an exploration of the resort, necessitating the use of an atlas to identify its location, the use of co-ordinates in map work, and planning routes to (and around) the town. Again this crosses subject boundaries and brings in knowledge, skills, and understanding from the subject areas of history, maths, and geography. The list of other activities that could be carried out here is vast but is narrowed down to the learning identified by the children and that which is indicated through prior assessment. The Year 5 children attending this residential wished to know more about Whitby as a holiday destination, and assessment had indicated that they needed to increase their use and understanding of data handling. The vehicle for addressing both of these needs was easily identified as a visitor questionnaire, asking passers-by if they were residents or visitors and the purpose of their walk in the town and asking about their knowledge of the work of the RNLI in Whitby. The skills needed for this activity were introduced in school, prior to the visit, with the questionnaire administered during the visit and the results handled and presented back in school. Again the topic provided a *real* reason to develop and use data handling skills, thus providing meaning for the children, and built on their own interests in the learning. Other purposeful and necessary learning opportunities contributed to the topic as it developed. These included an understanding of coastal erosion and the effects of water pollution, using primary sources of information in preference to secondary sources such as pictures or an internet simulation. The visit would be incomplete without carrying out field sketches, leading to artwork based on Henry Freeman and the coastal town itself. Following the visit, learning obviously continued by building on the experiences the children had whilst being immersed in life in modern-day Whitby.

Learning within the integrated topic

The short example detailed here demonstrates well that the integrated approach links together related work and so learning is not fragmented by being divided into subject lessons. For example, in a non-integrated curriculum, the features of a biography could be taught discretely and then practised by writing a biography of a known person, either a friend or a famous person. The features of a newspaper article could then be taught and practised by writing about a local event. The two literacy objectives will have been fulfilled – to know, understand, and use the features of a biography and a newspaper article – albeit discretely. It is not guaranteed that all children will have understood the features or their practical application using the discrete activities: however, by providing meaningful links through the use of a real-life context that is readily accessible and both well known and renowned within a town to be visited, the children have more reason to understand the usage. This provision of a meaningful context for learning and the blurring of subject boundaries are evident throughout the example presented here. It has demonstrated how history, English, geography, maths, and science can be studied concurrently to provide an in-depth investigation into an influential character from the past and the town in which he lived. It cannot be overstated how motivational this is for the children. It provides a purpose for their development of knowledge, skills, and understandings that they will use throughout their educational career and beyond. This is of significant importance for the more reluctant learners as they can see the purpose of the learning opportunities and have input into this themselves.

The integrated approach also caters for all learning styles; this obviously includes the visual, auditory, and kinesthetic learners (see the discussion in Jarvis 2005). Such activities as the use of pictures and the visits to the lifeboat station and the museum cater for the visual learner; the use of 'experts' to talk about Henry Freeman and Whitby itself cater for the auditory learner, and both the scientific investigations and the hands-on museum visit cater for the kinesthetic learners. Although these activities could be experienced discretely, the integrated approach ensures that individual learning styles are addressed together and the need for learners to make connections in their learning is met.

In addition, the approach encourages the development of skills that are transferable: for example, the skill of recording observations is essential in all subject areas, but, if it is taught only in the context of one subject, many learners will have difficulty using the skill in another subject as it will be internalised as relating only to the subject in which it is taught. Within this example of integrated learning, observations were recorded (in many forms) and used to provide reports that could be categorised as English, science, history, and geography, in addition to art and design. The records include biographies, newspaper articles, reports, and subject-specific records, e.g. investigation reports, field sketches, and questionnaires. The residential visit itself provided the perfect opportunity to use ICT in the form of photographs, to make film documentaries and podcasts, and to collect ideas in the form of a fact file or scrap books. All these were included as natural aspects of the learning but required knowledge, skills, and understandings across a range of subject areas to be both used and developed.

It is important to note that this way of working also develops the skill of working with others, both peers and adults – this accords with Kerry's (2002) work on setting learning objectives, in which he argues for five domains of objective that include the affective. The children are encouraged to work together throughout the topic, to share ideas and their developing knowledge, skills, and understandings. The adults whom the children work with include not only the class teacher but support staff, experts consulted on the visit, and visitors to the town being studied. The adults thus support the learning of the children, facilitating opportunities that are relevant to the children rather than delivering a prescribed curriculum through the provision of a ready-made series of lesson plans. Again this makes the learning meaningful and relevant to the child.

Reflection

It is essential in this way of working that you are able to identify the learning taking place. Try to list all skills that will have been used/developed in this short example of an integrated theme.

Conclusion

This chapter has presented a living example of the cross-curricular approach to learning in Key Stage 2. It has not diminished either the NC or subject disciplines. It has demonstrated that the cross-curricular approach is based on making meaningful links between subject areas in order to make the learning coherent and to be motivational, relevant, and real for the children. The example has set out how knowledge, skills, and understandings that cross subject boundaries are developed: it can be appreciated how this forms an excellent basis for the next stage of learning where subjects are taught discretely but shared skills need to be applied. An exciting element of the approach is that the learning is beginning to be initiated by the children and provides for both formal and informal learning to be recognised, again leading to relevance and ensuring deep learning by the children. The topic planning and delivery outlined within the chapter has also fully demonstrated that the approach is grounded within the ten key principles for effective teaching and learning identified by TLRP (Teaching and Learning Research Programme 2007). These principles are detailed in Table 5.2 and matched with their interpretation within the topic presented in this chapter.

This way of working is not a new approach to primary curriculum delivery but it is pleasing that it again features in the latest reviews into the primary curriculum – the Cambridge Review (Alexander 2009) and the Rose Review (DCSF 2009). These reviews have a common theme, that the curriculum is to be learner-focused, build on learner capacities and on prior knowledge and links together the learning from different subject areas. The illustrative topic here demonstrates these common themes in practice.

Table 5.2 Teaching and learning principles into practice

TLRP (Teaching and Learning Research Programme 2007)	
Teaching and learning principles	*Principles in practice*
Equips learners for life in the broadest sense.	Sets learning in the 'real world'
Engages with valued forms of knowledge.	Learning grounded in the requirements of the National Curriculum.
Recognises the importance of prior experience and learning.	Uses prior experience and learning, through assessment and using children's own interests.
Requires the teacher to scaffold learning.	Scaffolding is considered and provided throughout.
Needs assessment to be congruent with learning.	Assessment continued throughout the topic, leading to adjustments to the learning opportunities provided.
Promotes the active engagement of the learner.	The topic was chosen to provide a meaningful context for learning; to be motivational and to engage the children.
Fosters both individual and social processes and outcomes.	Throughout, individual, paired and group work was planned for, in addition to engaging with adults during the residential.
Recognises the significance of informal learning.	Opportunities for informal learning to be shared are provided, for example within the Fact Files and filming documentaries.
Depends on teacher learning.	Teacher knowledge is essential for identifying relevant learning opportunities within a topic.
Demands consistent policy frameworks with support for teaching and learning as their primary focus.	The use of the National Curriculum Orders and the Literacy and Numeracy frameworks are integral to the planning of the topic.

References

Alexander, R. (ed.) (2009) *Children, Their World, Their Education: final report and recommendations of the Cambridge Primary Review* London: Routledge

CEI (2007) *CEI Awards and the Excellence Network* http://www2.warwick.ac.uk/fac/soc/cei/awards/ (accessed October 2009)

DCSF (2009) *Independent Review of the Primary Curriculum: final report* Nottingham: DCSF

DCSF (2010) *A Guide to Enterprise Education* Nottingham: DCSF

DfEE/QCA (2000) *The National Curriculum: handbook for primary teachers in England* London: HMSO

DfES (2003) *Excellence and Enjoyment* London: HMSO

DfES (2004) *Every Child Matters: change for children* London: HMSO

Jarvis, M. (2005) *The Psychology of Effective Learning and Teaching* Cheltenham: Nelson-Thornes

Kerry, T. (2002) *Learning Objectives, Task Setting and Differentiation* Cheltneham: Nelson-Thornes

Plowden, Lady B. (1967) *Children and Their Primary Schools: a report of the Central Advisory Council for Education Volume 1* London: HMSO

QCA (undated) *Schemes of Work* http://www.standards.dfes.gov.uk/schemes3/ (accessed October 2009)

Shill, R. and Minter, I. (1991) *Storm Warrior* Birmingham: Heartland Press

Teaching and Learning Research Programme (2007) *Teaching and Learning Principles into Practice* DVD Available Light

Part 3

Supporting all learners

Chapter 6

Whole school approaches to engage learners

Natural inclusion

Alex Bedford and Karen Parsons

Introduction

This chapter looks at some issues concerned with special educational needs in the context of cross-curricular working. It takes a specific stance on special needs provision, one which is being progressively promoted by government and local authorities: inclusion. The text begins with a definition of inclusion. It sets out why inclusion is an important element in the education of all children and how achieving inclusion should affect the life of the school. It then moves on to consider the topic from a range of theoretical perspectives. In particular, the chapter draws a distinction between inclusion, on the one hand, and meeting special educational needs, on the other. From here, there is a look at some strategies that schools can adopt to make inclusion more of a reality. The relevance of working across the curriculum is considered as an integral part of this approach. The chapter ends with a case study of an 'inclusive' lesson, identifying how individual needs are met in the context of cross-curricular learning.

Background

The landscape of special needs education has changed in recent times. Increasingly the needs of a wide range of pupils – those with learning difficulties, physical disabilities, emotional and behavioural problems – are being met within a mainstream school environment. Government policy seems to be moving away from a notion of special schools and towards the idea of specialist education within all schools. Cynics might say that the move is funding-driven; but that is an argument beyond the scope of this book. The result of current trends is a move towards inclusion. This is well illustrated by the following extract from one local authority policy statement:

> All children within Wrexham County Borough have equal rights to the opportunities offered by education. The Authority is committed to supporting children with special needs within mainstream provision wherever possible, with appropriate support. They are also entitled to an education which ensures continuity and progression from pre-school to post-16. Wherever possible, we shall seek to meet the needs of children and young people within Wrexham schools and residential school placements will only be used where there is no suitable local provision.
> (http://www.wrexham.gov.uk/assets/pdfs/education/senpolicy_241007.pdf)

Definition

This chapter looks at the issue of inclusion – that is, at the right of all children, regardless of ability, to be educated in the same schools and in the same classes. Inclusion is more than catering for special educational need; it is a recognition that all children should learn alongside one another. As the Centre for Studies on Inclusive Education put it, as long ago as 1997:

> There is a growing consensus throughout the world that all children have the right to be educated together. In the last six years a number of major international statements have appeared, affirming the principle of inclusive education and the importance of 'working towards *schools for all* – institutions which include everybody, celebrate differences, support learning and respond to individual needs' (Salamanca Statement 1994).
> (http://www.leeds.ac.uk/disabilitystudies/archiveuk/CSIE/inclusive%20ed.pdf)

But the issue is far from unproblematic, and is open to some debate. This debate is reflected in Rose's work (http://www.isec2000.org.uk/abstracts/papers_r/rose_1.htm), and he is right to draw our attention not just to the philosophical issues that underpin that debate but to the practicalities of classroom teaching:

> It is evident that whereas much has been written about inclusion from a socio-political or human rights perspective, less attention has been afforded to developing a greater understanding of what works in inclusive classrooms. Dyson (1999) has described inclusion in terms of an issue of two discourses; the first of these, a discourse of ethics and rights, concerned to gain an understanding of pupils' rights and how they may best be addressed within the education system, is one which has received considerable attention within the inclusion debate. Dyson's second category, the discourse of efficacy, with a focus upon gaining a greater understanding of what might work in an inclusive school, has received less attention. Teachers faced with an overload of work resulting from a plethora of educational legislation express apprehension with regard to their ability to adequately meet the needs of an increasingly complex school population.
> (http://www.isec2000.org.uk/abstracts/papers_r/rose_1.htm)

The world around us is constantly changing. Society expects people with a range of special needs to be able to be increasingly independent, self-sufficient, and successful. As teachers, we have the responsibility for providing children with an education in tune with the world and one that can support them with skills to succeed and flourish in their future, as Cline and Frederickson (2009) point out:

> all the books that we read about special educational needs (SEN) and inclusion did not seem to us to reflect adequately the rapidly changing, increasingly diverse nature of the society we live in. What was once a relatively homogeneous and stable population has been transformed. Every aspect of society that affects the treatment of disabilities and learning difficulties has changed radically and continues to evolve – the cultural, ethnic and religious profile, patterns of family organization, economic and occupational structures, the relative status of men and women, and the perception of human rights and social responsibilities.

Pupils need to develop skills that allow them to be lifelong learners: to have the enthusiasm and ability to question and pursue lines of enquiry that interest and fascinate them. Social justice demands that these aspirations should not be limited to those deemed to be in the higher percentiles of achievement. We, as practitioners, should be pushing for these skills across the ages and all abilities.

Inclusion and cross-curricular learning

Our experience is that the cross-curricular approach to learning and teaching allows learners to be taught together; the gap between the abilities is narrowed and the opportunities it provides are so significant for pupils that it is hard to see why many schools still opt only for a traditional subject-based approach. Throughout life we group our skills and abilities without differentiation or deliberate exclusion. We use geographical and scientific skills with literacy, all immersed in the skills of enquiry. Cross-curricular learning allows learners to practise and mirror these life skills – a fact that is recognised by the Ministry of Education of British Columbia (Canada):

> Educators can assist in creating more inclusive learning environments by attending to the following:
> * activities that focus on development and mastery of foundational skills (basic literacy)
> * a range of co-operative learning activities and experiences in the school and community; and application of practical, hands-on skills in a variety of settings
> * references to specialized learning resources, equipment, and technology
> * examples of ways to accommodate for special needs (e.g., incorporating adaptations/ extensions to content, process, product, pacing, and learning environment; suggesting alternate methodologies or strategies; making references to special services)
> * a variety of ways for students to demonstrate learning, not just through paper and pencil tasks (e.g., dramatizing events to demonstrate understanding of a poem, recording observations in science by drawing, composing/performing a music piece)
> * promotion of the capabilities and contributions of children and adults with special needs
> * participating in physical activity.

(This summary is provided by the Province of British Columbia Ministry of Education derived from the *Handbook for Curriculum Developers* (February 1994) and *Special Education Services – a manual of policies, procedures and guidelines* (Response Draft, December 1994). It resonates with the themes of a number of chapters in this text.)

Inclusive means all

Ofsted (2001) defines an educationally inclusive school as 'one in which the teaching and learning, achievements, attitudes and well being of every young person matters'. It is important to remain open-minded about all learners in the school, but perhaps it is also important that we remember to take account of those learners who are considered to be gifted and talented (see Chapter 8), or those with dual or multiple exceptionalities. These learners, too, may be vulnerable, or may not be recognised as gifted or talented because their difficulty masks their true talents. A recent estimate suggests that 5–10 per cent of gifted pupils could have a learning difficulty and that 2–5 per cent of pupils with disabilities may also be gifted (one might think, for example, of Stephen Hawking) (http://www.teachingexpertise.com/e-bulletins/links-between-sen-and-gifted-and-talented-6636).

Thus, inclusion is a cultural and pedagogical stance, demanding high-quality experiences, achievement, and collegiality for all learners throughout the entire school and community. It is an entitlement for everyone who learns, works, and is influenced by the school.

Alexander (2009: 140) identifies the need for consistency within our schools stating that there is:

> evidence that the current curriculum – in terms of balance, content and progression – does not suit all children equally well, even though it is presented as an entitlement for all. The absence or marginalization of some activities and subjects raises the likelihood that some children will fall behind, misunderstand or opt out completely.

Consistency is defined by our relationships and values, enabling a shift from our historically driven desire to have a detailed constraining system into which to fit learners, to a set of reasoned approaches. Inclusive approaches fit learning *and* are applied humanely, with care, consistency, and professional judgements as the driving force.

Inclusion has implications for the ways in which schools are organised and staffed. Effective and well-trained Learning Support Assistants are undoubtedly one of the best resources to support learners with additional needs (see Chapter 7). It is important to ensure that they are supporting the learner by encouraging independence, communicating skills that will come into their own when the learners move to a different class or school. It is also important to build in familiar 'unfamiliarity' and ensure that different adults are deployed to support the learners so if their particular adult is away the learner is able to cope with that change and be supported by somebody else.

Inclusive strategies are formulated around high-quality pedagogical approaches, not distinct from but akin to mainstream strategies, engaging learning in a meaningful and social context. What is apparent is that the deployment of staff and the skills needed are complex, specific, and sometimes time-bound. To include learners with significant difficulties the school will need to draw on all the resources in the local community to work collaboratively in order to meet the needs of children. Inclusion is not an add-on, it is part of professional responsibility to build a more empathetic community that cares for its families.

How does inclusion, as a philosophy and approach, meet with social and moral expectations and stereotypes? In our experience, young learners are very supportive of those with specific difficulties. By giving more able pupils an opportunity to work alongside others it is possible to create an atmosphere of acceptance, one in which learners can take their experiences of school to the outside world too and share with society. Equally, it enables those learners with learning needs to access an ethos and environment where they can share social and emotional behaviours in a safe and secure place, alongside the quality of experiences to which all human beings are entitled.

Developing the inclusive school

Developing a wholly inclusive school is not an 'extra' or some kind of self-contained task that requires a member of the team to take a specific responsibility and to report on progress occasionally to the Governing Body. It is an integral way of working. It answers Claxton's (2008: xii) question: 'How do we organise schools so everyone will feel that they are there to improve something, and are able to do so, and not that they are constantly being reminded how "bright" or "weak" they are?' Developing successful inclusive practices means developing a whole school approach to learning. With success at being inclusive, the impact on a learner's attitudes, achievements and life chances substantially improves, as does the pedagogy. Teachers' professional development becomes focused on achieving the desired intentions of this philosophy. Inclusion needs a serious and articulated focus underpinned by common sense. However, inclusion should be challenged and be subjected to review like all innovation in order to discover how individual teachers and teams are facilitating learning. Daniels and Porter (2007) refer to overarching pedagogical approaches, rather than separate strategies focused on special needs, as being the key building block in achieving inclusion. Davis and Florian (2004) agree:

> We found that there is a great deal of literature that might be construed as special education knowledge, but that the teaching approaches and strategies themselves were not sufficiently differentiated from those which are used to teach all children to justify the term SEN pedagogy. Our analysis found that sound practices in teaching and learning in mainstream and special education literatures were often informed by the same basic research.
>
> (Davis and Florian 2004: 33–4)

Case Study 6.1 looks at the process which we went through at Abbots Green Primary School from 2005 to 2009 in order to make the transition from traditional approaches to special educational needs teaching to an inclusive philosophy that embraced all learning for all pupils.

Case Study 6.1 Making the transition to inclusiveness at Abbots Green

Abbots Green School, Suffolk, was built between 2004 and 2005. It opened in September 2005 to serve a growing and diverse population. Within the mainstream school nested a Specialist Support Centre for moderate and complex learning difficulties. Children between the ages of four and nine were supported at the school.

An inclusive journey began well before the school opened. Engagement with the community was a priority. Supported by local businesses and community establishments, the school was able to communicate its inclusive message. Maslow's (1970) hierarchy served as the guiding principle above all others – that physical and emotional needs were met first in order to secure effective learning. This was embodied in the practice of the staff and a set of expectations:

- Developing open, secure, and respectful relationships with children and their families by all staff at all levels
- Acknowledging that all children have a right to learning
- Teaching that learning alongside children with significant differences is empowering and a privilege
- Breaking down prejudice and misunderstanding. We know this is a crucial balanced life skill because parents and learners cited it as a positive experience in their time at the school
- Acknowledging that we learn from each other. The empowerment children and parents felt through learning Makaton sign language to communicate with a wide range of learners highlighted the power of inclusive strategies
- Accepting that children are developmentally at different stages and have different interests, just like adults
- Acknowledging that teachers and Learning Support Assistants are skilled in ensuring that learning across ages is effective.

Inclusive strategies are effective for all learners and not exclusive to children on the 'SEN register'. They should be seen as tools within the teacher's learning repertoire, deployed to maximise achievement. This is once again highlighted by Davis and Florian (2004: 33–4) with respect to a specific SEN pedagogy.

Over a period of five years, Abbots Green was recognised as a leading school for inclusive practice. The school had no choice but to be inclusive with 86 per cent of learners in 2005 being categorised as 'hard pressed' according to Acorn data. (Acorn data are a measure of social deprivation – a standard measure of family income etc.) There are five categories and 'hard pressed' is one of the most deprived. The school had an unprecedented level of children with significant special educational needs in the mainstream, coupled with a Specialist Support Centre at the heart of the school.

Staff skills were significantly developed over a period of time through focused CPD, performance management, and the expectation of living and breathing inclusion. The school became very effective in supporting a wide range of learners.

In 2009 the leadership of the school changed; the headteacher and deputy head took new roles within the local authority.

The school supported children and families in the local community and opened its specialist resources, such as sensory rooms, used by pre-school children with multiple and profound difficulties.

In 2008–2009, the school employed a Cognitive Behavioural Therapist with the brief to support families and learners from the immediate and wider community. To complement this strategy a Learning Support Assistant was deployed to be not the interface but the 'human face' between children, families, and staff. The barriers were well and truly being broken down as the school opened its facilities for wider uses.

Year on year parents told us that some of the most important experiences they and their children had were from being able to learn and socialise with children who had difficulties.

Some of the most challenging experiences at Abbots Green were with children who presented extreme behavioural, social, and emotional difficulties. Relationships, environments, and strategies were developed specifically to meet the needs of these 'exceptional' pupils.

To complement the journey a bespoke nursery was designed using Dr Kenn Fisher's principles of the pedagogy of space and built (opening in 2010) to ensure a smooth pathway from three years onwards. This facility ensures that high-quality early years learning is accessible to local families and also to young children with specific moderate and complex learning difficulties within a wider geographical area.

Given this outline of the development of the inclusive philosophy between 2005 and 2009 at Abbots Green, you might find it helpful to look at practice in your own school situation.

How ready is your school for inclusive practice?

Initiating an inclusive philosophy in the primary school introduces into the learning debate, then, many interrelated and complex factors. We are in a climate where mainstream schools are being called upon to take greater accountability for children with both specific and generalised, social and emotional, communication, physical, behavioural, and learning difficulties. As a result of this, schools have responded in a variety of ways. Positive approaches have enabled schools to learn a great deal and to apply their insights successfully to the whole school community: in other words, to practise inclusiveness. This process involves several interrelated factors, as shown in Figure 6.1.

Every school is unique in having its own staff, its own traditions, and its own ways of working, i.e. its own culture, people, and processes: or, to put it another way, we are dealing very much with the way we do things, the people who do it, and the systems that support them. These elements form the start of a working model. All these links are connected historically, systemically, emotionally, and physically. A good place to begin in examining your own school's inclusiveness is with the elements in this model. Successful schools that engage with effective inclusive practice have reviewed the impact that their culture, their people, and their systems have on their learners and wider community.

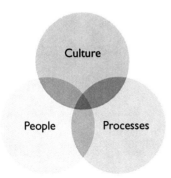

Figure 6.1 Culture-people-processes
(http://www.jiscinfonet.ac.uk/infokits/change-management/printable-version.pdf) (redrawn)

Reflection

Look at Figure 6.1. What can you say about your school under each of the headings? How do these elements work towards inclusiveness, or hinder it? How does your school compare to the elements described in Case Study 6.1?

It can be a challenge for school professionals and governors to analyse and align their school's culture, people, and process to improve learning outcomes. But consider the wider implications when this model is applied to groups of schools in a community cluster. How do the culture, people, and processes of disparate groups merge successfully without the uniqueness being diluted, compromised, or stifled? Change for the collective good of a community will happen only when the barriers of traditional thinking are removed, and schools, along with their children, are recognised as being part of a living community.

So far in this chapter we have looked at the development of the philosophy of the inclusive school, and have indicated that cross-curricular learning and teaching have a logical place within that development. In the rest of the chapter the intention is to revisit these two themes to add a little more substance to the arguments outlined above. First, we will look at the theory of inclusion and then examine a practical example of cross-curricular learning in an inclusive setting.

Readiness for inclusive practice

To throw some further useful light on the process of change to inclusiveness we suggest another model – the so-called 7S Model of Peters and Waterman (http://www.jisc infonet.ac.uk/tools/seven-s-model). Though the model is now quite dated it contains within it enduring insights. We can use this reflective tool (Figure 6.2) to analyse the complex links and interdependent factors within a school and its community to bring about change.

Here, the core item, Shared Values, must be realised every day in the school to ensure inclusiveness. These central values consist of: attitudes and relationships, a shared understanding of learning, and openness to accountability.

Reflection

- What are the inclusive values your school holds? Why?
- How strong are these values? What needs to be done to build upon them?
- What is the culture of the school? How do you know this?

Attitudes and relationships

Crozier has emphasised that, while everyone has a view about how education should be, it is a rapidly changing phenomenon, in which teachers – as professionals – need to keep

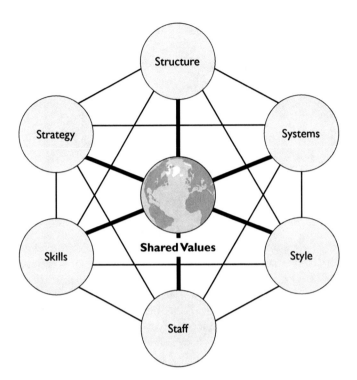

Figure 6.2 The 7S Model (redrawn) after Peters and Waterman (1982) (http://www.jiscinfonet.ac.uk/tools/seven-s-model)

parents on-side: to give them 'a sense of agency' (2000: 73). Teachers need to be the intermediaries who explain the learning process to other stakeholders. Watkins and Lodge (2007: 15) believe that there are three different models of learning in the modern class-room: reception, construction, and co-construction.

- *Reception*: effectively, the didactic mode
- *Construction*: individual sense-making – where learning is more open-ended and pupils are encouraged to make sense of learning through discussion and discovery
- *Co-construction*: building knowledge with others – here pupils find themselves learning through dialogue and collaboration with others with the teacher acting as facilitator.

Stakeholders need to understand, and share, the values of the classroom. Over the years other scholars, too, have put forward similar models of learning (some of these were rehearsed in Chapter 2; see also Jarvis 2005). How do these models impact on inclusive cross-curricular learning? The theory of the three models of learning could be very closely linked with the attitudes and beliefs of staff and, most importantly, parents. There is a danger that people expect children to be taught as they themselves were taught. Parents need to have an understanding of the benefits of constructionist and co-constructionist learning, and how they go hand in hand with cross-curricular teaching, to enable schools to have confidence and belief in these techniques with their pupils. Given the importance of parental support, it is vital that we consider the skills that learners need to access this style and to ensure that their learning is as effective as possible. Watkins and Lodge's study (2007) concluded that children learn best when:

- They take responsibility for their own learning
- They are actively engaged in their learning
- Learning is interactive
- They see themselves as successful learners.

This approach not only complements cross-curricular learning but defines it pedagogically. It demonstrates the importance of children understanding their own learning – a meta-cognitive process (Wilding 1997).

Shared understanding of learning

The ideal of the previous section is clearly supported in Alexander's latest work (2009: 282), which clearly articulates the need for a national change in teaching and learning approaches: 'The common strand, and it should be closely heeded, is that children want and need to know what they are doing and why, to be brought inside the thinking that informs the teacher's decisions on their behalf. Children, too, are interested in pedagogy.' Building on Alexander's thinking, that children 'are interested in pedagogy', we can review our teaching practices to engage them earlier and make more sense of the journey. Hart *et al.* (2004), in looking to engage learners and secure their involvement, define this transformability as a 'joint enterprise': but engaging learners, especially those who are 'turned off' and present what could be described as learning difficulties, is a high priority for schools. Successful and inclusive strategies make learning irresistible and hook those children who are not engaging and are therefore placing themselves at risk, their well-being at risk, their learning at risk, and ultimately their futures at risk. Consider the model below for engaging learning.

Reflection: a possible model for engaging pupils in learning

- Identify learning focus; children involved at this stage – existing understanding shared and questions raised.
- Construct planning around enquiry and needs.
- Apply experiences directly to learning.
- Ensure learning is validated, valued and communicated.
- Plan next steps collaboratively.
- Plan with children, listen to their interests and build meaningful, authentic experiences with them.
- Teach and explore with them, refer back to their enquiries, make the reasons for learning explicit – give them a cause.

Accountability

Everyone who has a role within an inclusive school is accountable for making inclusion work. But inclusion may demand a shift in public perspective concerning schools and their purposes. Standards are important in the learning process. The level at which these are achieved will affect learners' life chances and personal success. But translating Ofsted categories into crude accountability measures for schools does nothing to improve out-comes for pupils. Inclusion demands that we have to ensure that standards are aspirational, that all learners have realistic targets, and that all learners can be supported within this system. If learners have support and resources within the classroom we can create a cross-curricular learning environment, such as the one described in Case Study 6.2, that inspires learners and captures their specific needs.

One of the problems with the current approach to accountability is that measures are crude, and they are crudely applied. The mechanistic system of measurement through testing assumes that all pupils are the same and have the same potential, and that they can all reach the same levels of achievement. This cannot, logically, be true; but no allowance is made for this in applying the accountability measures. Effectiveness is much more than being able to deliver learning targets to pupils; it is an awareness of the bigger picture that enables learners to have a personalised and individualised curriculum and learning journey: a journey of knowledge and skills. This is embodied by Watkins, who boldly stated at Suffolk's Primary Curriculum Conference in 2010 that 'Coverage is the enemy of learning'.

Having examined the nature of Shared Values in the 7S Model in Figure 6.2, we can move on to look briefly at the other six components of the model. In effect, these build towards answering the question: what are the factors that are prerequisite for operating inclusive learning policies and practices in a school? Table 6.1 draws the insights of these components together into a series of questions that challenge educators – heads, teachers, administrators, governors, support personnel – to examine their own practice.

Table 6.1 An analysis of some components for ensuring readiness for inclusion

Systems

What demands does inclusive practice make on factors such as finance, professional training, staff, or parental commitment?

Do all staff, including administrative and school business managers, share the underpinning values? How do the ways they conduct themselves, their systems, and their activities show this?

What are the appropriate measures of success for this way of working?

How are these monitored, evaluated, and built upon?

What aspirations and markers does the school use to keep *learning* for all at the forefront?

Structure

How is the school organised to achieve the inclusive goals it aspires to?

Who leads? What is the structure of responsibility within the school?

In practice, what model of management predominates: e.g. collegial, distributed, the heroic?

How do different sub-groups form teams?

How do those teams communicate effectively, with common goals and through efficient processes?

Who makes the ultimate decisions and at what level are these shared?

Does every participant feel a part of the whole, and how well are they integrated into the communication structure?

Table 6.1 Continued

Staff

What roles within the school are needed to achieve positive outcomes for learners?

What positions need to be filled?

What kinds of people, with what range of skills, are needed to fill them?

Are there gaps in the skills staff need to meet the learners' needs?

What skills audits have been undertaken to drive this process?

Skills

Where are the school's strengths?

Are these shared professionally with others?

Are there skills gaps?

Who can support or reduce these gaps – e.g. by better use of existing staff or by bringing in outside assistance?

What is the school known for doing well? What evidence is there?

Are there any obvious weaknesses?

What is the evidence for these, and how can improvement be effected?

How are staff skills acknowledged, monitored, assessed, and celebrated?

What impact does monitoring and appraisal have, e.g. are identified needs genuinely met?

These and similar issues need to be examined and re-examined; and, of course, this process should be part of the regular updating of the school's Self-Evaluation Form and the headteacher's discussion with the School Improvement Partner.

Style

How do stakeholders see the physical environment of the school? Within the building, and outside?

How safe is the environment?

Does it present a climate that reflects psychological security and safety?

Is the school well and appropriately resourced?

Is learning collaborative?

Are the ethos and climate marked out by positive values?

Strategies

What is the school's inclusion strategy? Can everyone in the school community articulate it?

Is everyone committed to the strategy as a broad principle and as the beacon that guides day-to-day decisions and behaviours?

What can be done to make it come alive and be real for all the learners?

How does the school deal with parental, local authority, and government pressure which conflicts with the strategy?

How is the strategy communicated and celebrated within and beyond the school?

Pulling the threads together

So far this chapter has attempted a definition of inclusion. It has set out why inclusion is an important element in the education of all children and how achieving inclusion may affect the life of the school. In Case Study 6.1 we looked at the effect that introducing an inclusive philosophy had on the functioning of one school known to us. The chapter also considered the topic from a range of theoretical perspectives. The relevance of working across the curriculum was considered as an integral part of the inclusive approach.

An example in practice

The intention is to end the chapter by looking at how inclusion works in the context of a single lesson. To this end, Case Study 6.2 describes a 'typical' lesson, making explicit how the needs of all children, regardless of ability, are catered for in a cross-curricular context.

Case Study 6.2 Some elements in cross-curricular, inclusive learning

High-quality learning is naturally inclusive. To enable this, it is worth paying close attention to several key principles.

First, a rigorous and secure *assessment procedure* is embedded in the pedagogy of the teacher and school. This assessment allows the teacher to plan and teach at the appropriate pace, with challenge and level of achievement. One strand of this assessment is the use of the KWFL approach – what the children *Know*; what the children *Want* to investigate; how they will *Find* it; what they have *Learned* – which gives a clear picture of where the children are from a skills, knowledge, and understanding perspective.

Second, *communication*: once the *Know* and *Want* have been explored, the class engages with the planning and teaching phase. The aim is that learners must be prepared for their learning to start. Useful resources like whole class visual timetables support learners and focus them to become more aware of what they will be learning next and give them a broader understanding of the wider learning agenda. For SEN learners with specific difficulties, resources such as an individual visual timetable and a discussion before the learning commences give them an opportunity to question and prepare.

Third, capturing and linking the interests and *imagination*: the wow, the awe, and the wonder.

There are a myriad of ways to inspire learners, for example dilemmas, problems, and enquiry approaches. One might begin by telling the children: 'An Anglo-Saxon letter has been found and a local museum is organising an archaeological dig to gather information . . .' The right stimuli and context will have all learners enthusiastic, willing, and keen to take part. What is important here is to consider how the stimulus fits with the learning, providing a context for the children which allows them to have a purpose.

Children need ownership over their learning; they must feel that it is valued and they must feel confident to share their ideas. Giving them a range of ways to communicate their ideas independently (see Chapter 12) will enable the teacher and adults to make clear evaluations about those learners who need more input and those learners who are ready for a challenge. Learning support assistants (see Chapter 7) are vital in encouraging positive talk and questions, and in helping to correct any misconceptions in a supportive manner.

Mixed class of Y5/6 in an urban primary school – afternoon lesson in December for two and a half hours

Class 5UR are a fantastic class with a wide range of abilities, attitudes, and talents. They present a wide social spectrum and a range of learners with social, emotional, behavioural, and communication difficulties. Learning for these children has to have meaning, be in context, and stay active. Writing reluctance is common for many of these young people. The class teacher and I have been empowering their skills as learners using a model of high-quality communication, capitalising on respectful listening, engagement, and active learning built around trust and relationships that are intrinsically valued.

The skills of listening, empathy, interdependence, and collaboration are significantly challenged through the learning experiences extended by questions from their friends and adults.

One small example of this has been captured in what follows. Each learner has a single strip of plasticine. They are encouraged to play with it and mould it. The story *The Tunnel* by Anthony Browne is read and reread with the class and they are asked to shape the plasticine into anything that captures their imagination or feelings in the story. Learners have the choice of who they sit with and whereabouts in the class they do this, but the expectation is that if they make this choice then their learning reflects it.

Adults discuss and model the skill of interdependence (knowing when it is best to learn with others and when by yourself) and learners choose to create their model individually. They are naturally curious about each other's ideas and they talk with each other, asking increasingly deep questions about each other's creation. This is a routine within the class and has been made a natural part of the learning repertoire. Questions and observation lead to revisions to their own models; children have the opportunity and permission to broadcast these and share their learning with the class. Resources are an integral part of learning. Children know where the available resources are to capitalise and build upon their imagination. They use IT independently, capturing the design phases with digital cameras as a record for their synthesis and evaluation of the learning. Individual work, pairs, and small groups develop as each learner makes the personal decision about how they want to improve and build upon their learning. Some work collaboratively, others co-operatively, and some individually.

The story continues with learners using everyday class resources including books, textures, coloured papers, words to represent feelings, and 'what ifs' to inform the reader. This is personalised through the children's perspective of what's at the end of their own tunnel . . . what's it like?

All adults are briefed to extend the thinking by encouraging questioning, reflection that can lead to intuition. Children are required to challenge themselves and not rely on external motivation but move towards the inner want and desire to succeed.

Outcomes are differentiated by adult support and questioning, but the key driver here is that the learning is led by the children.

Outcomes focus on the most able including linking moral dilemmas and engaging in profound learning.

The quality of language, imagination, social skills, and constructive learning are assessed, and linked to the 'traditional' subjects of English and maths.

A clear strength of this inclusive practice is that the teacher is responsible for English and maths with the class. The adults have a personal, clear, and focused understanding of where to support, extend, and challenge pupils across the areas of learning.

Conclusion

Inclusion is challenging but reflects the realities of our developing society. It fulfils the intention to meet every individual's need; and to protect all children because, or regardless, of their abilities and aptitudes. It is the next logical step in the development of schools modelled on the best principles of social justice. As indicated in this chapter, cross-curricular approaches are particularly suitable for learning and teaching in these contexts.

References

Alexander, R. (2009) *Children, Their World, Their Education* London: Routledge

Claxton, G. (2008) *What's the Point of School?* Oxford: One World Publications

Cline, T. and Frederickson, N. (2009) *Special Educational Needs, Inclusion and Diversity* Milton Keynes: Open University

Crozier, J. (2000) *Parents and Schools: partners or protagonists?* Stoke on Trent: Trentham Books

Daniels. H. and Porter, J. (2007) *Learning Needs and Difficulties among Children of Primary School Age: definition, identification, provision and issue* Cambridge: Primary Review

Davis, P. and Florian, L. (2004) *Teaching Strategies and Approaches for Pupils with Special Educational Needs: a scoping study* London: DfES

Dyson, A. (1999) 'Inclusion and inclusions: theories and discourses in inclusive education' in H. Daniels and P. Garner (eds) *World Yearbook of Education: inclusive education* London: Kogan Page

Hart, S., Dixon, A., Drummond, M., and McIntyre, D. (2004) *Learning without Limits* Maidenhead: Open University

Jarvis, M. (2005) *The Psychology of Effective Teaching and Learning* Cheltenham: Nelson-Thornes

Maslow, A. (1970) *Motivation and Personality* New York: Harper Row

Ministry of Education for British Columbia (1994) *Handbook for Curriculum Developers* (February 1994) and *Special Education Services – a manual of policies, procedures and guidelines* (Response Draft, December 1994)

Ofsted (2001) *Evaluating Educational Inclusion – guidance for inspectors and schools* available on http://wsgfl.westsussex.gov.uk/ccm/content/curriculum/inclusion-and-equalities/educational-inclusion-general-issues/statements-about-educational-inclusion.en?/page=3

Watkins, C. and Lodge, C. (2007) *Effective Learning in Classrooms* London: Paul Chapman

Wilding, M. (1997) 'Taking control: from theory into practice' *Education Today* 47 (3): 17–23

Waterman, R., Peters, H., and Philips, J. (1980) *Structure Is Not Organisation*. Business Horizons. June. Indiana University: Foundation for the School of Business

World Conference on Special Needs Education (1994) *The Salamanca Statement and Framework for Action on Special Needs Education* Salamanca, Spain 7–10 June 1994 available on http://www. unesco.org/education/pdf/SALAMA_E.PDF

Internet sources

http://www.isec2000.org.uk/abstracts/papers_r/rose_1.htm
http://www.jiscinfonet.ac.uk/tools/seven-s-model
http://www.leeds.ac.uk/disabilitystudies/archiveuk/CSIE/inclusive%20ed.pdf
http://www.teachingexpertise.com/e-bulletins/links-between-sen-and-gifted-and-talented-6636
http://www.wrexham.gov.uk/assets/pdfs/education/senpolicy_241007.pdf

Chapter 7

Managing the contribution of support staff to cross-curricular learning

Pat Foulkes and Jill Wallis

This chapter argues that the role of support staff in schools' delivery of cross-curricular learning must be reviewed to ensure that their contribution is effective. Support staff have a range of areas of strength in a cross-curricular approach and some exemplary case studies are used to illustrate these. However, the chapter also warns that key issues recurring in the management and deployment of support staff must be addressed if their contribution is to be fully effective.

Introduction

The rise in the number of Teaching Assistants (TAs) in schools in the last decade has been well documented (Walton 2009: 18); in 2009 the *Education Guardian* reported a tripling in the number of TAs since 1997. Following workforce reform, their role has become increasingly educational and more embedded in classrooms as an integral part of the teaching team: the 'partner paraprofessionals' foreseen by Kerry (2001: 35).

Increased training and career progression opportunities are now available for those within the support role, including that of Higher Level Teaching Assistant (HLTA). The NFER research survey (Wilson *et al.* 2007: 91) concluded that the HLTA role was having a positive effect on pupil performance 'with almost three quarters of senior leaders identifying *supporting pupil learning* as the most significant impact of HLTAs in schools'.

However, more recent research by Blatchford *et al.* (2009) presents a less encouraging picture of the impact of support staff deployment: routinely working with lower-attaining pupils and pupils with SEN often means removing such pupils from the classroom for intervention support without the expected impact on pupils' learning. In fact, their findings indicate 'a negative relationship between the amount of additional support provided by support staff and the academic progress of pupils' (Blatchford *et al.* 2009: 129).

Blatchford *et al.* consider some possible explanations for this, including the TA's lack of 'preparedness' because of problems in ensuring sufficient time for planning with the teacher and gaps in the TA's subject and pedagogic knowledge. They conclude by stating that 'we do not want to give the impression that support staff do not have an important role to play' but feel that 'problems may have arisen from assuming that extra support will lead to positive outcomes for pupils without first establishing a clear understanding and view of the role of support staff' (2009: 140).

It is therefore imperative that, when reviewing the role of TAs in supporting the integrated curriculum, the contribution they offer should be re-examined and their role in the process of a cross-curricular approach should be carefully managed for that contribution to be fully effective.

In Special Schools there is already evidence of good practice both in valuing and managing learning support assistants (LSAs) and also in maximising productive learning time through a personalised and often thematic approach. As Halliwell (2003: 36) found, in Special Schools 'assistants are often the persons most frequently involved in the daily implementation of a programme or in the use of specific resources'.

The potential contribution of TAs and LSAs to an innovative cross-curricular approach is wide-ranging and multi-faceted. They can bring a wide range of personal skills and enthusiasms to the planning and delivery of integrated and thematic learning, building on and complementing the skills of teachers, and can foster positive attitudes to learning. With many having followed a different career path to that of qualified teachers, TAs and LSAs often have a different perspective and life experience to those of the class teacher, which may open up new ideas and possibilities. Simply having another adult involved in the planning process can generate ideas and encourage creativity. The workload in preparation and planning is also shared and can be distributed according to particular areas of interest. Kerry (2001: 75) highlights the fact that a TA in the classroom provides 'not just another pair of hands, but another pair of eyes, ears and an informed brain' which can be harnessed to advance learning.

Greater opportunities for interactive learning and activities such as role-play and practical experiments can be offered through the team work of teacher and support staff. Mindham (2004) has identified the positive impact of the wider range of experiences which these approaches may offer: 'By involving a variety of tasks and valuing skills beyond those associated only with the core curriculum we enable all children to feel a sense of pride in their achievements.'

During the learning activities the presence of another supporting adult also helps with behaviour management if an excitingly different activity is planned; and it allows the exploration of more potentially 'risky' activities, resources, and environments. In identifying the positive aspects of TA support, Blatchford et al. (2009: 2) found that, for less able pupils in particular, 'the more support received, the lower their distractibility and disruption and the better their relationships with peers, being independent and following instructions'.

The Teaching Assistant may also have a wide range of links with the local community and may be able to draw on a network of local support for visits or s/he may have an awareness of key personnel locally who could be approached for their involvement. 'The local community directly influences the pupils' lives and there is much to be gained from furthering closer interaction, links and liaison between school and community. The community is also a rich resource for support staff with valuable local knowledge' (Campbell 2005: 131).

Case Study 7.1 A history theme

When involved in planning a thematic approach in history through the Great Fire of London, the TA had the idea that a real fire would really engage the pupils' interest and she suggested creating a London street (D&T) and then setting fire to it (science). She was able to enlist the support of the local fire brigade for safety (her brother-in-law was a local fire officer) and thus the learning was extended to links to 'People who help us'. Learning objectives in art (painting the frieze of houses to be burnt), literacy (writing newspaper report) and ICT for historical research and presentation of the newspaper account were all developed. There was a key focus on involving all year groups in the themed project as part of vertical grouping, and pupils from Year 1 helped in the production of 'houses' while Year 6 interviewed and were interviewed through role-play as house owners and newspaper reporters. Parents were kept informed of the school 'fire' and were invited to attend. They were also canvassed for props and materials for D&T.

Kirtlan (in Walton and Goddard 2009: 129) recognises the importance of TA support in a creative curriculum and the guidance they provide for pupils to 'begin their learning journey'. However, she cites Watkinson's warning that TAs must 'provide the scaffolding, not build the complete tower'.

TAs often have more opportunity to personalise learning by getting to know each pupil's interests and being aware of potential barriers to their engagement in learning.

A child may well have more opportunity to confide in a TA who works more regularly with them or provides individual support so the TA can plan ahead to remove any possible barriers to inclusion in integrated learning. Their awareness of the quiet, 'invisible' child can ensure an appropriate strategy is planned to provide them with equality of access to learning experiences and to enable them to demonstrate skills in a range of learning. A TA's potentially greater awareness of a pupil's home background can also minimise potential barriers to an interactive learning experience.

Case Study 7.2 Inclusion

The school was planning a Book Week with themed characters involved in drama, in literacy (by developing the characters and story lines), and in art through display work. The first day in Reception Class was planned for pupils to dress up as characters from *Peter Pan* and talk about them and then enact the story for the rest of the school. The TA was aware that some pupils might not have support at home for creating the costumes and so she produced a spare set of basic costumes (pirates and fairies) which could be offered to any pupils who arrived without their own costumes, enabling them to be fully included in the learning activities.

The TAs can themselves be a valuable resource of unexpected skills and interests. A passion for music, art, or cookery can be exploited to support a range of integrated learning opportunities. TAs may also be more representative of the local community than many of the teaching staff in terms of their ethnic and cultural backgrounds. Thus they may be more aware of cultural issues and become a valuable source of advice.

Case study 7.3 Multiculturalism

A TA who was originally from Poland was working in a multicultural urban primary school and she suggested that as part of an integrated approach the school should plan a year-long celebration of languages represented by the school community. She offered to plan a calendar so that each week represented a different global or community language and she involved any pupils fluent in that language to teach the rest of the school basic greetings for registration, polite exchanges, and numbers 1–5 which were to be used throughout the school for that week. The TA researched key phrases on the internet and produced displays which were changed weekly to reinforce the vocabulary. She also copied photographs and taped music from the part of the world represented to be played in the school entrance.

Case Study 7.4 Bilingual Teaching Assistants

In a large primary in an inner-city area, with a multi-ethnic student intake, bilingual teaching assistants were deployed to work with recent arrivals and those with significant vocabulary issues as a result of having English as an additional language. In one unit, the book *The Mousehole Cat* was being used as the basis of a range of cross-curricular lessons. These included drawing maps of the area in the story, with accurate placing and labelling of key places; measuring distances between some of these features; writing diary entries for key characters; and writing recipes for characters' favourite foods.

One teaching assistant for this series of lessons was bilingual and was allocated to a group of pupils whose mother tongue she spoke. In addition she and the teacher had designed a range of visual aids to assist pupils. For example, illustrations from the book were copied and laminated, with labels, for key features in the story such as the harbour, various characters' houses, and key geographical features. These were always available as props on the table, and the TA also asked or answered questions in the mother tongue to ensure pupils could understand the tasks. Thus the key learning objectives could be met by students provided they understood the vocabulary being used. The use of TA language support and the visual prompts made the lesson accessible to them.

TAs may be creative and skilled in producing learning materials or displays to celebrate pupils' work. They may have more time available than teachers for designing and producing interactive displays throughout the school to support school themes. They can help in the production of props and costumes. A TA, once trained in ICT and aware of the wide range of resources available to support learning, can become a real enthusiast and may choose to explore school themes in integrated learning for personal development and understanding.

Potential pitfalls to be managed

Planning

While earlier examples highlight a range of ways TAs can contribute to the effectiveness of integrated learning, their role in the process needs to be carefully managed.

It is even more essential in the potentially more complex creative curriculum sessions that TAs are fully involved in planning processes for integrated learning. They may be able to cope with individual discrete lessons in particular subjects without being involved in the planning but merely being told their role in a brief aside prior to the lesson, although this should not happen in a professional relationship. As mentioned earlier, Blatchford *et al.* (2009: 133) identify a lack of *preparedness* as one of the key facets in limiting TA effectiveness in advancing pupils' learning: 'a lack of meaningful time for joint planning and preparation before, and for feedback and reflection after, lessons . . . means the potential for effective pedagogical involvement [is] reduced'. Moreover, the complexity of the learning objectives in integrated learning means that a TA who has not been part of the planning cannot be expected to support the learning to greatest effect. TAs need to understand the underpinning skills and range of learning objectives in order to support pupils in developing those skills.

There could be a danger that the TA has a rather superficial view of an integrated learning activity and, in some instances, may lack the necessary breadth of subject knowledge and understanding of the key aspects on which pupils need to build. It is the role of the class teacher to make the learning explicit for the TA and in doing so to facilitate pupil learning.

Resources preparation

An enthusiastic TA, particularly one who has contributed a key idea to the planning, may go to extremes in researching and preparing materials: enthusiasm needs to be tempered with a realistic view of the impact on learning. A TA may not share the teacher's professional training, experience, and judgement in such matters. A TA may feel partly responsible for the success of a planned activity and may focus heavily on the stimulus and excitement rather than the learning outcomes. Thus, discussions of assessment criteria and learning outcomes should also be part of the initial shared planning. In addition, one activity, even one in which a period of integrated lessons has culminated, should not require an unrealistic amount of advance preparation and should be balanced against the other curriculum needs of the school.

Similarly, a TA may volunteer to be involved in arranging trips and recruiting visitors to support an area of integrated learning such as a museum trip or a geography field trip or inviting a visitor to school to talk about their occupation. The administration and organisation of such visits can be onerous, and occasionally the learning intention can be lost in the search for an exciting out-of-school experience. Pupils may remember the drama of the event, or sometimes even the gift shop, rather than the intended learning. Again it is important for the manager of the TAs to remind them of the need to keep the focus on the learning intention, which can sometimes be met more effectively by a simple activity.

TA strengths, skills, and enthusiasms

Campbell (2005: 128) highlights the importance of playing to everyone's strengths in school and the value of flexibility. She quotes one headteacher:

> You can't afford for teachers not to have strengths in core areas of maths and literacy but with support workers like Miss X you can use her expertise in sport and community work almost exclusively. You have a lot more flexibility about using the expertise of support workers.

A TA can gain considerable job satisfaction from the feeling of contributing expertise to a topic and from recognition of that expertise by professional colleagues. The HMI report (2002: 18) reviewing the impact of the work of TAs concludes 'making the most of [TAs'] abilities should certainly not threaten the professionalism of teachers; rather it should be encouraged and developed to the full'.

Case Study 7.5 Using TA skills effectively

In an average-sized urban primary school a Year 4 group experienced a cross-curricular week in which teachers and TAs worked together to provide a range of experiences with a new school garden as a central resource. One TA who was a keen gardener brought in a range of plants for a science session, demonstrating directly the key aspects of plant biology by allowing children to remove plants from their pots and examine in detail their parts, matching these with the diagrams they had been given. The plants were later planted out in the garden and monitored, to extend pupils' knowledge of the cycle of growth and life-cycles.

While an enthusiastic TA with a passion for creativity and a desire to be involved in resource preparation can be a much-appreciated asset, occasionally enthusiasms need to be curbed and this has to be managed sensitively by the class teacher, otherwise it will place a strain on this important relationship. A careful teacher overview is needed to rein in enthusiasm and keep the focus on learning though experience, rather than just the experience.

Special Schools and the integrated curriculum

One setting where the creative curriculum, topic-based learning, and extensive integration of support staff can often be seen at its best is in the Special School. There are a number of reasons for this.

First, most, if not all, pupils have Individual Education Plans and very fully defined needs and targets. Inevitably, the range of their skills and academic achievement is narrower, and progress much slower and more precisely defined, and thus, perhaps, easier for staff to monitor. For less academically qualified staff, as many TAs are, curriculum subject knowledge is less likely to be a stumbling block than in mainstream classes, although this is more than balanced by the medical and SEN understanding and expertise they may need to have.

However, the severity of those very needs often means that TAs in Special Schools are more likely to have had specific training for working with the pupils for whom they are responsible and are often working more closely with teaching colleagues. As Murray (2009: 14) comments, TA work in Special Schools 'can require in-depth knowledge and understanding of a wide range of learning and physical disabilities'. She points out that such TAs are also more likely than mainstream TA colleagues to have teaching responsibilities.

Second, because pupils' learning is so often severely constrained by their needs and difficulties, considerable ingenuity is needed to design activities which meet the curriculum requirements yet are accessible to the pupils.

Third, short concentration spans and significant loss of teaching time for medical or toileting interventions mean a need to be creative about using activities not necessarily obviously academic in focus for curriculum delivery.

Fourth, pupil targets are often focused on personal development and early communication or engagement skills at the bottom or middle of P-levels, and these tend to lend themselves to a wider range of activities than more curriculum-specific learning objectives.

Finally, in some settings, the needs of the children can lead to there being one member of staff for every child in a group, with those staff members, be they teacher or TA, taking significant responsibility for their pupil during the lesson as the teachers cannot leave their own charge unsupervised to monitor all the other pupils and staff. This also means TAs are more closely involved in training, planning and curriculum and assessment meetings, decisions and implementation than is the norm in mainstream settings. Murray quotes a Special School TA who comments, 'You're part of a classroom team where everyone has specific skills to offer' (2009: 14).

All of these factors lead to lessons where many curriculum areas and skills may be covered, albeit at a limited level, and where consolidation may occur even when the intended activity breaks down or is suspended to allow for pastoral or medical care to be administered. Special School staff in the observed setting had often developed, or even planned, excellent spur-of-the-moment adaptations to the original plan to maximise learning when things change.

In addition, because of the need to capture small achievements and keep close records of these, and because the one-to-one work makes this possible, Special Schools often have well-developed informal as well as formal assessment methods. These may include photographs (as some skills being recorded may be physical or related to facial expression), post-it notes quickly written and later attached to pupil records, and shared achievement feedback during plenaries. These are often the only way in which such students can have some experience of self-assessment – or at least of assessment in which they can take some part, as the comments are usually made by the TA, referring to what the child has done, for example, 'Tim managed to do all the actions for that song, didn't you, Tim?' Also, during activities, teachers and TAs frequently make very specific assessment for learning and give formative feedback directly to students, such as 'Good signing, Abdul'; 'Good watching, Louise'. Halliwell emphasises the need for TAs in Special Schools to be trained to support, differentiate, assess, and record progress, and indeed suggests that experienced TAs may well be used to 'model how to deliver an intervention programme or use a specific resource' (2003: 15).

In each of the following case studies, some at least of the elements above were in evidence.

Case Study 7.6 Maximising learning experiences

In School A, a student also studying for a part-time degree completed her research project into the time 'lost' to curriculum delivery because of breaks for medical or toileting care. She found that those staff who felt most satisfied with their ability to deliver the curriculum were those who had developed strategies to extend learning into those areas; for example, by counting the tiles in the toilet area to continue a mathematics session, or identifying colours of clothes, or continuing to sing the songs being used in the main lesson, or practising fastening clothing. As it was often TAs who did toileting tasks, this had become a well-developed skill in those whose teachers had seen the advantage of working in this way, or who had themselves seen the opportunities. The research recommendation was that the school should formalise this by identifying explicitly in planning ways in which such intervals in the school day could be used, and linking key skills to specific activities.

Case Study 7.7 Capturing TA expertise

In the same school, a TA with musical skills was invited to attend a session in Foundation Stage to play songs for the children to engage in. Songs with interactive components and repetitive refrains were used to maximise pupils' engagement and to assess their ability to predict, to make deliberate movements and choices, and to engage with others. Pupils were also encouraged to take turns to communicate, in some cases using electronic methods, or signing whether they wanted the songs to be loud or quiet or to be fast or slow. TAs worked with each child, in some cases holding them on their laps to assist or control movement, and ensured that each was encouraged and supported to take part. Further skills such as turn-taking and listening to others were also developed. It would not have been possible for the children to be engaged and enabled in this way without the one-to-one support of the class TAs or the musical skills of the visiting TA. Very specific assessment was also possible because of the close observation, including of small voluntary movements, each could make of their pupil.

Case Study 7.8 Personalised learning and assessment

In a lesson with a focus on 'pushing and pulling', a group of Key Stage 1 children functioning at low P-levels were enabled to take part in a range of interactive and kinesthetic activities by the presence and support of several support staff. Thus, one child who could not walk or do active tasks was helped to pull brightly coloured materials through a tube, emphasising through signing the actions of pushing and pulling, and was able to demonstrate her understanding by changing her actions. In addition, communication skills and colour recognition were developed by continuous and repetitive commentary, with signing, by the TA. Meanwhile another TA worked with a child who was mobile but who required close monitoring, having epilepsy and AHDH amongst other special needs, to assist him to use a seesaw, ride a bike, and roll on a large ball, again using the key vocabulary and being assessed through his actions and signs. The teacher worked with two other children with other special needs to help them use the seesaw, which they could not do without support. Yet another child, able to work with some independence, was pushing a pram and being monitored and interacted with by whichever staff member she came towards.

Case Study 7.9 Use of space and detailed assessment

In a another activity with the same group of children with Profound or Moderate Learning Difficulties, the class was divided into two groups by ability and moved into separate rooms to allow less distraction, and to provide smaller spaces for staff to supervise. The teacher mainly worked in one room with a TA but also supervised the work in the adjoining room where two TAs supported pupils. As a result these children, several of whom had mobility problems as well as short concentration spans and limited or no communication skills, were enabled to develop their mathematical skills in the area of data handling. They used playdough, tea sets, bags of varied objects, and other resources to work on colour, counting, sorting, and other related tasks, while also working continuously on their communication skills, following instructions, and, where possible, signing or speaking key words. With these children, learning takes place in tiny increments and may consist of a recognisable, but momentary, attempt to reproduce a recognised sign such as 'more' or 'red'. It is only the close one-to-one work which not only allows the opportunities for these pupils to experience learning opportunities but also allows for their small and intermittent increments of learning to be observed and recorded. It is common policy also for a TA to take photographs of activities to capture children's engagement and achievement, not only for recording purposes but also to share with parents and carers.

In mainstream schools, the role of TAs may differ somewhat, although Blatchford *et al.* (2009: 1) found that 'the vast majority of support provided by TAs, both in and out of the classroom, was for low attaining pupils and those with SEN' and so much of the experience of Special School TAs will be similar to that of TAs in mainstream schools. Hughes adds that other aspects of the difference between the role of the teacher and the TA can have an impact on pupils' learning, as TAs can be more relaxed in their interaction, and can act as 'valuable providers of help; promoting opportunities for collaborative work . . . and creating a secure setting for the pupils to reflect on what is being learned' (1997: 108), free from the whole class management issues that may prevent the class teacher from providing this for all pupils.

Conclusions

Whether in a mainstream or Special School setting, there seem to be some criteria linked to success which might be pointers for all schools to consider when planning both the use of a creative curriculum and good deployment of support staff. Key issues seem to be:

- Close involvement of TAs in planning, assessment, and lesson delivery. The effective implementation of this is identified as a key difficulty by Smith *et al.* (2004): 'The main difficulty associated with working with teaching assistants was the lack of time teachers and teaching assistants had to prepare together'. Little progress seems to have been made in this area to date, as evidenced in the research cited earlier by Blatchford *et al.* (2009). The fact that TAs are typically part-time staff can aggravate the situation and they may find that they are present for parts of the initial planning but miss key elements because of their timetabled hours.
- A perception of the valued status of support staff. We are now well distanced from Balshaw's (1999) description of the 'spy in the classroom' teacher perception of the TA; this is confirmed in Smith *et al.*'s (2004) research identifying the 'considerable level of support for teaching assistants' as illustrated by a quotation from a primary teacher: 'teaching assistants are so valuable. I find the children get huge benefits.'
- Appropriate high-quality training for TAs in relevant skills and subject knowledge. A further key finding from Blatchford *et al.* (2009: 134) was that 'more often TAs' subject knowledge did not match that of teachers', and the TAs' 'wider pedagogical role' needed to be supported by training and continuing professional development.
- Close analysis of pupil skills and needs, leading to good personalised learning with the information and processes shared among all staff.
- Detailed curriculum mapping against activities in order both to identify opportunities for delivery and also to ensure clear understanding by all of exactly what is or can be delivered.
- Detailed and highly informed summative assessment of progress by staff who know their pupils very well and are very clear about the opportunities offered by the lesson or series of lessons, including spotting incidental or unplanned learning opportunities.
- Clear success criteria for attainment and achievement which feeds into self- and peer assessment of learning with assessment systems which allow for quick and on the spot recording of achievement, and continuous sharing of this with other colleagues.
- Explicit management of staff involvement with a realistic appraisal of cost effectiveness of effort involved in some thematic projects.
- Awareness of the impact of differences in contractual arrangements. Support staff may have a range of diverse roles or job descriptions and different line managers: for example, they may act as classroom support, learning mentor, cover for planning, preparation and assessment (PPA) as an HLTA, mid-day supervisor, or after-school club manager. This diversity in roles can militate against easy line management and clarity of priorities in supporting learning.
- Continuing changes in the school culture. Schools have largely now adapted to the workforce remodelling and will be changing to accommodate the new approach to a creative and integrated curriculum, which may necessitate a review of roles and responsibilities between support and teaching staff.
- Training for teachers in working with TAs as identified in Blatchford *et al.* (2009: 133) as a contributory factor in problems in ensuring pupil attainment under TA support.

They recommend that 'a substantial component of all teacher training courses should involve ways of working successfully with support staff' and stress the need to 'consider in a systematic way the management of TA deployment in relation to managerial, pedagogical and curriculum concerns'.

Special Schools may be able to address some of these management issues more easily as they tend to be facilitated by low pupil/adult ratios and by very small teaching groups. There may be more of a challenge in mainstream settings, but approaches which work should not be rejected out of hand just because they are difficult to deliver, or, indeed, adopted in situations where key success predictors cannot be met. On the other hand, they do identify some of the areas of potential challenge for the effective deployment of support staff in the creative curriculum design, delivery, and assessment. If, however, these issues are managed in a constructive and developmental way, the creative curriculum for the twenty-first century is more likely to meet Rose's view (2009), recognising that 'the new curriculum must be underpinned by an understanding of the distinct but interlocking ways in which children learn and develop'. This needs to be understood by all those involved in the delivery of that curriculum to ensure a holistic approach to advancing learning and utilising the skills of the whole school workforce through a well-managed approach and shared understandings.

References

Balshaw, M (1999) *Help in the Classroom* London: David Fulton

Blatchford, P., Bassett, P., Brown, P., Martin, C., Russell, A., and Webber, R. (2009) *The Deployment and Impact of Support Staff in Schools* London: Institute of Education DCSF Research Report DCSF RR148

Campbell, A. (2005) 'All different, all equal' in A. Campbell and G. Fairbairn (eds) *Working with Support in the Classroom* London: Paul Chapman Publishing

Education Guardian http://www.guardian.co.uk/education/2009/sep/04/teaching-assistants-classroom

Halliwell, M. (2003) *Supporting Children with Special Educational Needs* (2nd edn) London: David Fulton

HMI (2002) *Teaching Assistants in Primary Schools: an evaluation of the quality and impact of their work* London: HMSO

Hughes, M. (1997) 'Managing other adults in the classroom' in I. Craig (ed.) *Managing Primary Classrooms* London: Pitman Publishing

Kerry, T. (2001) *Working with Support Staff* Harlow: Pearson Education

Mindham, C. (2004) 'Thinking across the curriculum' in R. Jones and D. Wyse (eds) *Creativity in the Primary Curriculum* London: David Fulton

Murray, J. (2009) 'Special people' *Learning Support Journal* I (Autumn Term): 14–15

Rose, J. (2009) *Independent Review of the Primary Curriculum: final report* (Rose Review) London: DCSF

Smith, P., Whitby, K., and Sharp, C. (2004) *The Employment and Deployment of Teaching Assistants* (LGA Research Report 5/04) Slough: NFER

Walton, A. (2009) 'Support staff as professionals' in A. Walton and G. Goddard (eds) *Supporting Every Child* Exeter: Learning Matters Ltd

Walton, A. and Goddard, G. (2009) *Supporting Every Child: a course book for foundation degrees in teaching and supporting learning* Exeter: Learning Matters

Wilson, R., Sharp, C., Shuayb, M., Kendall, L., Wade, P., and Easton, C. (2007) *Research into the Deployment and Impact of Support Staff Who Have Achieved HLTA Status* Slough: NFER

Monitoring the work and progress of the most able within an integrated curriculum

Carolle Kerry, John Richardson, and Sue Lambert

In this chapter we attempt to bring four distinct approaches to the issue of teaching gifted and talented pupils in primary schools, and to do this in the context of an actual school setting. First, we argue for an approach to analysing learning that depends on assessing cognitive demand. Second, we promote the cross-curricular theme by looking at the school's 'themed weeks', which bring learning together across subject areas. Third, we discuss the teacher/headteacher/governor partnership which reviews our work with gifted and talented pupils. Fourth, we pursue our normal policy in the school of listening to pupils' voices, and how the young people themselves view the cross-curricular approach. In the process we look at the rigour of how to audit the progress of the gifted or talented pupil and we link the processes to debates about identification, lifelong learning, and the nature of knowledge. Throughout, the chapter shows the headteacher, teachers, and governors working together to provide the best educational experience for these pupils and how that may impact on other pupils in the class or school.

Introduction and definition

Over the years there has been a variety of 'labels' to describe those children of higher ability. For the present purpose the government-favoured 'gifted and talented' will be adopted and the following broad definitions are offered:

> Gifted young people are those 'who have the ability to excel academically in one or more subjects such as English, drama, technology'.
> (DCSF quoted in CfBT / Lincolnshire County Council 2007a: 4)

> Talented young people are defined as those 'who have the ability to excel in practical skills such as sport, leadership, artistic performance. These students may well follow a vocational pathway to accreditation and employment'.
> (ibid.)

Challenging the most able children in the classroom is at the heart of an effective learning environment and is every teacher's, and every school's, responsibility (CfBT / Lincolnshire County Council, 2007b). The most able pupils need to be presented with work that challenges them, stretches and excites them, motivates them, and which, at the same time, caters for 'their social and emotional needs . . . Motivation, high aspirations and good self esteem are key to fulfilling potential' (DfES 2006a: 15). For many people, providing education for the most able pupil smacks of elitism, but, in an environment in which the cognitive stakes are high, raising the thinking level for able pupils benefits all pupils regardless of ability (Manuel 1992).

Since 1988, teaching and learning have been set within the boundaries of the National Curriculum, a curriculum straitjacketed into core subjects (English, mathematics, and science) and foundation subjects plus religious education. The social and emotional aspects of learning were, it may be hypothesised, constrained by the necessity of schools conforming to the rigour of assessment, reports, league tables, and Ofsted Inspections. This strait-jacketing effect of the National Curriculum across primary school education was noted by Kerry and Kerry (2000a); and more recently by Bolden and Newton (2008) even in the context of mathematics teaching. A wind of change appeared to be blowing across the country's primary schools, when, in 2009, *The Independent Review of the Primary School: the final report* (DCSF 2009) was published. A change of political masters in 2010 determined the Report's abandonment together with plans for a new curriculum in 2011. However, some of the Report's recommendations still resonate with the present argument and are worthy of consideration:

> [S]ubject disciplines are grouped into six areas of learning that have at their heart the essential knowledge, understanding and skills that all primary-aged children need in order to make progress and achieve. Teachers will be able to make links within and across areas of learning to help children understand how each distinctive area links to and is supported by others.
>
> (ibid.: 2.23)

The earlier *Interim Report* (DCSF 2008a) had entered the debate of subject disciplines versus cross-curricular studies and noted: 'when observed in practice by the Review, the approach which attempts to teach skills as entities disembodied from a coherent core of worthwhile knowledge has not been convincing in securing children's understanding of important key ideas' (ibid.: 1.46) and

> There will be times when it is right to marshal worthwhile content into well-planned cross-curricular studies . . . because it provides ample opportunity for [children] to use and apply what they have learned from discrete teaching, for example, in mathematics, English and ICT.
>
> (ibid.: 1.47)

However, the *Final Report* (2009) draws back somewhat and only dips a toe into the debate of subject disciplines versus cross-curricular studies:

> Consultations before and after the interim report showed widespread support . . . for explicit opportunities for children to benefit from subject teaching *and* cross-curricular studies that cover the principal areas of our history, culture and achievement and the wider world.
>
> (DCSF 2009a: 2.12) (emphasis original)

And of the potential of cross-curricular studies *per se*:

> Areas of learning provide powerful opportunities for children to use and apply their knowledge and skills across subjects . . . While it is usual for primary schools to think of mathematics, English and ICT in this way, virtually all subjects serve more than one purpose: they are valuable as disciplines in their own right and add value to cross-curricular studies.
>
> (ibid.: 2.35)

It is argued elsewhere (Chapter 2 above) that Rose has merely mirrored Gardner's (2007) developing work on multiple intelligences, and has done so without Gardner's careful analysis of the chosen intelligences, thus producing a rather poor imitation of them. None the less, Rose's aspirations for the nation's primary children are set out in his letter to the Secretary of State that accompanies the Report:

> I hope the review will help our primary children to build on their success so that all our children benefit from a curriculum which is challenging, fires their enthusiasm, enriches and constantly enlarges their knowledge, skills and understanding and, above all, instils in them a lifelong love of learning.
>
> (DCSF 2009a: 5)

Some critics of cross-curricular learning infer that with the abolition of subject-focused teaching will come a diminution of learning across the board (Woodhead 2008), with the concomitant effect of special disadvantage to pupils of higher ability. This contention is disputed in the present volume (Chapter 1). Given that, however spuriously, subject-specific approaches are linked indissolubly in some minds with 'quality', the challenge for teachers in an era of increased school and teacher autonomy will be to ensure that our most gifted and talented students perform to the best of their ability within the parameters of the now legitimised cross-curricular approaches and more open curriculum decisions.

During the 1950s exploration into the levels of cognitive demand made upon pupils in class was summarised by Bloom (1956) in the chapter on 'The cognitive domain'. Bloom identified six levels within the cognitive domain, from simple recall or knowledge of facts previously learned, through comprehension, to application, analysis, synthesis, and evaluation – these last being higher-order thinking skills. Bloom's classification (see Chapter 2 above) provides an easily implemented, differentiated model for categorising learning in the classroom, a model which can be applied both to core subjects and to the linking of subject content through cross-curricular studies (see case study below). Within the Bloomian model pupils are given the opportunity to experience learning which requires all levels of thinking, not just the basic recall or comprehension that research indicates (Kerry and Kerry 2001) is the everyday experience of many young people.

In reviewing the work of gifted and talented children in the school we make a conscious effort to establish and take on board the implications of exposing children to higher-level thinking and to improving cognitive demand. Children's articulation of their learning in these terms helps to determine the assessment process.

Reflection

Consider the tools and strategies which are used in your school or class to:

*   Differentiate levels of thinking
*   Ensure that gifted and talented pupils, and all pupils, have the chance to operate at each cognitive level
*   Provide cross-curricular learning opportunities as well as those which are narrowly subject-based.

Having looked in general terms at the provision of cross-curricular work and at the possibility of using higher-order thinking as a marker for the gifted and talented (and incidentally for all children), we return to look in a little more detail at the vexed question of identification – specifically in the non-core subjects.

Identification issues relating to gifted and talented pupils in non-core subjects

Defining what is meant by the terms gifted and talented is challenging, particularly within areas of the curriculum with less direct or less standardised forms of monitoring and assessment than are prevalent in the core subjects, i.e. testing and close assessment. For the gifted and talented, abilities may be more skills-based than subject-based. But the caveat is: more able pupils may, none the less, have diverse needs, and their abilities may not be obvious. It is important to recognise, for example, that emotional intelligence may support or inhibit learning and that children from vulnerable groups are more likely to under-achieve or perhaps not have their gifts or talents easily recognised (DCSF 2008c, 2009b; Goleman 1996). Frustration, low self-esteem, lack of challenge, physical ill health, and the expectations of others can all impact on the identification of abilities and achievements for gifted and talented pupils (Headington 2003; George 1995).

The Report of the Teaching and Learning in Review Group (DfES 2006b), commenting on under-achievement, noted that gaps persist in achievement, and factors that contribute to these are complex and interrelated; they include the individual attitudes, beliefs, and expectations of pupils, parents, and teachers.

It is also important to say, right from the outset, that what is reflected here is a philosophy of learning. If we adopt the stance described with our pupils, then as teachers it is useful for us to be aware of our own expectations, values, and beliefs. How far are we willing or able to be flexible and open to ideas in our responses to gifted and talented children, or their alternative ways of working and learning, when these may not be what we planned for, expected, or understood? Do we reflect on our own teaching and learning, as Pollard (2005: 14) suggests, so that **we** develop skills through a cyclical process in which teachers monitor, evaluate, and revise their own practice continuously? The Cambridge Review (Alexander 2009) also emphasises the need for teaching to be informed by research which helps to clarify conditions for effective teaching and learning, and Sousa (2003: 7) also notes that teachers may need training to recognise any stereotypical views they may hold which may impact on effective teaching and learning.

The emphasis of government and public perception on logical and linguistic intelligence still, arguably, determines how schools are judged (Sousa 2003). This is acknowledged in the Cambridge Review (Alexander 2009), where the importance of separating this assessment for accountability from the need to report on attainment in all areas of education is noted. Certainly mathematics and English form the basis of formal assessment for identifying gifted and talented children through testing; if the definition is narrow then certain gifts and talents will not 'fit' the indicators or measures. Those talented in sport or music can often, arguably, be identified through their performance; but those with ability to work collaboratively, who demonstrate leadership skills or a perceptive appreciation of artwork, may be less easily identified or supported. This point is illustrated in Case Study 8.2 later in the chapter.

Guidance and information about how to identify, monitor, and assess children who are gifted and talented in non-core areas are often vague and, as the DCSF (2008b) comments, it is schools themselves that have the discretion to decide how best to identify gifted and talented pupils. The DCSF does acknowledge that identification should encompass, as well as academic subjects, a range of talents such as leadership or areas of vocational skill, and that this identification should be a continuous process, based on a portfolio approach, part of school life, and involve open communication with educators, pupils, and parents and carers. But guidance is still very much open to interpretation, which makes it especially difficult for young teachers or those in schools which do not prioritise work in this area.

A further challenge here is that one of the criteria in identifying gifted and talented learners is ability rather than achievement (DCSF 2008c) – in other words, scores are not the whole story (Sousa 2003). The gift or talent may be skills-based, linked to particular intelligences (Gardner 1993) that transfer across subjects rather than being subject-specific, or it may be in areas where quantifying the ability is difficult and arguably not applicable. Lazear (2004: 86) would argue that any testing should include the development of intelligence as well as mastery of the academic curriculum. Although multiple intelligence is a matter for debate, it does highlight the need to consider the range of activities in which pupils can show their abilities and that opportunities need to be given for such gifts or talents to be observed (White et al. 2003).

Debate within research about whether intelligence is fixed or changeable, and even its exact definition, remains active; but contemporary research findings seem to indicate that intelligence can be taught, learned, developed, and enhanced, so fixed identification is perhaps inappropriate or at best unhelpful (Lazear 2004; White et al. 2003; DCSF 2008b; Hymer 2002). This affects how we approach learning and teaching in terms of their being seen as a linear or cyclical process (Smith 2005). If intelligence is seen as changeable, then more weight should be given to continuous process-based identification of children rather than reliance on tests or exams (Hymer 2002). The learning needs to be more interactive, be less about right answers, and should encourage collaborative work. Identification of gifted and talented pupils should be by multiple criteria so teachers should not become too reliant on one method (Smith 2005; White et al. 2003; Hymer 2002). This highlights one of the challenges for teachers in identifying and supporting children who are gifted and talented – there is no homogeneous group, so approaches to identifying, monitoring, and supporting the learning of gifted and talented children needs to be diverse; personalised to the individual. It is also difficult for teachers to define how indicators are used. Does one indicator suggest a gift or talent, or should children exhibit a number of indicators to be considered gifted or talented?

DCSF (2008c) also notes the essential part that teacher observation and informal assessment play in identification, monitoring, and assessment of gifted and talented children, but again professional development to do this effectively and consistently is often lacking. Although it could be argued that experienced class teachers are good at using ongoing assessment, observation, and questioning to address learners' needs and plan next steps in learning, this is not specific to meeting the needs of the gifted and talented. Observation on which judgements are based needs to include: noting how children verbalise or write their evidence, and through a skilled teacher asking high-level challenging questions (Headington 2003). However, too often, teachers are not formally educated in a range of observation and questioning techniques that might help focus their monitoring and assessment of children.

Consideration of how we help learners to invest in the learning, know the purpose of the learning, and have ownership of it is also important. Research led by Rudduck and Flutter (2004) shows that consulting pupils and involving them in teaching and learning approaches lead to higher pupil engagement and attainment, particularly through assessment for learning. The use of assessment for learning strategies enables all children, but particularly gifted and talented children, to have ownership of learning, engage in self-reflection and target setting, evaluate and check work, negotiate with staff, use their own initiative, and attribute success or failure to their own decision-making rather than to the teacher or curriculum (Wallace *et al.* 2007). This clearly requires a flexible approach to teaching and learning, which a review of research by White *et al.* (2003: 18) found was one of the most important characteristics of teaching gifted and talented children.

Reflection

How do you identify the gifted and talented children in your school or class? What could you do to do this more effectively?

Teachers need to build opportunities for children to set the success criteria, be involved in self- and peer assessment, and have opportunities to give and receive feedback from the teacher. Children (all children, not only the gifted and talented) need to be actively engaged in the process so that targets can be set for future learning to aid motivation (Headington 2003; Smith 2005). Helping children to develop as autonomous, lifelong learners who are able to direct their own learning and work independently on investigative or problem-solving activities that challenge and allow creative thinking should be the aim of all those in education.

The identification of, and provision for, gifted and talented pupils

In recent years the identification of and provision for pupils deemed as gifted or talented has received its highest profile ever in the National Curriculum era, i.e. since 1988. This is evident not least of all in the wealth of government publications designed to support identification and provision (DfES 2007; DCSF 2008c). With this increased emphasis has come relativity in the definition of what makes a child gifted or talented, with DfES

Guidelines suggesting that schools identify 5–10 per cent of pupils as 'gifted and talented' in each year (Mouchel Parkman 2007: 10–11). This relativism is not without controversy, not least because of pupil mobility. Does a child become gifted and talented in comparison to the relative attainment of his or her peers and, crucially, does he or she require any provision above and beyond the differentiation already evident in classrooms where good practice is observed?

At South Hykeham Community Primary School children are defined as gifted and talented when it is deemed that they cannot have their needs met by in-class differentiation alone.

Identification in the core subjects of English, mathematics, and science is heavily supported by summative assessment data, for example optional SATs and end of unit assessments. However, as we have seen, the non-core subjects do not lend themselves as easily to a data-based model of identification. For this reason the school has begun to use cross-curricular or (as we call them) 'themed weeks' both to support the identification of children with gifts and talents and to extend provision for such learners. This is consistent with research suggesting that integrated learning is deemed to support the learning of gifted or talented students (Van Tassel-Baska and Brown 2007).

Reflection

- What provision is in place in your school to cater for the specific needs of individual gifted and talented children?
- How is their progress recorded?
- What are the respective roles of teachers, the head (or designated person for gifted and talented), and governors in this process?

The use of cross-curricular themed weeks in meeting the needs of gifted and talented students

In the last two academic years themed weeks have taken place on a termly basis primarily to enhance the curriculum, and to provide increased breadth and enrichment. Subjects have been selected to reflect the school's monitoring programme. In addition to the themed weeks, TASC (Thinking Actively in a Social Context) weeks have also been used which take children outside the confines of the National Curriculum and its school-based interpretation to address real-life issues. These are based on the widely acclaimed work of Wallace et al. (2004). The two TASC themes used to date have been planning healthy Christmas parties and preparing all aspects of summer productions from tickets to props. These provide opportunities for staff to confirm or challenge their understanding of a pupil's gifts and talents and also to identify new gifts and talents that are less likely to be seen in single-subject teaching and within the context of objective-driven focused lessons.

South Hykeham is a small school (NOR 136) where subject leadership falls on a limited number of staff and typically teachers lead more than one subject. Assessment for Learning (AfL) strategies are in place and ensure that teachers have a good grasp of levels of attainment and our themed weeks have revealed few surprises in terms of identification of pupils – our register of gifted and talented students has not been altered as a result.

However, confirmation that pupils are working at higher cognitive levels can be made through themed weeks.

To ensure that meaningful time is given over to each curriculum area, core subjects are a focus for one half-term each year. Non-core subjects are focused in a three-year cycle.

The cross-curricular themed weeks do not only support identification of needs, however, nor do they benefit the gifted and talented alone. They are also a powerful tool for the development of gifts and talents for all children. In our art and RE week for instance, children developed abilities within a variety of media quickly and were able to have a greater choice over which media to use because of the focused nature of the week. The ability to link concepts from different curriculum areas also allowed for enhanced learning, and an outcome of the art and RE week is developed below. Planned themed weeks for the current academic year include a 'money week' which falls within the mathematics monitoring part of the cycle and a 'multicultural week' which embraces PHSE.

Themed weeks are being implemented across our curriculum primarily to enhance learning for all students, but the intensity of focus lends itself to clearer assessment by staff of what individual children can achieve. From this, provision at other times during the school year can be more closely linked to gifted or talented individuals as well as to other children. This supports our philosophy that enhancing learning for the most able enhances it, too, for all students (Kerry and Kerry 2000b). An example of work carried out in a themed week appears as Case Study 8.1. The case describes something of the content of the week. Interviews with the subject leader and with a pupil, Jonathan, are described; subsequently an analysis of Jonathan's interview draws out aspects of the learning that has taken place.

Case Study 8.1 A themed approach: art and RE

Art and religious education were the subjects of exploration by pupils at South Hykeham Community Primary School, Lincoln, during a themed week in which they studied 'Creation'. The art and RE subject leader described the week as 'a purposeful cross-curricular learning opportunity' engaging the whole school. Normal lessons were set aside, and all staff were involved in the planning and execution of the week's activities. Staff had previously attended a painting workshop at a local secondary school in which they learned first-hand about progression in painting skills and what they could expect from their children. During the RE sessions the children learned about and from the story of Creation from a Christian perspective and that of other faiths and cultures, and, through the medium of art, applied this learning. They learned first-hand from visitors and second-hand through stories and myths. Throughout the week the subject leader monitored the children's work to ensure that each child worked purposefully and that differentiation, where applied, was appropriate. Observer governors noted the enjoyment and engagement of the children, and the subsequent artistic outcomes were displayed throughout the school

---

Within these parameters it is pertinent to ask: what evidence does the school have that this method of cross-curricular learning develops the skills and understanding of the able pupil, and, second, how can this learning be assessed?

To try to ascertain the levels of learning that took place, it was necessary to understand the planning, execution, and reflection processes that took place. A semi-structured interview with the subject leader was undertaken (extracts below), and to triangulate this process the authors had access to taped interviews between her and pupils that took place within a few days of the art/RE themed week.

Interview with the subject leader

The subject leader (SL) was asked about the motivation and planning behind the cross-curricular art/RE themed week.

We are continually looking for purposeful cross-curricular learning opportunities throughout the school. To ensure that we can monitor progression and continuity throughout the school we try to adopt whole school approaches where relevant. The motivation was based on looking at the two subjects that I co-ordinate, asking how we measured progress in the two subjects, knowing where the school was at in RE and art, knowing what we were doing on a daily basis and asking: 'Where do we go from here?' . . . Our planning for the themed week revolved around a document which shows the basic skills in art . . . We all work on a basic skill at one time . . . so all of the teachers were teaching painting at the same time. The document breaks up where the children should be at in each year group . . . We know where the children should be at, where they are supposed to be and we know the next step and the one below.

But how did this work in practice? The subject leader's interview with a nine-year-old Y4 pupil – Jonathan – provided clues.

Case Study 8.2 Jonathan's understanding of creation

Jonathan was asked to look at a selection of photographs and artwork and asked whether, by looking at the pictures, he could make any link between the Christian story of creation and the aboriginal story of creation:

Well, we say that God created the sun, moon, and the stars, and it is sort of the same for the aboriginals because they thought it was, they thought it was the ancestors who created the sun, moon and stars . . . Christians think that there was one person who created all of it whereas some other religions believe there are a series of different people or things who created different things and like, for example, with the aborigines, they had like ancestors, they could be snake, they could be human, they could be emu, they could be whatever animals that are in Australia. Well, we say that God then rested but they say that they just turn themselves into something different, and they slept. And they also think that dream time is for ever, and they don't think, whereas we think that Creation ended once God created the earth, the sun, and the moon and the stars and the planets, they don't. They think dream time is still happening and that it is always happening just like trees grow, that's their explanation . . .

Jonathan was then asked whether he believed God created the world in six days:

I personally think, I believe He created the world of course. I personally think it might have taken Him a bit longer than six days. Perhaps instead of six days, there might have been six weeks, six months or six years. One year for each of them, 'cos God is eternal living, so days to Him are different from days to us. Like a day to Him would be like a second. To us, a day is 24 hours, hours to Him are weeks or months . . .

He then returns to the aboriginal creation story:

I would like to have found out exactly why they believe there were ancestors, though I respect other people's religions . . . I'd like to know how they believe that ancestors had magic. . .

He ponders further about aboriginal magic in the story:

And also I do find that having a sacred digging stick which made things appear would be a bit dramatic, perhaps where they dug they just dropped seeds in. But I do find that a bit, well, how exactly would that just spring up?

Analysing the learning in a cross-curricular themed week activity

In a follow-up interview, the subject leader saw Jonathan as 'using higher order thinking skills . . . that he had the ability to compare and contrast two differing cultures and he was able to give his own opinion about them'. But in order to confirm or refute the teacher's assessment, and to try to understand in greater depth the thinking that Jonathan was undertaking, it was necessary to conduct a small-scale content analysis deconstruction of his conversation.

Content analysis determines the presence of certain words or concepts within, in this instance, language. Researchers quantify and analyse the presence, meaning, and relationships of the words or concepts and then make inferences about the messages that the conversation conveys.

From the outset Jonathan's ability to make comparison across cultures was apparent: '*We say that God created the sun, moon and the stars . . . the aboriginals . . . thought it was the ancestors who created the sun, moon and stars*'. He compares and contrasts: '*Christians think . . . one person created all of it . . . with the aboriginals they had ancestors . . . snake. . . human*

. . . emu. We say that God then rested but they say . . . [the ancestors] slept'. He muses that for aboriginals *'dream time is for ever . . . we think that Creation ended once God created the earth, the sun . . .'*.

Within this paragraph Jonathan rehearses in great detail the knowledge he acquired during the lesson. But his knowledge is not just repetition of fact, i.e. data recall: he evaluates and applies the knowledge: *'We say . . . but the aboriginals thought . . .'*.

Jonathan then turns to the abstract and discusses Creation, both Christian and aboriginal. He analyses what he has learned: *'I personally . . . believe He created the world'*, but within that belief there is a dimension that causes him reflection: *'. . . it might have taken Him a bit longer than six days'*. Speculation creeps in: *'. . . it might have been six weeks, six months or six years'*. He evaluates and makes judgements about the Creation story suggesting that *'God is eternal living, so days to Him are different from days to us'*.

Jonathan's account of the aboriginal story of creation causes him to think deeply – he wants to know answers to questions: why aboriginals believe in ancestors, why these ancestors had magical powers. The *'sacred digging stick'* causes him problems and he tries to solve this issue with a rational explanation: *'Perhaps where they dug, they just dropped seeds in'*.

Reflection

How might you use the idea of a cross-curricular themed week in your own situation to help meet the needs of all children and specifically those of the gifted and talented?

How could you use Bloom's *Taxonomy*, as described above and in Chapter 2, to help you understand the levels of thinking in your own classes?

The use of audit tools to support the needs of gifted and talented children

The Quality Standard for Gifted and Talented Education, jointly developed by the DfES and the National Association for Gifted and Talented Youth (NAGTY), is a self-evaluation and planning tool for schools wishing to improve their gifted and talented provision (DfES 2005). School leaders and teaching staff are able to assess their school's provision through a series of statements indicating whether, in their perception, the school is at 'entry' (readily achievable by most schools), 'developing' (provides extra challenge), or 'exemplary' level (designed for centres of excellence). The 'exemplary' level of the Quality Standard and the more recent Classroom Quality Standards (DCSF 2008d) should be useful tools in the teacher's armoury for understanding and enhancing the learning of gifted and talented pupils in an integrated curriculum.

Consistent use of the Quality Standards enables schools to assess where they are located on the three-tiered scale and allows for provision in all of its forms, from policy to classroom practice, to be identified. Once current practice has been identified, the Standards can then be used for effective action planning to secure enhanced provision for gifted and talented pupils. This has been the case at South Hykeham, where a cycle of audit, action plan, and review has taken place over the last two years involving teachers, the headteacher, and a group of governors. This audit tool also allows for comparison of provision between all learners and those identified as having gifts or talents, the implication being that there should be equality of opportunity, i.e. no mismatch in provision.

The use of this tool has also been discussed at length in gifted and talented meetings between the head (also leader of gifted and talented provision at the school) and those governors with the gifted and talented remit. Once an accurate picture of existing provision has been agreed, the tool supports improvement by identifying the next phase for development. An example of this is in *identifying* children with gifts or talents.

- 'Entry' provision enables schools to identify gifted and talented pupils and have a shared understanding of what gifted and talented means in terms of local and national contexts.
- At the 'developing' phase pupils are screened annually, and the 'exemplary' aspect of the audit tool practice involves using multiple criteria and sources of evidence to identify children. At South Hykeham the tool was used to identify next steps in developing identification – the register of children with gifts or talents is now updated termly.

The challenge for the school now is to move to 'exemplary practice' and develop the range of evidence used to determine a child's gifts and talents. This may be through, for example, greater involvement with parents and clubs that children may be involved in as well as extending the use of assessment for learning procedures across the school.

The discussion above notes that tracking of pupils in core subjects is a relatively easy task. Such subjects lend themselves readily to hard data analysis resulting from testing, and the majority of schools use data to track under-performance against targets. It is in non-core areas that tracking of pupil performance is typically more difficult, as argued earlier.

Tracking progress using a cross-curricular approach

Typically at South Hykeham non-core subjects such as art have been assessed using expectations of achievement at the end of a unit of work. Each unit of work has a designated series of learning outcomes. Where children have exceeded or not met these outcomes they are recorded as having done so. Children who are consistently recorded as exceeding expectations may be considered as gifted and talented within that subject area, and their needs may not be met by differentiation alone.

This approach to assessment can be used when adopting a more themed approach to curriculum planning as long as all relevant outcomes are identified and importantly children are assessed accurately. Themed approaches of themselves do not cause assessment and tracking difficulties. It is the need to provide a curriculum framework with a high regard for continuity and progression that allows for accurate assessment to ensure that future learning builds on prior skills and knowledge. Children with gifts or talents may best exhibit these within the context of integrated learning and indeed may learn best within such a framework, but it is also necessary to assess and track progress by subject in order to tailor provision to needs. With the advent of Assessing Pupil Progress (APP), assessment of pupils, within the core subject of the National Curriculum at least, is changing. If its principles were extended to other aspects of the curriculum, it would support the assessment and tracking of progress of talented children further.

The pupil voice on cross-curricular learning experiences

Having discussed in some depth the way the curriculum for gifted and talented pupils is constructed both from the perspective of government policy and from the school's interpretation of that policy, it is pertinent to pause and ask: is what we present to the children as a way of learning something that they can own and enjoy?

A distinctive feature at South Hykeham is its readiness to hear the pupils' voices. We have a long tradition of school council activity, and a strong commitment to meeting pupils' own expressed needs. In order to discover the answer to the question posed above, the authors met with four Y5/6 pupils: Tara, Scott, Olivia, and Michael. The findings from this discussion are presented as Case Study 8.3.

We decided to conclude our discussion of themed weeks by giving a voice to the pupils by interviewing a cross-section of them. Here we record some responses, though the printed word hardly does justice to the way in which they articulated 'fun', 'exciting', and 'enjoyable'.

Case Study 8.3 The pupil voice in cross-curricular working

The children were invited to consider what they learned during the cross-curricular, themed weeks and how that was different from normal lessons:

> We learned things that we wouldn't have learned during ordinary lessons, because you didn't have time to go on to them, . . . take for example during the Money week, if we had not had a themed week we would probably have brushed on the currencies, we would have had say a single lesson [on currency] but during the themed week we had a whole time to study the currencies, so we were able to look at lots of currencies, not just one. (Michael)

They returned to the RE/art week when his class had studied the creation story from the perspective of the First Nations people of America:

> We looked at their tribes and we looked at totem poles and then we looked at maps on the smart board to discover where the different tribes lived. We learned their story about creation, which is different from ours . . . (Scott)

> I knew nothing about the First Nations, so what I learned was new and different. It gave me ideas of how other people lived. (Olivia)

> We learned about something we knew about, creation, from someone else's point of view. We discovered about how they saw the world . . . and in their art they left their mark behind so that we can learn about it. (Michael)

The pupils also called to mind, with great enthusiasm, their science week during which time they 'built' water rockets (science), had visits from the local water company (environmental issues), and a talk from a dentist who, after getting a couple of children to rinse their mouths with special liquid, showed how plaque had settled on teeth.

> In normal lessons we get a piece of text, we copy it down, we look in the book all the time. During themed week we **discovered** how to do things rather than be told about how they were done. And it stuck in my brain more, I can't remember page 65 of the book, but I remembered how to make a water-powered rocket. It sticks in your brain. (Scott)

The children were then asked about skills they had learned to use during a themed week – first when they worked on their own, and second when they worked in groups.

> You use your heads instead of your mouth because you keep your ideas to yourself because you don't want people to take your ideas. On your own you are thinking of every possibility. It's harder on your own than in a group because you have to think of every possibility, the answer to the question, you've got to kind of rocket your brain about. (Michael)

> In the groups you've got to kind of teamwork, work together as a group because you'll just fall out if you don't. (Scott)

> If you work as a group and you are stuck for ideas, you can work with the other people and they can help you. (Tara)

> In a group you can divide out the jobs whereas on your own you've got to do everything, you can share ideas and work out which idea will work the best. (Olivia)

We asked the pupils: did themed weeks excite you as a way of learning? Which themes would you like to investigate in the future? The children's enthusiasm shone through:

> They are a lot more fun, they make you want to do it right and it's going to be good and so you get stuck in. It can be a bit stressful if it's hard. (Scott)

> If it goes wrong it makes you want to do it again, because it is fun. It inspires you. (Olivia)

> You can learn about something different, something you didn't know about and maybe if you enjoyed it you could go on and do it for your work. (Michael)

So 'inspiration' and 'fun' seemed to be the watchwords. But there were other kinds of learning, like empathy:

In road safety week we learned about road safety, safe biking, travelling to and from school but we also learned about it through literacy when we made up a road safety game – we had to write the instructions for that. We made up maps of the local area, so that was geography . . . (Tara)

I found that quite difficult because you have to try to picture the area in your mind. I could probably walk it blindfold but putting it down on paper, that was difficult. (Michael)

They then turned to topics they might like to pursue in future. They agreed that a heroes week could provide a focus on subject areas that have not been covered in previous themes. Interesting philosophical discussions emerged about whom they would class as a 'hero'. Initially pupils concentrated on the Superhero theme, discussing which elements of the curriculum could be incorporated into the theme:

Design and technology could be incorporated into making costumes.

Drama in the form of an end-of-week presentation could be one outcome.

You could link it in with PE as well because of the running around that you would need to do as a Superhero.

You could write a descriptive paragraph about what they are like.

Of the everyday people who might be regarded as 'heroes' the children were keen to involve them through in-depth visits or visitors:

Fire Service, Police Service, Hospital people, ambulance, paramedics. These people could be asked to come into school to talk to the children about how they work and what they do. We could learn about their job, what they do in their job.

This scenario would not be new in any way, but it is interesting that the children wanted to learn 'in more depth': which revisits Michael's opening comment about time.

Having listened to the discussion between the pupils, the headteacher finally raised the issue of choosing future cross-curricular themed weeks. This suggestion was received with great enthusiasm and what follows are their collective thoughts:

You would have a say in what you were doing.

Some children can get to choose the theme, not everyone can but some can.

You can do the theme most people agree on.

> If we go back to the heroes theme every year group could do a different type of hero.
>
> Different year groups might need to have different Themes – Y5/6 are more mature, would probably want to hear from the fire and police service, but Y2/3 might want to do something else.

From the discussion it is clear that the cross-curricular approach of South Hykeham's themed weeks are not just popular, but children see the value of their learning potential, confirming Rose's comment in his Final Report (2009: 8) that 'the appetite and zest for learning of children in their primary years is unrivalled' – perhaps with the proviso that pupils are provided with work that challenges, stretches, excites, and motivates them.

References

Alexander, R. (ed.) (2009) *Children, Their World, Their Education: final report and recommendations of the Cambridge Review* London: Routledge

Bloom, B. (1956) *Taxonomy of Educational Objectives* London: Longman

Bolden, D.S. and Newton, L.D. (2008) 'Primary teachers' epistemological beliefs: some perceived barriers to investigative teaching in primary mathematics' *Educational Studies* 34 (5): 419–32

CfBT (Council for British Teachers Education Trust/Lincolnshire County Council) (2007a) *Gifted and Talented: strategy for supporting gifted and talented pupils incorporating policy and guidance for schools* Lincolnshire School Improvement Service

CfBT (Council for British Teachers Education Trust / Lincolnshire County Council) (2007b) *G&T Update to Governors* South Hykeham School (November)

DCSF (Department for Children, Schools, and Families) (2008a) *Independent Review of the Primary Curriculum Interim Report (The Rose Report)* Nottingham: DCSF

DCSF (Department for Children, Schools, and Families) (2008b) *Effective Provision for Gifted and Talented Children in Primary Schools* Nottingham: DCSF

DCSF (Department for Children, Schools, and Families) (2008c) *Identifying Gifted and Talented Learners – getting started* Nottingham: DCSF

DCSF (Department for Children, Schools, and Families) (2008d) *Gifted and Talented. Classroom Quality Standards (CQS) Guided Resource: a subject focus* Nottingham: DCFS Publications

DCSF (Department for Children, Schools, and Families) (2009a) *Independent Review of the Primary Curriculum Final Report (The Rose Report)* Nottingham: DCSF Publications

DCSF (Department for Children, Schools, and Families) (2009b) *Gifted and Talented Education: guidance on addressing underachievement – planning a whole-school approach* Nottingham: DCSF

DfES (Department for Education and Science) (2005) *National Quality Standards for Gifted and Talented* Nottingham:DfES

DfES (Department for Education and Science) (2006a) *Effective Provision for Gifted and Talented Children in Primary Education* Nottingham: DfES Publications

DfES (Department for Education and Science) (2006b) *2020 Vision: Report of the Teaching and Learning in 2020 Review Group* Nottingham: DfES Publications

DfES (Department for Education and Science) (2007) *Gifted and Talented Education* Nottingham: DfES Publications

Gardner, H. (1993) *Frames of Mind: the theory of multiple intelligences* (2nd edn) London: Fontana Press.

Gardner, H. (2007) 'Multiple lenses on the mind' in C. Huat and T. Kerry (eds) *International Perspectives on Education* London: Continuum

George, D. (1995) *Gifted Education Identification and Provision* London: David Fulton

Goleman, D. (1996) *Emotional Intelligence: why it can matter more than IQ* London: Bloomsbury Publishing

Headington, R. (2003) *Monitoring, Assessment, Recording, Reporting and Accountability: meeting the standards* (2nd edn) London: David Fulton

Hymer, B. with Michel, D. (2002) *Gifted and Talented Learners: creating a policy for inclusion* London: David Fulton

Kerry, C. and Kerry, T. (2000a) 'The effective use of school time in the education of the most able' *Australasian Journal of Gifted Education* 9 (1): 33–40

Kerry, T. and Kerry, C. (2000b) 'The centrality of teaching skills in improving able pupil education' *Educating Able Children* (Autumn): 13–19

Kerry, T. and Kerry, C. (2001) 'The Celtic Park challenge of excellence' *Education Today* 51 (2): 10–15

Lazear, D. (2004) *Multiple Intelligences Approaches to Assessment* Carmarthen: Crown House Publishing Ltd

Manuel, G. (1992) 'Talents that need special nurturing' *Times Educational Supplement* 21 February

Mouchel Parkman (2007) *Institutional Quality Standards in Gifted and Talented Education* London: Mouchel Parkman

Pollard, A. (2005) *Reflective Teaching* London: Continuum

Rose Report (2009). See DCSF (Department for Children, Schools, and Families) (2009) *Independent Review of the Primary Curriculum Final Report (The Rose Report)* Nottingham: DCSF Publications

Rudduck, J. and Flutter, J. (2004) *How to Improve Your School* London: Continuum

Smith, C. (2005) *Teaching Gifted and Talented Children in the Primary School: a practical guide* London: Paul Chapman Publishing

Sousa, D.A. (2003) *How the Gifted Brain Learns* Ventura, California: Corwin Press Inc.

Van Tassel-Baska, J. and Brown, E. (2007) 'An analysis of the efficacy of curriculum models in gifted education' *Gifted Child Quarterly* 51 (4): 342–58

Wallace, B., Maker, J., *et al.* (2004) *Thinking Skills and Problem-Solving: an inclusive approach* Abingdon: Fulton

Wallace, B., Fritton, S., Leyden, S., Montgomery, D., Pomerantz, M., and Winstanley, C. (2007) *Raising the Achievement of Gifted and Talented Pupils within an Inclusive School Framework* Oxford: NACE, and London: Gifted and Talented

White, K., Fletcher-Campbell, F., and Ridley, K. (2003) *What Works for Gifted and Talented Pupils: a review of recent research* Slough: NFER

Woodhead, C. (2008) Another fine mess http://timesonline.co.uk./tol/news.uk/education/article 5336233.ece (accessed 5 February 2009)

Part 4

Issues, skills, and approaches

Chapter 9

Curriculum planning and preparation for cross-curricular teaching

Judith Laurie

This chapter asks why planning is at the heart of successful teaching and, by analysing feedback from educationalists, HMI, and Ofsted on past cross-curricular approaches, suggests principles for more successful topic planning, especially at medium and short term. It emphasises that schools, whilst following selected principles, should feel confident to use an appropriate planning model for their circumstances and children. Through a practical case study example, it illustrates how a medium-term plan may be devised.

Introduction

Effective planning provides the foundation upon which high-quality teaching and learning can be built. Although teachers can often recall outstanding lessons that were taught 'off the cuff', in reality these are the exception not the rule. Most teachers will agree that equally vivid in their memories are the lessons which failed because of inadequate planning and preparation.

Planning is the manifestation of a teacher's thinking about what (and how) she hopes children will achieve and learn by the end of the lesson, week, or unit of work. Ideally, there will be a degree of collaboration with colleagues, which will result in planning that draws on a range of skills and expertise in different subjects. Certainly, Ofsted regards collaborative planning and good subject knowledge as positive features of outstanding teaching and learning (Ofsted 2009b, 2002). 'Planning is the process of thinking, consultation and developing ideas that leads to the production of plans which act as a guide for your lesson' (Hayes 1997: 54). Hayes's notion of planning as a process, which involves consultation with others, reminds us that this should, of course, include the children. Other steps in the process involve consideration of children's prior learning and achievements and how to make the learning relevant, leading to a final plan which is a 'guide' to what is going to happen in the classroom. The word 'guide' reminds us to adopt a flexible approach that will allow for the unexpected, or changes in children's interests.

Whether for discrete subject teaching or integrated learning, effective planning is the key to success (Kerry 2010), and the overall features of effective planning apply to both approaches.

What are the features of effective curriculum planning?

The answer to the question will be influenced by which type of planning is being discussed. It is commonly recognised that there are three main 'levels' of planning:

- Long term – setting out learning for between one or two years or a whole key stage
- Medium term – setting out the learning for a term or half term
- Short term – setting out the learning for a unit of work, normally between one and four weeks' duration. In addition, short term refers to planning for a specific lesson or session.

This chapter does not take further the individual features of these levels; this topic can be more fully explored in several sources (Jacques and Hyland 2003: Arthur *et al.* 2006; Hayes 1997; PNS 2004). However, it is relevant to highlight the importance of achieving coherence between the levels, whilst avoiding repetition or overlap. Experience of working with student teachers shows that a common error in the early stages is to provide too much detail at medium term, much of which is then repeated in short-term planning. The golden rule is that each level of planning should not repeat information from the previous stage but provide detail *additional* to what has already been planned.

Focusing on what features will be present in effective planning at the medium and short term, authorities on education express notably similar views, and common features include:

- Clear objectives, related to the statutory curriculum
- Plans that focus on developing skills and concepts as well as knowledge
- Planning that takes account of children's prior learning
- Short-term planning that is informed by assessment for learning
- Planning that involves children in the process
- Planning that is flexible
- Planning that makes the learning relevant to children
- Strategies for inclusion and differentiation
- Activities well matched to objectives
- Opportunities for first-hand or investigative learning
- Links made between subjects.

This list, while not exhaustive, applies to planning equally for discrete subject teaching and for integrated learning through cross-curricular approaches. That said, there are specific challenges in planning for integrated learning upon which the remainder of this chapter will now focus.

Issues related to successful planning for integrated learning

Integrated learning is a term used to refer to a range of learning experiences; here the context is cross-curricular learning, often referred to as thematic, project, or topic approaches. In such approaches a number of different curriculum subjects are brought together to structure learning through a common 'topic'.

After the news of the Independent Review of Primary Education, led by Sir Jim Rose, began to filter into schools during 2008, older primary teachers were often of the view that his proposals were, at least in part, a return to pre-National Curriculum approaches to primary education when teaching through topic was common in most schools. However, Rose (DCFS 2009) has emphasised that this is too simplistic a view. He is sharp in his response to the 'nothing new' opinion of the review and claims that it is aiming for *quality* rather than *novelty*, and that with regard to 'best practice' 'it would certainly be "new" if many more of our schools were as good as the best' (DCFS 2009: para. 18). It seems that there is a sense of frustration about effective pedagogy in schools; and a key message from the review, that the curriculum should include 'challenging subject teaching alongside equally challenging cross-curricular studies' (Rose 2008: 4), is remarkably similar to what was said by Sir Jim Rose, and his colleagues Alexander and Woodhead, in 1992:

> There is clear evidence to show that much topic work has led to fragmentary and superficial teaching and learning. There is also ample evidence to show that teaching focused on single subjects benefits primary pupils. We see a need both for more sharply focused and rigorously-planned topic work and for an increase in single subject teaching.
>
> (Alexander *et al.* 1992: 3.4)

The second major report of 2009 is the Cambridge Review led by Robin Alexander. Whilst not in agreement with all of Rose's justifications for cross-curricular approaches, in particular using it to address aspects of curriculum overload, he recognises that integration is important and suggests that 'schools think carefully about which aspects might be taught separately and which combined, which need to preserve disciplinary integrity and which are amenable to thematic treatment' (Alexander 2009: 55). He is quite clear that a 'domain', his equivalent to Rose's 'areas of learning', has a thematic coherence and integrity, but is not 'an invitation to low-grade topic work' (2009: 43, 44).

Reflection

What aspects of literacy or numeracy benefited, or might have benefited, from being taught as part of a topic you have taught or planned?

Strengths and weaknesses of cross-curricular approaches

It seems reasonable to conclude that a cross-curricular approach should have a central place in primary teaching and learning (see Chapter 1 in this volume). It is widely accepted (Katz and Chard 2000; Barnes 2007; Dean 2001; DfES 2004; Ofsted 200? ~~~h to offer for successful teaching and learning, including:

- Coherence in learning between different subjects
- Making learning more relevant
- Building and reinforcing key concepts and skills
- Providing contexts for using and applying subject-specific skills

At the same time there have been, over many years, identified thematic teaching. As long ago as 1978 a survey by HMI recor topic or project teaching lacked progression in learning and res mented, and repetitive teaching, especially in subjects such as geo 1978); Barnes (2007: 179) referred to the danger of 'watering Alexander *et al.* (1992: 2) spoke of 'fragmented and superfici whilst Dean (2001: 155) was concerned about how well teacher learning or achieve continuity in the context of topic work.

These concerns of fragmented learning, lack of coherence, repetitive and superficial teaching will be used, in what follows, to consider how a more rigorous planning approach can support effective cross-curricular learning.

Fragmented learning or *lack of coherence* can be the result of selecting aspects of subjects somewhat randomly and bringing them into a topic for reasons that are not entirely related to children's learning. Criticisms have been made of planning for a topic that makes only tenuous or spurious links between subjects. Ofsted (2003: 18) identified that although some of the most creative work seen in schools was interdisciplinary, simply making spurious cross-curricular links could be a barrier to creativity, especially if teachers had a lack of subject knowledge in the arts.

Making tenuous links might be described as using the 'key word approach'. For example, a topic on the theme of water may lead to topics that happen to have the word 'water' in the title or involve water in some way. For example, choosing stories such as Charles Kingsley's *Water Babies*, John Burningham's 'Come Away From the Water, Shirley' or Noah's Ark; history work on how Victorians did their laundry or geography work on the water cycle; whilst Handel's *Water Music* is chosen for listening and appraising. It should be said at once that possibly there are meaningful links to be made between *some* of these aspects and, indeed, very good learning to come from studying all of them, although not necessarily in the context of a topic on water. The literature examples would make excellent contributions to children's literary experiences and are too important to be left to chance inclusion in a topic. Selecting them merely because they have some relationship with water misses the true meaning of cross-curricular learning. It fails to support coherence in teaching history, geography, literacy, or music, or the development of key skills and concepts.

A strategy for a more successful starting point is to consider key questions such as 'what do we want children to gain from this work?' or 'what do we want the children to learn?' (Ofsted 2009b: para. 30). Furthermore, when these key questions have been answered, it helps to then identify focused topic questions such as 'why is water important in our lives?' The answers to such questions will begin to direct and guide the choices of what to include in the curriculum plan. Taking the importance of water as a specific topic question and key concept, we may now begin to see how some of the original choices may not advance the children's learning about water. Although work about the Victorian laundry may well have a place here, perhaps there are other literature choices that can offer starting points for more pertinent discussion – for example, the aboriginal legend of the water-holding frog 'Tiddalik' which, amongst other things, illustrates the effects of drought.

As well as seeking coherence across subjects, Pollard (2002: 199) noted that there should also be consideration of coherence *within* individual subjects in order to avoid *superficial or 'watered down'* learning. He notes that coherence is 'only partially amenable to planning, for it derives its force from the sense, or otherwise, which the children make of the curriculum which is provided'. It seems reasonable to suggest that children can be helped to make sense of the curriculum if the teacher has a secure understanding of the subjects. However, an expectation that individual primary teachers can have in-depth expertise in all subjects of the statutory curriculum is unrealistic. Furthermore, what is meant by 'subject knowledge' and its relationship to effective teaching has been a matter of debate for many educationalists (e.g. Blenkin *et al.* 1992; Alexander 2009). There is a particular concern here that there is a difference between *mastery* of knowledge and simple knowledge of facts. Pollard (2002: Chapter 8) provides a useful overview of this debate.

Using the expertise of subject leaders who can support colleagues and monitor the coherence of planning for 'their' subject contributes to progression and coherent learning within and across each subject. The role of subject leaders has been one that Ofsted has repeatedly referred to in relation to effective planning and supporting teachers' subject knowledge (Ofsted 2002, 2009a). Most recently, in a report focusing on the particular demands that different subjects make on teachers' subject knowledge, Ofsted recommended that schools should develop access for teachers to 'an expert subject leader'. Recognising that it is unrealistic to expect that primary schools will have experts for all subjects, they encourage making links with other local schools, Advanced Skills Teachers (AST) and 'other' experts such as museum staff or members of the community (Ofsted 2009b). This is certainly an option which schools might actively consider to boost the quality of their work.

One aspect of teacher subject knowledge that may seem obvious but is key to success in planning is knowledge and understanding of the National Curriculum (NC) programmes of study and levels of attainment. Being able to recognise where meaningful and coherent links can be made across individual subjects and which transferable skills and concepts are relevant necessitates confidence in working from the National Curriculum documents. My work in Initial Teacher Training (ITT) since 1995 has shown how much more difficult it has become to ensure that student teachers develop this familiarity. In many schools student teachers are directed to plan, sometimes entirely, from sources other than the National Curriculum, most commonly the revised frameworks of the Primary Strategy, commercial schemes, and internet sources. Of course, experienced teachers are likely to be able to make the links between the NC and the resources being used, but if ITT providers do not ensure that student teachers experience planning from the statutory documents we may be educating teachers who will find it difficult to plan confidently and creatively for cross-curricular learning.

Reflection

How confident are you in your knowledge of National Curriculum programmes of study and levels of attainment, and the links between them?

Planning for coverage of the statutory curriculum content

The problem of *superficial* teaching and learning within cross-curricular planning may be linked to the matter of coverage of the statutory curriculum. Some schools use long-term planning to ensure that NC content for all subjects is mapped out in detail for each year and term over the key stage. They may, or may not, also plan for the NC key skills and cross-curricular themes. Although this approach can be very successful, especially as it provides a context in which effective links across subjects can be made, there are potential problems if 'coverage' is the driving force.

Some of our student teachers report that, in their own planning, they are required not to change any aspects of the school's planning – even down to individual lesson activities; this is because some schools insist that all children in parallel classes must have identical experiences. This approach seems to arise from a view that there is a 'coverage' issue if children in parallel classes, even if working towards the same subject objectives, do so through different tasks and activities. Such a rigid approach disregards the fact that schools are encouraged to employ flexibility in planning. Schools were reminded, in *Excellence and Enjoyment* (DfES 2004: 17), of important 'freedoms' available to them even within the statutory requirements. These include the freedom to decide which aspects of a subject pupils will study in depth and how long to spend on each subject, as well as how to teach the subjects.

If schools map out the detailed content of each curriculum subject, allocating equal time and attention to most aspects, there is a danger of superficial coverage and what Dadds (in Pollard 2002: 173) described as the 'hurry along' curriculum. In this case 'coverage' will become a more dominant planning and teaching issue for teachers than learning itself (Kendall-Seatter 2005: 10). Equally important, within such tightly prescriptive planning, is the possibility that the place of Assessment for Learning (AfL) is diminished and that there are reduced opportunities for children's interests to be drawn into the planning (Kendall-Seatter 2005: 12).

An alternative and more flexible approach involves long-term planning that identifies only broad themes taken from the NC 'Breadth of Study' guidance for each subject – for example, from geography themes of 'Water' or 'Settlements', or from history 'Local History' or 'Romans'. Details of subject content are identified at the medium-term planning stage and will be matched to the specific topic headings chosen within the broad theme. So, for example, under 'Local Study' a topic focusing on 'People' may lead to aspects of history subject content chosen for in-depth study that may be different from those chosen if the topic heading was 'Transport'. This does not mean that the key knowledge, understanding, and skills of the Local History project cannot be successfully met. Some of these issues are revisited in Chapter 10 of this volume.

An interesting approach was explained to me in a primary school which is regarded by Ofsted and local authority advisers as very successful, with outstanding features. The teachers' perceptions of planning are reported as Case Study 9.1.

Case Study 9.1 Flexible planning

The teachers emphasise that their more flexible approach reflected the school's values and aim to provide a *broad and balanced* curriculum *relevant* to their children. They believe strongly that having tight, pre-set topic headings taught repeatedly year after year adversely affects the possibility of making the curriculum relevant by responding to changes in the children's needs, as well as their interests (not to mention the teachers' interests and expertise!). Furthermore, they can also heed local opportunities such as, in their case, the building of a new airport close to the school. They are confident in taking the 'freedom' to decide which aspects of each subject will be covered in depth, thus avoiding the danger of 'superficial' teaching. Within a two-year cycle of broad topics, owing to mixed-age classes, there is also variety for which aspects may be covered in depth from one year to the next. Self-evidently, in this more flexible approach there is a need to ensure that appropriate coverage of the statutory curriculum is achieved. In this particular school there is careful monitoring of medium-term planning by the subject leaders and senior staff so that over the two-year cycle they can ensure that all aspects are included at some level of study.

Such an approach is valued by the Nuffield Primary History (NPH) organisation which quotes Marjorie Reeves, an Oxford historian, as saying she would like pupils to sit down in 'a good rich patch of history and stay there for a satisfying amount of time' (Reeves 1980: 53). NPH goes on to emphasise the importance of avoiding fragmentation, not by giving equal time to all elements of the history curriculum but by making clear links (connecting threads) between each of the selected topics studied in depth. They suggest that this can be achieved by 'planning a couple of lessons at the end of the year or key stage (and certainly at the end of Year 6) where you review and pull together the discrete units of history the children have studied' (Nuffield Primary History accessed on 30 September 2009).

The Rose Review proposes further reduction in subject prescription and content in order to give schools more flexibility to select curriculum content according to local circumstances and resources. He emphasises the support of subject associations for reduced content and notes that those who 'champion' subjects 'acknowledge that forcing primary schools to teach too much curriculum content in the time available will lead to superficial treatment that is detrimental to their subject' (DCFS 2009: 1.15).

A skills-based approach to planning

In contrast to planning that starts with subject content is an approach adopted by some schools that places key transferable skills at the centre of planning. There is no doubt that the NC Programmes of Study and levels of attainment reflect the importance of key transferable skills. One need only look at how strongly the development of communication skills is shown through the vocabulary of all subjects, with repeated references to 'explain', 'describe', 'recount', 'express views'. Equally strong is the emphasis on subject-specific skills and understanding, included in all Programmes of Study.

However, there are those, including Alexander (2009: 18), who dispute the view that children need a primarily skills-based curriculum rather than one focused on subject knowledge. He discusses at length the polarised views taken by some on this matter and argues that 'setting them [skills versus subject knowledge] in opposition is foolish, unnecessary and epistemologically unsound'. He argues that we must define which skills are important, whilst also understanding that knowledge is far more than facts to be learned. He concludes that skills must 'complement knowing and understanding rather than supplant them' (2009: 18) and that educationalists must define what is meant by 'skills' or there is a danger that 'we shall carelessly lose not only knowledge and understanding, but also skill itself' (2009: 19).

What might be described as a 'balanced' approach is supported by Rose, who proposes keeping elements of the existing structure – a statutory curriculum organised under knowledge, skills, and understanding, albeit within his proposed six areas of learning rather than separate curriculum subjects (DCFS 2009: Recommendation 5). Decisions about precisely which skills should be developed have been made on the basis that there are commonly recognised skills 'essential for learning and life' that will form the new 'core': literacy, numeracy, ICT. Communication skills and Personal Development have been highlighted as of primary importance (Recommendations 9 and 13) and should be developed across all subjects. For other areas of learning the subject associations and 'learned societies' have been asked to advise on essential subject-related skills. There are dangers in this approach, of course, as we saw in the initial stages of NC planning: notably, that organisations that have a particular subject remit will, inevitably, be concerned to fight a corner. Analysis of the Programmes of Learning in the final report (DCSF 2009: Annexe B) shows clear evidence of transferable skills in all areas. The report does not favour either a skills-based or a subject approach to planning; rather it encourages that such decisions remain within the control of schools. The important message is that well-planned and rigorous cross-curricular learning will ensure that skills *and* knowledge can be developed *across* subjects.

Suggested principles for planning integrated learning

In the light of the points discussed above, effective planning for 'rigorous' cross-curricular teaching and learning can be supported in the following ways:

- Cross-curricular topics should include a limited number of subjects, chosen because of meaningful links between them and the broad aims for learning.
- Cross-curricular topics may involve a lead subject (or two) which drives the topic and provides opportunities for in-depth study.
- Medium-term planning should identify selected subject knowledge and transferable skills that will be the focus of particular attention for teaching and assessment.
- Topics should begin with key questions related to the intended broad aims for the children's learning.
- More specific questions, including some suggested by children, should help structure the choice of subject content and activities.
- The statutory curriculum programmes of study and attainment levels (this terminology may change in 2011 when the revised statutory National Curriculum is introduced) should be the starting points when planning cross-curricular objectives and assessment.

Reflection

Which of the suggested principles do you feel could be more fully developed in your planning?

A possible model for planning integrated learning through topic

The threads and debates of this chapter are drawn together in what follows by use of an example of cross-curricular planning (Table 9.1). The example will be used to illustrate the principles articulated to this point, whilst also briefly addressing some additional issues that apply to all effective planning. These include:

- Relevance of teaching and learning
- Developing attitudes and dispositions
- Children's involvement in planning.

The example is not intended to suggest that all medium-term plans should be presented in this way; it offers only one model. However, it does attempt to show how some of the weaknesses identified by critics might be avoided through effective planning.

The plan is for a hypothetical school in an industrial town in Lancashire, and is for up to a term's study with a Year 3/4 class, although the planning could be adapted for a shorter period. It has arisen from a long-term plan identifying broad themes linked to single subjects. For the term in question the lead subject is geography focused upon study of a locality in the United Kingdom and a country that is less economically developed. The specific topic is Houses and Homes, which can provide some experience of study at a local and regional level.

It is structured into three sections, with, first, study in the local area, followed by study in another area of the North West region that provides some contrast but is still close enough for fieldwork visits. Finally, there is a third section that focuses on houses and homes in a less economically developed country. The time spent on each of the three sections may vary according to the teacher's decisions, influenced by the balance of other geography work over the whole year and factors such as children's interests and pace of learning.

Making decisions about subject knowledge, skills, and concepts

As suggested, the plan begins with an overarching question 'Why are houses different?' which immediately begins to inform decisions about subject content and aims for the children's learning. The question suggests that meaningful links can be made with history, whilst opportunities to study building materials inspire potential links with science and art.

This process could be approached in reverse, with broad aims for the topic being the starting point from which the key question(s) are identified. Thus, if the school long-term planning approach begins with key skills and concepts and, in a given term, the concept is: '*change in the context of how settlements differ in size and character*', this may inspire a different starting point question.

Taking the first suggestion of starting with a key question, the theme of Houses and Homes, alongside the identified question, has led to the selection of geography subject content from the NC Programme of Study (POS) for Key Stage 2 related to geographical locations; differences and similarities in environments including weather and climate; environmental features, and change. The first column in Table 9.1 shows that not all elements of the geography POS have been chosen but, even so, there are a significant number. This demonstrates that in most topics it is possible to touch on many POS elements of both the lead subject and indeed related subjects. However, as noted earlier, choices can and should be made about which aspects will receive in-depth attention.

In this plan the emboldened objectives are those selected for most attention in teaching and assessment; those not in bold will be 'covered' but with a 'lighter touch' and may not be part of planned, focused assessments. Some objectives, for example, asking geographical questions and using geographical vocabulary, will appear, albeit with differences in the precise vocabulary, as 'ongoing' objectives in all geography topics.

The key question has also influenced the choice of selected geography subject skills such as fieldwork and mapping skills; whilst the links with history and science prompt choices of transferable skills such as collecting, recording, and interpreting evidence, and classification and explaining similarities and differences all of which have links across these subjects.

The choice of cross-curricular objectives should also be selective, focusing upon closely linked skills across several subjects. In the example, shown in italics, are objectives from geography, history and science POS related to skills in using a range of information sources. (Table 9.1: geography 2d, history 4a, science 1b). To reflect this aspect of the plan, a key learning and assessment objective is recorded as '*to be able to show how information from a range of secondary sources, including ICT, has been used to answer research questions*' (Table 9.1 column 3).

The final point to be made is that all choices should be made in the context of the school's long-term plan and feedback from subject leaders monitoring individual subjects. This will ensure that over the year or key stage children are receiving a broad and balanced curriculum, which meets, as a minimum, the requirements of the statutory curriculum.

Table 9.1 Medium-term planning for a Year 3/4 class: overarching theme – Houses and Homes

Context: School in industrial town in north-west England, from Industrial Revolution, with many brick-built houses.
Comparisons with Pennine small town/village, with many stone-built houses; homes in India – rural/urban, rich/poor

Lead subject: Geography
Main linked subjects: History, science, art

Key question
Why are houses different?

What do we want the children to learn and get out of the topic? (Aims)
- To understand that houses are different owing to availability of materials, local environment, climate, and history
- To develop geographical skills – Geographical Enquiry (geographical vocabulary/questions, use secondary sources of information, express views about environments; Fieldwork Skills (sketching, photography, mapping)
- To develop aspects of all NC key transferable skills but particularly: communication, application of numbers, IT
- To develop a range of transferable NC subject skills but particularly: use and interpret sources of evidence; classify, collect, present and interpret data, use simple texts to retrieve information, identify and comment on similarities and differences

NC Geography objectives (selected)	Cross-curricular links	Learning objectives/ assessment	Starting point questions	Exemplar activities
Geography Enquiry and skills	**History**	**To be able to:**	**1st focus in local area:**	
1a Ask geographical questions	1a Place changes into correct period of time	Use appropriate geographical vocabulary to ask questions, express views and findings	What are houses like in our town or area of school (style, materials, sizes)?	Walk in locality to look at houses – styles, ages, materials.
1b Collect and record evidence	4a Find out about changes from a range of sources of information, including ICT	Explain some reasons for differences in houses	What are older houses like or built of?	Visit other parts of town for different examples
1c Express views about people, places, and environments	4b Ask and answer questions, and select and record information ...	Use maps to identify features in local area	Are newer houses different? In what ways?	Class survey of house types observed and/or children's houses
1d Identify and explain different views that people, including the children themselves,	7 How an aspect in the local area has changed over time	Comment on similarities and differences	How are our houses heated and lit?	Visit to building site or visit by architect or builder
	Science	Carry out a fair test and use	How have houses changed over time in our area?	Investigations into house building in local area, including related traditional local

hold about topical geographical issues

2a Use appropriate geographical vocabulary

2b Use appropriate fieldwork techniques and instruments

2c Use globes, maps, and plans

2d Use secondary sources of information

Geography knowledge and understanding

3a Identify and describe what places are like

3b The location of places and environments

3c To describe where places are

3d To explain why places are like they are

3e To identify how and why places change

3f To describe and explain how and why places are similar to and different from other places in the same country and elsewhere in the world

---

Sc1

1b Test ideas using evidence from observation

1b Consider sources of information, including 1st hand experience and range of other sources to answer questions

1f Use systematic observations and measurements, including use of ICT for data logging

Sc3

1a Compare everyday materials and objects on basis of their material

1b See that some materials are better thermal insulators than others

Art

1a Record from first-hand observation

1c Collect visual and other information to help them develop their ideas, including using a sketchbook

4a Visual and tactile elements, including colour, pattern and texture, line and tone, shape, form and space . . .

---

data logging skills

Record information in different ways, e.g. sketching, photography, graphs, tables

To offer opinions on environments and ways to improve or sustain

To evaluate personal skills in use of pencil, paint, or pastels and adapt or improve own art work

To show how information from a range of secondary sources, including ICT, has been used to answer research questions

Explain some effects of climate and economic factors on the building of homes

Offer some reasons for similarities and differences between homes in England and India

To use globes and maps to identify countries of the world

2nd focus in another part of UK

What are houses like in the Pennine village?

Why are there fewer brick-built houses?

How are they built, heated, lit?

What sort of houses do we like best?

How and why are the houses different from our area?

3rd focus in less economically developed country

What are houses like in India?

How are they built, heated, lit?

How and why are the houses different from ones in our country?

---

building manufacture (opportunities for children's choices of focused study, e.g. brick-laying, brick-making, brick-bonds, joinery, window styles, etc.)

Science investigations into insulation

Talk to older people about changes in houses

Walk in locality to look at houses – styles, ages, materials

Record findings

Talk to local builder or older local residents

Compare similarities and differences with houses in home area

Investigate reasons for differences in building materials – i.e. stone instead of brick. Visit to stone quarry

Investigate why some new houses are still built of stone (environmental issues)

Use sketch book material as starting points for pencil drawings, painting, or pastel work related to colour, pattern, texture, shape

TABLE 9.1 Continued

NC Geography objectives (selected)	Cross-curricular links	Learning objectives/ assessment	Starting point questions	Exemplar activities
3g To describe and explain how places fit within a wider geographical context	**Mathematics** **Ma1** 1e, 1i, *Using & applying – reasoning & communicating* **Ma3** 1e, 1f, 2a, 2b, 2d *Shape, space, & measure*			Make links by email with school in India. Share information on local areas
5b Recognise how people can improve the environment or damage it and how decisions about places and environments affect the future quality of people's lives	**English** **En1** – 1, 2, 3, 10, Sp. & Lis. Including group discussion **En2** – 3, 5a, c, f, g 7, 9b Reading for information using range of non-fiction texts **En3** – 1, 9b, 9c, 12 Compose writing for information or to persuade **ICT &** **PSHE & Citizenship** Range of opportunities available			Use photographs to compare different types of homes in India Use internet to research houses in urban and rural settings in India Research selected (chosen) aspects of different types of house building from those found in UK

Learning objectives and assessment foci

As already noted, in this example objectives from other subjects have been chosen selectively to link closely with the main, geography, theme. Selected literacy, numeracy, and ICT objectives, an essential part of all topics, provide real contexts for using and applying appropriate 'core' skills. The suggestions in the example are not prescriptive and other options might have been chosen. Needless to say, a wide range of literacy and oracy skills will be used throughout and the focus on developing information retrieval and non-fiction reading and writing reflects the nature of the topic. None the less, selecting fiction genre for writing would be equally valid. The teacher will, of course, ensure a balance across the year of opportunities for different types of reading and writing. Assessment of key objectives *in context* provides evidence for teacher assessments against National Curriculum levels (APP), whilst also providing feedback on teaching to inform further planning both within and beyond the topic.

A final point to note is that the objectives on the medium-term plan are not *lesson* objectives and will need, in most instances, to be 'broken down' into smaller, more precise objectives at the short-term planning stage. For example, a geography-based objective about using maps to identify features in the local area may be adopted across more than one lesson; on a lesson plan the objectives will identify which particular mapping features will be focused upon. You can find detailed guidance on learning objectives and how to set them in Kerry (2002).

Moving from objectives to activities

It is common at the start of a topic for teachers to use a 'mind mapping' approach for possible activities, ideally involving children in the activity. Such an activity might be the next step, using the key question as the prompt to trigger ideas pertinent to the topic. Completing a mind map earlier in the process, using 'Houses and Homes' as the prompt, could result in an unmanageable range of possibilities. Even so, all mind map suggestions should be evaluated and discussed to select the best options in relation to the broad aims, as well as ones that have particular interest for the children.

It is from this process of mind mapping that more focused starting point questions and exemplar activities may be extracted and planned for. The precise details of study questions and activities will be refined in short-term planning. For example, knowledge of what is available in the local area of the school may lead to a particular focus on different styles of houses, whilst in another environment the ages of houses may be of particular interest. An activity to conduct a survey of differences in houses may include children's own houses, but a teacher who is aware of sensitive diversity issues may choose to 'depersonalise' this activity by carrying out a survey of houses observed during fieldwork.

Making the learning *relevant* to the children should begin at the medium-term planning stage and is related to making the learning *meaningful* for children. This picks up the need to scaffold learning, to begin from children's own experiences and what is familiar. For the topic in the example, the starting point is houses in the local area. This will allow children to relate what they already know to new learning about houses and homes in other regions and countries. However, Barnes (2007: 186) asserts that planning for relevance is not only about selecting an 'entry point from everyday life'. He proposes the importance of 'the emotional setting of learning' in order to establish meaningful links by using shared or personal experiences to support relevant and meaningful learning. In the example (Table 9.1) the teacher may seek emotional relevance through aspects related to children's own homes, or experiences arising from a child who has recently moved house, or by using literature or drama to engage children's emotional responses to aspects of the theme.

A danger when seeking relevance is that planning may remain solely within the immediate scope of children's personal experiences. Although children's experience is a good starting point, it is important for children 'to understand and know about phenomena distant from their own first hand experiences' (Katz and Chard 2000) – this theme is picked up again in Chapter 8. Ofsted (2009b: 18) recognises that a feature of planning that results in 'achieving excellence' is that topics start in familiar contexts but quickly move the learning on. This is particularly true in schools regarded as being in challenging circumstances, with children whose home experiences may be very limited. In these cases, providing opportunities for learning beyond the immediate environment is vital.

The concluding point to be gleaned from Table 9.1 is that *relevance* becomes very important when learning about houses in India, a more distant concept. As well as good choices of resources, for example high-quality and recent photographic and internet sources, which are used well by the teacher, relevance must be achieved by comparisons with children's own homes to help them make sense of the learning. This key point is sometimes missed in topic work, when the study of India, Romans, or Aztecs is focused only on researching and recording factual information, without opportunities to make the knowledge meaningful.

Teachers always need to articulate and ensure achievement of the key concepts that underpin the planning. An appreciation of this in the present example can be gained through exploration of a key concept such as change over time or, in a geography-led Houses and Homes topic, through the different effects, in the UK and India, of environmental, economic, or climatic influences. Such conceptual understanding of differences and similarities will also provide vitally important opportunities for expanding relevance in learning by developing children's personal, social, and citizenship values.

Short-term planning

The medium-term plan is deliberately not detailed or tightly linked to individual lessons in the topic. Some teachers would want to include other aspects at the medium-term planning stage such as lists of resources or suggestions for how differentiation and inclusion will be achieved. There is no problem about any of this, only a matter of what works best for individual schools or teachers. However, whatever is included should not take away the flexibility of the planning by including too much detail. Activities in the example medium-term plan (Table 9.1) are described only at a very general level to allow for further involvement of children in raising questions and selecting specific aspects of study. This helps to develop positive attitudes to learning through ownership of work that is of interest to them. Needless to say, teachers must monitor carefully children's choices to ensure that they are part of a coherent learning experience overall.

Teachers unfamiliar with this way of working may wonder, when planning individual lessons within a cross-curricular topic, whether they should always aim to progress learning in more than one subject. There is not a simple yes or no answer to this question. Certainly the lesson may, like the topic, have a lead subject, and a good lesson plan will have one primary learning objective, which could be related to one subject area.

It is common to have a secondary objective that highlights opportunities for a transferable skill such as data-handling or group discussion. Alternatively, the primary objective might be related to a key concept such as 'change' and this could involve learning that includes both geographical and historical change. When planning at short term, teachers should constantly be alert to overall key concepts and skills, and include in the lesson teaching points pertinent to them. This approach has similarities to the one from Nuffield Primary History described earlier, whereby lessons are planned at the end of the year to make links between the various history study units. For short-term planning this approach could be interpreted as planning specifically to make explicit links between subjects, for example through teaching points or key questions used during the introduction or plenary of a lesson.

Above all, it is vital to bear in mind that children's learning should not be constrained by planning. Identifying and sharing with children clear learning objectives or intentions for a lesson is important, but teachers must expect some learning to occur outside the initial planning.

In general, the essential aspects for effective short-term planning, whether for weekly or daily lesson plans, include:

- Information on previous learning or experiences
- Specific questions and learning objectives – knowledge, concepts, or skills
- Outline of any planned assessments to be made of key objectives, often related to focused work with small groups
- Teaching points, both subject-specific and cross-curricular
- Plans for what will be assessed and how
- Key questions, especially for the introduction and plenary, including some that are differentiated for the range of ability in the class
- Tasks and activities similarly differentiated
- Notes on organisation of the whole class, small groups and individuals
- Plans for roles of adults
- Resources
- Key vocabulary.

Reflection

- How does the model in Table 9.1 compare with other medium-term and short-term planning approaches you have used?

Conclusion

It is indisputable that children's learning is supported by opportunities that cross subject boundaries. However, a cross-curricular approach will be effective only if the teacher's planning makes meaningful links across subjects and through experiences that allow the connections to make sense to children. Cross-curricular planning could be construed to be an advanced skill for teachers, requiring enhanced understanding and skill about classroom processes.

Past and recent reports and initiatives have emphasised that schools should exercise flexibility in planning, and have the confidence and imagination to take ownership of the statutory curriculum by planning programmes that will meet the needs of their pupils. This will result in a range of different approaches to long-, medium-, and short-term planning, rather than one model. However, as has been discussed in this chapter, effective cross-curricular planning needs to take heed of key principles that have arisen from previous criticisms of ineffective approaches to topic or thematic planning.

The examples in this chapter use history and geography as the lead subjects, but this should not suggest that the humanities should always be at the forefront. It is important, over time, to have the creative and expressive arts, English, mathematics, or science and technology as lead subjects in planning. Above all, over the whole primary phase, children should receive a broad and balanced experience of all subjects or areas of learning.

Progression in learning within discrete subjects or areas of learning does not need to be sacrificed within an integrated approach. Through planning, effective teachers ensure balance between activities that develop conceptual understanding of the subject and those that allow children to simply practise subject or transferable skills.

Finally, at this time of detailed analysis and review, it is heartening to note that there is continued support from government and educationalists for cross-curricular approaches to learning. In schools where this approach has always been successfully in place, and for those who are in the process of developing planning for integrated learning, we can be confident that children will experience high-quality and coherent learning overall.

References

Alexander, R. (2009) *Towards a New Curriculum. Cambridge Primary Review Interim Report Part 2: the future* Cambridge: University of Cambridge

Alexander, R., Rose, A.J., and Woodhead, C. (1992) *Curriculum Organisation and Classroom Practice in Primary Schools: a discussion paper* London: DES

Arthur, J., Grainger, T., and Wray, D. (2006) *Learning to Teach in the Primary School* London: Routledge

Barnes, J. (2007) *Cross-Curricular Learning 3–14* London: PCP

Blenkin, G.M., Edwards, G., and Kelly, A.V. (1992) *Change and the Curriculum* London: PCP

DCFS (2009) *Independent Review of the Primary Curriculum: Final Report* www.teachernet.gov.uk/publications

Dean, J. (2001) *Organising Learning in the Primary Classroom* (3rd edn) London: Routledge/Falmer

DfES (2004) *Excellence and Enjoyment: a strategy for primary schools* Nottingham: DfES Publications

Hayes, D. (1997) *Success on Your Teaching Experience* London: Hodder & Stoughton

HMI (1978) *Primary Education in England: a survey by HM Inspectors of Schools* London: HM Stationery Office http://www.dg.dial.pipex.com/documents/hmi/7805.shtml (accessed 21 October 2009)

Jacques, K. and Hyland, R. (eds) (2003) *Professional Studies: primary phase* (2nd edn) Achieving QTS Series Exeter: Learning Matters

Katz, L. and Chard, S. (2000) *Engaging Children's Minds: the project approach* Stamford, Connecticut: Ablex

Kendall-Seatter, S. (2005) *Reflective Reader: primary professional studies* Achieving QTS Series Exeter: Learning Matters

Kerry, T. (2002) *Learning Objectives, Task Setting and Differentiation* Cheltenham: Nelson-Thornes

Kerry, T. (2010) 'Plotting compelling lessons: framework for inspiring quality learning and teaching' *Curriculum Briefing* 8 (2): 10–15

Nuffield Primary History http://www.primaryhistory.org/leadinghistory/planning,270,SAR.html (accessed 30 September 2009)

Ofsted (1999) *A Review of Primary Schools in England, 1994–1998* http://www.ofsted.gov. uk/Ofsted-home/Publications-and-research/Browse-all-by/Education/Key-stages-and-transition/Key-Stage-1/Primary-education-a-review-of-primary-schools-in-England-1994–98 (accessed 19 October 2009)

Ofsted (2002) *The Curriculum in Successful Primary Schools* http://www.ofsted.gov.uk/Ofsted-home/Publications-and-research/Browse-all by/Education/Key-stages-and-transition/Key-Stage-1/The-curriculum-in-successful-primary-schools (accessed 19 October 2009)

Ofsted (2003) *Expecting the Unexpected* http://www.ofsted.gov.uk/Ofsted-home/Publications-and-research/Browse-all-by/Education/Providers/Primary-schools/Expecting-the-unexpected (accessed 19 October 2009)

Ofsted (2009a) *Improving Primary Teachers' Subject Knowledge across the Curriculum* http://www.ofsted.gov.uk/Ofsted-home/Publications-and-research/Browse-all-by/Documents-by-type/Thematic-reports/Improving-primary-teachers-subject-knowledge-across-the-curriculum (accessed 26 October 2009)

Ofsted (2009b) *20 Outstanding Primary Schools Excelling against the Odds in Challenging Circumstances* http://www.ofsted.gov.uk/Ofsted-home/News/Press-and-media/2009/October/20-outstanding-primary-schools-excelling-against-the-odds-in-challenging-circumstances (accessed 19 October 2009)

Pollard, A. (2002) *Reflective Teaching: effective and evidence-informed professional practice* London: Continuum

Primary National Strategy (PNS) (2004) *Excellence and Enjoyment: learning and teaching in the primary years. Planning and assessment for learning: Designing opportunities for learning. Professional development materials* London: DfES http://nationalstrategies.standards.dcsf.gov. uk/node/88541

Reeves, M. (1980) *Why History?* Nuffield Primary History http://www.primaryhistory.org/leading history/planning,270,SAR.html

Rose (2008) *The Independent Review of the Primary Curriculum: interim report* London: DCFS http://publications.teachernet.gov.uk

Chapter 10

Assessing cross-curricular learning

Kathleen Taylor

Introduction

This chapter recognises that learning in primary schools is changing, and that assessment for learning techniques have to change in order to match these movements in educational thinking. Key concepts that teachers need to bring about effective assessment are considered: in particular, feedback and dialogue. The role of marking and its associated skills are discussed. The chapter then moves on to examine cross-curricular issues in assessment. A case study provides a practical example of assessment in its dynamic role, guiding learning. The chapter concludes that assessment works best when children adopt it as part of the integrated classroom experience.

Background

The purpose of this chapter is to consider how the integration of assessment for learning might work in a climate of changing practices and curriculum design in primary education. The idea of new 'freedoms' in primary education has motivated schools to base their long-term planning to suit their ethos such that subject-based curriculum design is being replaced by cross-curricular designs (DfES 2003: 16, 17). Some schools have adopted the six areas of learning in the Early Years Foundation Stage, others key skills and thinking skills, and still others are choosing to base the curriculum in contexts such as topics and projects leading to plans that are much more cross-curricular and integrative.

Key skills and thinking skills are identified in the National Curriculum (NC) for 'promoting across the National Curriculum' because of the integral role they play in learning. (DfEE 1999: 20) They are embedded in the NC Programmes of Study and related attainment targets and are the skills children need to gain knowledge and understanding of a subject; by using and applying the skills children gain knowledge and understanding of the skills themselves. In the more recent Primary National Strategy (2004) both key skills and thinking skills called 'aspects of learning' are defined as 'cross-curricular learning skills' (Primary National Strategy 2004: 9).

The advantage of a curriculum based on cross-curricular learning skills is that children can revisit skills and continually build upon them such that a skill learned in one subject can be used and applied in another. Bruner (1963: 52) described this type of curriculum as a 'spiral curriculum'. He believed that curriculum design should allow children to revisit their ideas and build on knowledge and understanding and, at the same time, allow them to practise previously learned skills (http://www.gtce.org.uk/teachers/rft/bruner0506).

The main point about such skills is their transferability, i.e. their ability to be used and applied across the curriculum. For example, skills associated with 'enquiry', which is defined as a thinking skill, can be seen in many subjects: science, art and design, history, geography, English, physical education (Primary National Strategy 2004: 15), thereby providing opportunity to link subjects. Enquiry, in particular, is seen as 'embedded in the National Curriculum' (Primary National Strategy 2004: 15), and for this reason is a focus for learning in the Programmes of Study and summative assessment in the attainment levels.

Many theorists have advocated the enquiry approach to learning because it is a vehicle to gain knowledge across subjects. This was particularly true in the case of the seminal education thinker John Dewey, who believed the object of school was to 'arouse curiosity and investigation, to train the powers of observation and to instil a practical sense of the powers of enquiry' (Dewey in Garforth 1966: 71). A starting point for learning, for example, beginning with first-hand experience and close observation of natural objects in the local environment, might lead initially to art – where observation is deepened by drawing and painting. But, ultimately, it could lead to other subjects in the effort to find patterns, make comparisons, pursue questions, and make connections, all skills associated with enquiry. This theme is explored further in Chapter 8 in this volume.

Equally transferable across the curriculum is the 'discourse' associated with the skills so that the child learns the structures of enquiry that can be applied across subjects. A teacher who models such discourse is in effect providing the language that enables the child to work equally well in various subject domains. The word *discourse* is used to distinguish it from other types of talk because it relates to the language that is specific to a subject, in this case the language of enquiry. Though Mercer (1995: 77–83), in explaining discourse as the 'frames of reference' by which children can be helped to construct knowledge and understanding, is predominantly referring to subject disciplines, the concept is adaptable to cross-curricular contexts.

Indeed one of the main criticisms of cross-curricular design lies in the balance between breadth of study and depth of study such that children are sufficiently empowered in the 'structures' of a subject from which they can build further knowledge and understanding (Bruner 1963: 12). Assessment for learning provides the opportunity for children to practise using the discourse associated with the skills and subjects, and for this reason is integral to cross-curricular planning. As we have seen in previous chapters (especially Chapter 1), subject-learning and cross-curricular approaches are complementary, not mutually exclusive.

The 'aspects of learning' identified in the Primary National Strategy, along with their associated discourse, form the major elements in curriculum design to which assessment for learning is integrally linked and which will be further explored in this chapter.

Some key terms

The term assessment for learning (AfL) is often associated with formative assessment and refers to the continual or ongoing process of the review of learning and progress. Vygotsky saw assessment, and what we would now refer to as assessment for learning, as a 'dynamic' process: not one that occurs only after having learned something, but as parallel with the learning (see Drummond 2003: 136). So assessment for learning is about focusing not on what children have already learnt but rather on what they are about to learn, i.e. in the 'zone of proximal development'. Drummond (2003: 136) says that a teacher who is 'enlightened by this form of assessment is in a good position to support each child's learning as it happens'. Indeed, Ofsted inspectors expect to be able to watch this process in operation in classrooms.

Research into classroom assessment, conducted by Black and Wiliam (1998), put children at the heart of assessment for learning, and as a consequence practices in assessment have indeed become much more *dynamic*, with greater emphasis being given to the child's role in assessment. This has led to the phrase 'assessment AS learning' (Briggs *et al.* 2008) being used to describe assessment's integral role in the ongoing process of teaching and learning. By contrast, assessment *of* learning describes a summary of the overall assessments of the child to date and is referred to as summative assessment.

The current Qualifications and Curriculum Authority's (QCA) key message about assessment is:

- The learner is at the heart of assessment.
- Assessment needs to provide a view of the whole learner.
- Assessment is integral to teaching and learning.
- Assessment includes reliable judgements about how learners are progressing; these are related, where appropriate, to National Standards and expectations.

The first three points (above) refer to the 'close-up' view of the child where reflection on learning occurs as it is happening, feedback is immediate, and relevant next steps identified. This relates very much to assessment AS learning, as well as assessment for learning (but as the distinctions between the two are not clearly defined as yet in the new strategies for assessing pupil progress, and other related QCA support guidance, reference to such practice in this chapter will remain within the more generic term – assessment for learning). The final point in the list above, whilst providing what QCA calls the 'public view' because it indicates formal recognition of achievement, nevertheless contributes significantly to the day-to-day judgements a teacher makes about progress (Anwyll 2008). Knowledge of the National Standards (i.e. the National Curriculum Attainment Targets and the new Assessing Pupils' Progress Attainment Criteria) provides the teacher with a view of the over-arching educational goals at which the teaching is aimed. James (in Mansell *et al.* 2009) claimed that formative and summative are not different types of assessment but rather describe how assessment is used. She talks about assessment in the classroom being summative if it is used merely to establish where pupils are, rather than helping them to know how to achieve. Conversely, formal tests and exams can be used formatively when the teachers help children to analyse their performance and find ways to improve.

Reflection

How do National Standards inform your planning? How do you use these formatively?

Assessment as the active agent in teaching and learning: feedback and dialogue

We can now take a closer look at the formative day-to-day assessment that lies at the heart of teaching and that sits equally well in both subject-bound planning and cross-curricular planning. Assessment is not a passive process: it is active because of its integral role in the process of teaching such that the teacher's reflection on children's learning involves inter-action and intervention. In this way, assessment for learning serves to reinforce, consolidate, and extend learning. Black and Wiliam (in Pollard 2002: 314), in their seminal work on assessment, concluded that formative assessment is the 'single most powerful tool we have for raising standards and empowering lifelong learning'. They pointed to five specific features of assessment for learning that they saw as the most instrumental in improving achievement, namely:

- Positive feedback focusing on the quality of the child's work and advice about how to improve
- Children trained in self-assessment
- Opportunities for children to express their understanding designed into *any* piece of teaching, for this will initiate interaction whereby formative assessment aids learning
- Dialogue between children and teacher that is reflective, thoughtful, and focused to explore understanding
- Children given the opportunity and help to improve following feedback from tests and homework.

(Pollard 2002: 314–15)

These points are used to begin the discussion here because, when looked at as a whole, they form the basis of enabling practice for both teachers and children, and one that transcends government demands.

Implicit in the ethos of a good classroom is a teacher's and children's shared appreciation of a positive approach and attitude to their work and efforts. Indeed Black and Wiliam make the point that 'entering a dialogue' with a child or children about a piece of work (the word 'work' here means any classroom task, and is not confined to something which is written) should be from a 'positive' perspective by focusing on the 'qualities' of the work (Pollard 2002: 314). It is all too easy to lower a child's self-esteem by feedback that is negative or vague or feedback that appears positive but is in effect dismissive.

Black (1998: 133–4) argues that 'vague and incomplete' feedback is an indication to the child that their work is poor, and that in time the child will come to believe success is unachievable. He goes on to say that children's feelings about their work are 'key deter-miners' in whether they perceive themselves as good learners or weak. Indeed, what a child experiences in terms of feedback may well determine his or her success or failure. The idea of 'entering a dialogue' is key as it rightly denies any dismissive responses by the teacher such as a glib 'that's fantastic', in preference to a response that gives the children the oppor-tunity to explain why work is good and what the next steps might be.

Of course such dialogue takes time. For this reason planning for such opportunities needs to be built into lessons. For example, a lesson can contain more than one plenary. It may have 'mini-plenaries' strategically placed throughout the lesson, or tasks that are organised with set times for reflection. A crucial aspect of such plenaries and reflective tasks is for children to be clear about the purposes of their learning and the related criteria for assessment, so that they can relate them to their learning efforts. In this way children come to know the conventions of dialogue and how to assess their work, because they see how it is done, learning from one another and practising the associated skills. Black and Wiliam (Black 1998: 130) refer to this as children being 'trained in self-assessment', and building self-assessment activities into classroom practice is one way of doing this.

Dialogue is a word that has taken up greater significance in primary education in the twenty-first century because of renewed emphasis on its central role in learning (Alexander 2000, 2004, 2008; Mercer 1995, 2000; Primary National Strategy 2003). What is special about dialogue is that it involves a search, a journey with a quest, wherein the participants are all seeking to find knowledge and understanding. Dialogue is not loose, but guided by a teacher who actively encourages children to make connections, correct misconceptions, and justify their views. It leads to deeper understanding and new knowledge, and brings about insights of oneself as a learner and teacher. Alexander's and Mercer's ideas, on dialogic teaching and discourse respectively, link well with assessment for learning because both require the teacher to be the 'reflective agent' (Pollard 2002: 312) who steers and directs the dialogue in a purposeful way and in light of what is being said. The teacher simultaneously responds, interacts, reflects, initiates, and leads such that the reflections are active.

Black and Wiliam (Pollard 2002: 315) make a strong case for dialogue that is 'thoughtful, reflective, focused to evoke and explore understanding, and conducted so that pupils have the opportunity to think and express their ideas'. For the dialogue to remain focused on assessment for learning, both teacher and children need to know that their evaluations are based on known educational goals including objectives that are part of a planned sequence of learning. If this does not happen, assessment becomes a limited exercise in opinion rather than one where the children have to explain and justify what they think. However, such reflective dialogue should not be designed only to see that objectives are being achieved. Undoubtedly, for some children this may be a hurdle in itself, but rather the dialogue can extend learning beyond the objectives. Dialogue that helps the child reflect will reinforce and consolidate learning as well as extend it. For this reason planning should take account of what teaching is involved in working below, within, and beyond the expected levels of attainment to ensure the teacher is prepared to extend the dialogue to support learning beyond expectations (DfEE 1999: 17). The theme of support of learning beyond expectations is taken up also in Chapter 8 above. Hart *et al.* (2004) warn, though, that children can become labelled by levels of attainment such that the teaching is then governed by the label rather than by knowledge of the child.

Assessment for learning is the way to know the child, and the level descriptors may be used as an aid to direct the teacher to the next steps rather than providing a boundary at which to stop. Socio-constructivist models of how 'knowledge is co-constructed' (Mercer 1995) suggest that learning can surpass levels of expectation through talk 'scaffolded' (Bruner in Mercer 1995: 73) by the teacher that maximises the potential for learning, i.e. the zone of proximal development (Vygotsky 1978: 86 quoted in Pollard 2002: 142).

A difficulty for teachers, and especially new and beginning teachers, is the demand that socio-constructivist models place on their knowledge of practice and knowledge of the subject. Purposeful talk used for 'steering classroom talk with particular educational goals in view' and 'cumulative' talk where 'teachers and children build on their own and each other's ideas and chain them into coherent lines of thinking and enquiry' are relatively rare (Alexander 2004: 34). One of the most difficult aspects for those new to teaching to achieve is actively to pursue a line of enquiry with a single child, because it is high on demand about knowledge of pedagogy and knowledge of the subject; its very rarity means that beginning teachers may not have seen this modelled in the classroom.

One of the criticisms concerning cross-curricular activities is the danger of losing sight of educational goals pertaining specifically to knowledge of a subject. Furthermore, beginning teachers may not be entering a situation where the relationships with the children have been established; as the co-construction of knowledge lies heavily upon these relationships, this may pose another difficulty (Mercer 1995: 61). Nevertheless the contention of all the research cited here is that dialogue for learning should be given greater prominence in classroom practice.

Whilst the argument here is for assessment for learning to be integral to dialogue and classroom talk, an attempt has been made to identify some of the difficulties for beginning teachers, especially in terms of knowledge about practice and the subject. In this context, however, a further point Black and Wiliam make regarding tests and homework is one worthy of further examination and one to which we turn in the next section.

Marking and feedback

Marking and the associated feedback for homework, unlike day-to-day assessment for learning, may not be tied tightly to the immediacy of classroom practice. Considering the child's work away from the classroom provides time for the teacher to think about what best to do next. Teachers in training, and newly qualified teachers, often gain much from marking children's work and designing feedback, because it is in this situation that there is time to think about the quality of the questions or instructions they set for the piece of work and in doing so they learn to modify what they ask in order to elicit more useful responses. Also, they are able to think carefully about what comments might best enhance learning and what implications their comments have in relation to providing opportunities to enable the children to put into practice their suggestions (see also Pollard 2002: 315). All teachers need time to reflect on what children's work tells them about the pupils' progress on the one hand, and about what it tells them about their own teaching on the other.

Marking homework is a reflective process and is one of the most strategic ways for a teacher to improve practice. It is like a dry run for assessment for learning in the classroom, whereby the implications of pursuing a line of enquiry with a child can be tried out at a distance. For the feedback comments to be of value, future planning needs to take on board the time needed for the child to address the feedback, and exactly how and where this will be achieved. This process may be cross-curricular in nature: thus a pupil may address issues and learning points in feedback about measurement in maths through geography or design technology. Information gathered through marking, together with noteworthy insights collected through oral feedback during teaching, should form the basis of any necessary modifications on day-to-day planning. Again, these judgements will operate across the curriculum, and feed from one subject area to another. In practice, the outcomes often take the form of annotations on lesson plans that show the modifications made to practice and the growth of the teacher as a reflective practitioner.

Reflection

How do you plan for child–teacher dialogue that gives the opportunity for the child to reflect and build upon what has been learned?

Planning for assessment for learning: national criteria that connect the curriculum

Black and Wiliam make clear that planning for 'any piece of teaching' should provide 'opportunities for children to express their understanding' (Pollard 2002: 315). Planning for assessment for learning was designated a key principle in a set of ten principles identified by the Assessment Reform Group (2002). The following features of planning for assessment for learning were identified:

- Opportunities for both learner and teacher to obtain and use information about progress towards learning goals
- Planning that is flexible to respond to initial and emerging ideas and skills
- Strategies to ensure learners understand the goals they are pursuing and the criteria that will be applied in assessing their work
- How learners will receive feedback, how they will take part in assessing their learning and how they will be helped to make further progress.

Recently, new QCA (2009) guidance on planning for assessment for learning, whilst continuing to advocate the ten principles identified by the Assessment Reform Group (2002), has further defined the principles and added to them such that teachers need to produce plans with:

- Emphasis on learning intentions and on sharing these with pupils and other adults in the classroom
- Assessment criteria for feedback and marking, for peer and self-assessment
- Differentiated classroom groups
- Built-in review time and flexibility
- Notes of pupils who need additional or consolidation of work
- Time for guided group sessions for explicit formative assessment opportunities should be provided
- Adjustments highlighted or crossed out: with what did and did not work and why.

(http://www.qcda.gov.uk/4338.aspx)

The advice and guidance available for assessment for learning have never been greater. Indeed, prior to the wealth of new information to be found on the National Strategies website was the Primary National Strategy *Excellence and Enjoyment* pack of professional development materials that was delivered to schools and Local Authorities for dissemination in 2004. This contained two sets of materials specifically for training teachers in assessment: *Assessment for Learning* and *Designing Opportunities for Learning*. In the main, however, much of the advice concerning assessment in the primary school is subject-specific and, as a consequence, is in need of interpretation in cross-curricular settings. Cross-curricular planning relies heavily on overarching educational goals that need to be carefully articulated by the teacher, and the learning objectives teased out from these in order to inform the assessment planning.

Promoting skills across the curriculum is not new and was advocated in the National Curriculum (DfEE and QCA 1999: 20), where some skills were identified as more closely subject-related (for example, *painting in art and design*), while others were seen as common to more than one subject area (such as *enquiry skills in science, history and geography*). Therefore, to plan effectively about how subject knowledge is addressed requires an in-depth understanding of curricular design, especially in terms of long-term planning and the related medium-term planning.

One of the advantages of cross-curricular planning is the way it moves teachers to contemplate the connections between overarching goals in the National Curriculum and discrete assessment criteria identified for lessons or a series of lessons. Beginning teachers sometimes find making the connection extremely difficult but, when they do, it is as if a light has been switched on: suddenly they find a relevant context upon which to base anonymous learning objectives and outcomes, and develop a better sense of direction with the children.

Sue Hackman, Chief Adviser on School Standards, in her foreword to *The Assessment for Learning Strategy* (DCSF 2008) makes clear that 'one of the key objectives of the strategy is to link classroom assessment reliably to National Curriculum levels in order to track the progress of individual pupils'. She concludes by reiterating that: 'The bottom line is that when you make a judgement, you use national criteria, and keep a note of the judgements made over time so that you can see how pupils progress. That's it.' Teachers who are knowledgeable about the way in which discrete assessment criteria relate to the summative levels of attainment ('national criteria') have the confidence to be more flexible and creative with the curriculum, because they know where their planning is leading.

Reflection

How do you convey to children how the discrete criteria by which they assess their work relate to the bigger educational goals?

Assessing Pupils' Progress (APP)

The problem of relating overarching educational goals to short-term assessment criteria is in some way being addressed by the tables of assessment criteria being produced by the National Strategies for APP (QCDA 2009). It is interesting that in the new APP the Assessment Foci for reading are organised by the elements of reading, i.e. literal, reorganisational, inferential, evaluative, and appreciative (Barrett's taxonomy, in Crisp 1978) rather than incrementally as in the NC levels of attainment. The arrangement makes explicit the *spiral* nature of the way skills and knowledge and understanding in reading are gained (*pace* Bruner, see above). For example, reading for inference, Assessment Focus 3 in the recently published APP for reading, does not appear in the NC attainment descriptors for reading until level 4. Yet children have already experienced reading for inference from an early

age. Children learn inferred meaning very early from the environment around them, and through the traditional stories and fairy stories they are told. They quickly come to recognise all is not what it seems: evil is often clothed in kindness, foolishness hides wit, weakness is really strength, and so on. Children's early reading books are packed full of inferred meanings, initially conveyed by the adult reading to the child, but often picked up by the children as their expectations of how texts work grow in response to their reading repertoire.

This point is easily seen in such commonly used books as *Rosie's Walk*, where the text relates the hen's journey but the pictures tell that what was incidental to the hen was catastrophic to the fox. The same kind of phenomenon recurs in *We're Going on a Bear Hunt* where repeating the phrase 'we're not scared' actually indicates the reverse. The organisation of the taxonomy of reading in APP clearly recognises reading for inference in Assessment Focus 3, as an early skill to be developed through seven level descriptors from level 2 to 8. Consequently the other aspects of reading, literal AF2, reorganizational AF4, evaluative AF6, and appreciation AF7, are similarly represented by an ascending order of descriptors.

Although the organisation of level descriptors is different in the NC from that of APP they are nevertheless arranged hierarchically. In APP the level descriptors are often accompanied by examples of what happens in order to meet the intended achievements of pupils. Teachers will go on debating the relative merits of APP and NC descriptors. This can be where an understanding of some of the underpinning theories that guide education can be useful. Making links between theoretical ideas on curriculum design is helpful in understanding, and sometimes critiquing, government guidance. The General Teaching Council is right to say: 'The best teaching and learning today builds upon knowledge and understanding of how children learn [gained] from research over time including work of educational theorists' (http://www.gtce.org.uk/teachers/rft/vygotsky1203/) http://www.gtce.org.uk/teachers/rft/bruner0506).

Cross-curricular contexts for learning and assessment for learning: key skills

In what follows we move on to look at a context for learning that promotes cross-curricular learning, and where assessment for learning is totally integrated. Links are made between the more theoretical models from earlier in the chapter and practice drawn from classrooms. The following is an example drawn from several enterprise projects undertaken with children in school and student teachers in training. The original plans are adapted to the present purpose but the principles remain the same.

Case Study 10.1 Assessment in integrated contexts

The context for the project is a small-scale enterprise based upon *Promoting other aspects of the school curriculum* from the section 'Enterprise Education' in *The National Curriculum* (DfEE and QCA 1999: 22). The overarching educational goals are based on the NC Key Skills: communication, application of number, information technology, working with others, improving own learning, and performance and problem solving (1999: 20–1; DfES 2003: 9).

The project is appropriate for Key Stage 2 pupils and can be easily modified for KS1. The medium-term plan for the enterprise draws upon the KS2 programmes of study in a variety of subjects with key focus on the core: especially speaking and listening skills, group discussion and drama in English, and problem solving in maths, SC1 and 2 (nutrition and health), ICT, and design and technology and PSHE.

The overarching aims are:

- To engage in structured learning experiences leading to the development of a school healthy food shop that will be economically viable in a competitive field (the competition was often the existing tuck shop)
- First-hand experiences in National Curriculum key skills and their identification in talk for learning and assessment for learning activities
- Understanding of the significance of reflection in learning to learn
- Communicating the joy of learning.

The enterprise involves children in:

- Meeting with the bank to organise funding and discuss money issues (the main source of funding was a starter sum as part of a government enterprise initiative with the bank; another way of raising money is to fund-raise for the project)
- Visiting a whole-food bakery, their mill and restaurant, to see what a healthy food shop looks like
- Conducting a healthy food survey in school to determine what would sell well
- Setting up a 'pantry' of ingredients for making the food
- Organising the working areas and arranging equipment
- Organising a site for the shop and equipping the shop
- Promoting the shop and healthy eating
- Working out ongoing costs
- Practising skills to make the food, supply and run the shop
- Managing the shop
- Accounting.

The descriptions of the key skills in the NC can be modified or emphasised depending upon the needs of the children in the class and used to underpin the enterprise. It is important to share the descriptions with the children as these will inform them when they analyse their own and each other's skills, knowledge and understanding and attitudes as part of the reflective activities planned into the lessons. Placing the key skills on cards that were then laminated provided a useful resource that could be used for reference throughout the enterprise and helped both children and teacher keep track of where they were going with the project in terms of their learning. The lesson plans are devised from the medium-term plan which sets out the matrix of objectives from the programmes of study, the associated assessment criteria in relation to attainment level, and the sequence of contextualised activities.

The task (below) is one of several that make up the enterprise project. It is aimed to address skills, knowledge, and understanding and attitudes across the curriculum for Year 5 and 6 children. Assessment activities for the children are built in to address both NC key skills and the appropriate programmes of study. The organisation for the task is for all the children in four or five groups to engage in the task over the period of four days and in preparation for the presentations on the fifth day. A group representing the managers (from another class) taste the scones as they are made, write a comment on the quality of the scones, and assign a score 0 to 5 for reference at the presentations. The organisation for making the scones determines the timetable for the other parts of the task to take place. It should all take place within a week. The taught sessions that accompany the task are in parentheses.

As part of the organisation for the task, children's assessment of their own and each other's learning is built in. For example, one group makes scones whilst another group observes and assesses using child-friendly sets of questions to help them. Table 10.1 shows how NC descriptors for key skills can be adapted so that children can use them as part of their observations and assessments. The NC references are included here, but these need not be part of the information given to the children. Similarly the questions for the managers to help judge the presentations are adapted from the programmes of study pertinent to the presentation task. Debriefing time and plenaries provide crucial opportunities for the groups to reflect on their observations, discuss the skills they have used, the knowledge they have gained, their attitudes to the various elements of the task, the insights they might have gained of themselves as learners, and what implications there are for their development as learners. Often a group will add to or modify the original questions aligned to 'children's assessment criteria' in order to convey meaning more clearly.

The task

As a result of a survey showing wholemeal scones to be the most popular choice for morning break-time, the managers of the healthy food shop have decided to buy in their scones on a daily basis. The optimum number of scones needed per day calculated from survey figures is 28.

You are invited to tender for the contract to supply the healthy food shop with 28 scones per day Monday to Friday.

Your task is to:

- Decide a company name and logo (group work ICT).
- Consider how to meet the requirements of supplying the shop with 28 scones per day (maths and design/technology taught sessions and group work).
- Design and cost the scones (design/technology and maths taught sessions and group work/ ICT).
- Make a sample of scones for tasting (supervised group work).
- Put in writing your costings and at the presentation hand them to the healthy food shop managers. You will need to consider the profit you need to make to ensure you can remain in business (maths teacher-led sessions and group work).
- Prepare a three-minute presentation to the managers of the healthy food shop trialling the scones (ICT/English speaking and listening, writing and drama).

Key skills for the task

National Curriculum key skills	Children's assessment criteria
Communication • Speak effectively to different audiences • Listen, understand, and respond appropriately to others • Participate in group discussion	• Were the group members able to ensure everyone was listened to and how did they do this? En1, 2e • What did you see happening that encouraged people to join in? En1, 3a • Was the communication always verbal or did you notice other means of communicating such as facial expression or gesture and what effect did this have? PSHE 4a
Application of number • Solve increasingly complex problems and explain the reasoning used set in real life contexts	• What did the group need to know to work out costings for the supply of scones to the shop? Ma2, 1a • How did they identify problems and resolve them? Ma2, 1b • How did they check for accuracy? Ma2,1e
Information technology • Use a range of information sources to analyse, interpret, evaluate, and present information for a range of purposes in a creative way	• What sources of information technology did the group draw upon and how were they useful to the group? ICT 1a, b, c • Why did the group use information technology to support their work for the presentation? ICT 5a, b • How did the information technology make the presentation more innovative? ICT 4a, b, c
Working with others • Contribute to group tasks and discussions • Be aware of other people's needs • Co-operate with others • Appreciate the experience of others • Benefit from what others say and do	• How did the group decide who does what? En1, 3a • How did the group make decisions and how was agreement reached? En1, 3b, c, d, e • How did they help each other? En1 3d, PSHE 4a
Improving own learning and performance • Reflect and critically evaluate your work and what you have learnt • With the support of others identify ways to improve your learning	• Were you clear about the purposes of the task in terms of what it helped you to learn? En2, 3c • Can you identify aspects of the task where you felt you learned the most? PSHE 1b • What obstacles hindered your learning and how did you overcome them? PSHE 4A
Problem solving • Identify and understand a problem • Plan ways to solve it • Monitor the solution and review the situation	• How did the group find out about, and decide upon, a recipe for the scones? ICT1a, 5a • How did the group resolve problems such as cost versus health? PSHE 3a, b, Ma2, 1d, DT 5a. 1a, b, c, d, 2a, b, c, d, e, f • What problems did the group experience and how did they overcome these problems? DT 1c, 3a Ma2, 1dk

Presentations

The presentation which forms one of the outcomes of this task is the cumulative result of the peer assessment and debriefing activities integral to the project; it provides a further means by which the children can make explicit learning that is implicit. For this reason it is a very useful assessment tool. Barnes (2007: 224) makes a distinction between presentation and performance, where presentation is defined as work in progress. The presentation in this project, whilst it forms an end-point in terms of the tender, occurs relatively early in the project and is one of several presentations for a real-life purpose that can be built in, for example presentations that address the cost versus health issues. The questions for the managers, like the questions used to assess key skills, speaking and listening skills, and skills in ICT elsewhere in the project (Table 10.1), ensure that the assessment of presentations remains focused and relevant and is yet another means of educating children in assessment for learning (see Table 10.1).

The value of such a project is the high level of motivation it stirs in the children and the exciting and joyful learning environment highly motivated children create. The review and assessment for learning built into the project are there to serve the child first and foremost. Children come to see that criteria for assessment, whether as statements or questions or both, are there to help them understand why they are learning what they are learning and, importantly, how to move their learning forward. The cycle of learning which the task follows is very much aligned to Kolb's cycle of experiential learning, where learning is rooted in first-hand 'concrete experiences' that are 'observed and reflected' upon and lead to the 'abstract conceptualisation' or how we think about things, all of which is achieved by being actively involved, which Kolb calls 'active experimentation' (http://www.business balls.com/kolblearningstyles.htm).

So what is being suggested here is that assessment for learning, conducted by the children, using questions aligned to assessment criteria, gives focus to the reflection such that it is what Vygotsky called 'dynamic assessment' (Drummond 2003: 136). In other words, the teacher is equipping the children with the *discourse* that provides the language of assessment and equally the language to learn. Children gaining familiarity with the language for assessment by engaging in assessment for learning activities are able to pose further questions or modify questions to make them clearer which helps them to redefine the original problem and analyse solutions more thoroughly. Sternberg (2007) suggests that in the process of redefining a problem is a 'willingness to grow' and a willingness 'to persevere in face of obstacles'.

Table 10.1 Assessment criteria for the presentation

Were the points of their argument in a sequence that was easily understood? En1 1c, d, PNS Spkg Y5, 2
Were the group able to defend points in the presentation by referring to evidence? En1 1a, 2d, 2e. PNS Spkg Y5, 2
What aspects of the presentation were most persuasive and why? En1 1b, d. 4a, b, c. PNS Spkg Y5, 2. En3 9b, c
Were the ICT innovations they used in the presentation effective? How were they effective? ICT 3b and 5a
What is the single most effective feature of the presentation and why is it most effective? ICT 4b, c, En 4a, c, En3 1e

However, this may not be the case for every child. Some will falter in the face of problems, and whilst a 'recognition of their limitations' (Sternberg 2007) might help one child, for others it is daunting. For this reason, one should not underestimate the collective strength of the group – just as in the enterprise case study, where assessment for learning is not directed at the individual but rather the group. The group structure does not exclude individual assessment; and indeed, observations made by the teacher should result in adaptations in teaching to individual needs. But essentially the group is mutually supporting, and targets for improvement are collective.

Integral to the project's design are the ways and means of providing evidence of children's learning from which the teacher can construct records for future summative reports, and in the more immediate teaching situation modify planning to meet children's individual needs. In this project, assessment for learning is not an add-on or something that happens after the main teaching: it is part of the teaching. As a consequence, it is not about 'training' children in self-assessment but educating them about the value of assessment to their learning and the learning of others.

Assessment for learning pushes the boundaries of conventional forms of teaching. So, too, do adventurous contexts for learning across the curriculum. Together these elements set the tone for exciting and adventurous classrooms. Their combination leaves room for much future research into their dynamics and inter-relationships.

References

Alexander, R. (2000) *Culture and Pedagogy: international comparisons in primary education* Oxford: Blackwell

Alexander, R. (2004) *Towards Dialogic Teaching: rethinking classroom talk* (3rd edn) York: Dialogos

Alexander, R. (2008) *Essays in Pedagogy* London: Routledge

Anwyll, S. (2008) *Development of Assessment and Primary Curriculum Review* NaPTEC Conference October, University of Oxford for the QCA

Assessment Reform Group (2002) *Assessment for Learning: 10 Principles: research-based principles to guide classroom practice* Cambridge: Cambridge Institute of Education Assessment Reform Group

Barnes, J. (2007) *Cross-Curricular Learning 3–14* London: PCP

Black, P. (1998) *Testing: Friend or Foe? Theory and practice of assessment and testing* London: Falmer Press

Black, P. and Wiliam, D. (1998) *Inside the Black Box: raising standards through classroom assessment* London: King's College

Briggs, M., Woodfield, A., Martin, C., and Swatton, P. (2008) *Assessment for Learning and Teaching in Primary Schools* (2nd edn) Exeter: Learning Matters

Bruner, J. (1963) *The Process of Education* New York: Vintage Books

Crisp, F.M. (1978) 'Questioning children's reading – an application of Barrett's taxonomy' *Reading* 12 (1) (April): Summary

DCSF (2008) *The Assessment for Learning Strategy* National Strategies, QCA / Chartered Institute of Educational Assessors Nottingham: DCSF

DCSF (2009) *Getting to Grips with Assessing Pupils' Progress* National Strategies, QCA / Chartered Institute of Educational Assessors Nottingham: DCSF

DfEE (1999) *The Review of the National Curriculum in England: the consultation materials* London: DfEE

DfEE and QCA (1999) *The National Curriculum: handbook for primary teachers in England. Key stages 1 and 2* London: DfEE and QCA

DfES (2003) *Excellence and Enjoyment: a strategy for primary schools* London: DfES

Drummond, M. (2003) *Assessing Children's Learning* (2nd edn) London: David Fulton

Garforth, F.W. (1966) *John Dewey Selected Educational Writings* London: Heinemann

General Teaching Council – Research for Teachers: Bruner, J. (0506) *Jerome Bruner's Constructivist Model and the Spiral Curriculum for Teaching and Learning* http://www.gtce.org.uk.teachers/rft/bruner0506 (accessed 28 October 2009)

Hart, S., Dixon, A., Drummond, M.J., and McIntyre, D. (2004) *Learning without Limits* Maidenhead: Open University Press

Mansell, W., James, M. and the Assessment Reform Group (2009) *Assessment in Schools. Fit for purpose? A commentary by the Teaching and Learning Research Programme* London: ESRC, TLRP (accessed November 20009 on http://www.tlrp.org/pub/commentaries.html)

Mercer, N. (1995) *The Guided Construction of Knowledge: talk amongst teachers and learners* Clevedon: Multilingual Matters

Mercer, N. (2000) *Words and Minds: how we use language to think together* London: Routledge

Pollard, A. (2002) *Reflective Teaching: effective and evidence-informed professional practice* London: Continuum

Primary National Strategy (2003) *Speaking, Listening, Learning: working with children in key stages 1 and 2* London: QCA and DfES

Primary National Strategy (2004) *Excellence and Enjoyment: learning and teaching in the primary years. Learning to learn: progression in key aspects of learning* Professional Development Materials London: DfES

QCA (2009) *AfL Checklist*. http://www.qcda.gov.uk/4338.aspx

QCDA (2009) *National Strategies: assessing pupils' progress* (accessed on http://nationalstrategies.standards.dcsf.gov.uk)

Sternberg, R. (2007) *Creating Creative Thinkers for a Changing World* Cambridge: Assessment Conference, October, University of Cambridge

Vygotsky, L.S. (1978) *Mind and Society: the development of higher psychological processes* Cambridge, Massachusetts: Harvard University Press

Internet sources

http://www.businessballs.com/kolblearningstyles.htm
http://www.gtce.org.uk/teachers/rft/bruner0506
http://www.gtce.org.uk/teachers/rft/vygotsky1203/
http://www.qcda.gov.uk/4338.aspx

Chapter 11

Using a range of media in cross-curricular teaching

Trevor Kerry

Introduction

The chapter looks at the increasingly creative use of a variety of presentational media, through which individual children or groups can access learning and – importantly – express their learning outcomes. It covers such topics as ICT, video presentation, photography, video-conferencing, role play and dramatic productions, and media reporting. Examples are drawn from the real world of schools and classrooms and analysed for their practicality and effectiveness as learning tools.

Background

There is no intention here to claim that the days of the exercise book are numbered or that children producing work orally in the form of answers to the teacher are undertaking an outmoded activity. But the fact remains that, just as variety of approach keeps teachers' lessons fresh and stimulating, so utilising and encouraging a variety of responses from pupils by employing a range of media provides most effectively for individualising learning and meeting preferred learning styles. Further, we argue here that cross-curricular thinking is most pertinently encapsulated using appropriate media – whatever these happen to be. We use examples to show how innovative lessons often lead to innovative presentations by pupils of what they have learned and that, through that process, learning is better anchored in the pupils' consciousness. A brief example will suffice to move us into the debates.

An art lesson lends itself well to pupils exploring a number of different media. Most of us would not expect art to be constrained by a single approach or interpretation – unless, of course, the intention of a specific lesson was simply to teach a designated skill such as modelling clay or drawing an object from life. So, in the case study that follows, what the teacher sets is the theme; what the pupils do is to interpret the task as they see fit.

Case study 11.1 Pattern

The teacher wants the pupils to explore the concept of pattern

She provides them with some ideas from everyday life as stimulus: paving stones, a roll of wallpaper, the natural patterns of lichen on the school wall, the shape of the soil

---

moved by the plough on a distant field which is visible through the classroom window.

They discuss the essential nature of pattern. That it is repetitive. That it makes shapes. That sometimes the shapes it makes break up the outlines – e.g. the camouflage pattern on Tony's jacket. That it can be bold or subtle. That it can deceive the eye.

When they have explored the idea, the teacher suggests they begin to think about the medium in which they might best express the idea of pattern. She says they can work alone or in small groups of up to four.

The task is the same, however they choose to work: to create or discover patterns and bring the outcomes to the next lesson to show everyone else. Then they will show their patterns, explain them to their peers, and tell everyone why they chose the medium they did in order to demonstrate their chosen patterns. Here are some of the outcomes.

Sharon and Tracey decided to make their own patterns. They wanted to make their own wallpaper, so they got a roll of plain paper and traced out some designs on it, which they then coloured in.

Tony liked the camouflage pattern on his jacket so he made a three-dimensional model of a jungle and put some of the toy zoo animals (tigers, leopards) in it to demonstrate how they disappear from sight because of the patterns on their coats.

Janet and John took out a digital camera and looked round the school site for potential patterns. They came back with photographs of the hopscotch court, the concentric rings of the tennis target, the loops in the goal nets and the diamond shapes of the wire round the school field.

Niall took a scraperboard and etched out the patterns in a feather he had found.

Rick and Ally got excited by natural things and made models of ladybirds and of butterflies with mirror-image wings using folded paper and mirrors.

Jo and Sandra face-painted a panda face on Kelly trying to capture the slightly lop-sided pattern of panda markings.

A group of four took the video camera and ran it round the outside of the school building looking at the patterns made by building bricks when they are laid, the patterns of flower heads in the school garden, and the cracking of paint on an old wooden shed.

Rodney, who is averse to some of the more practical aspects of art and prefers reading, took the view that words make patterns, for example in poetry. So he made up a poem:

Bumble bee
Mumble bee
Rumble bee
Buzz
Honey bee
Money bee
Sunny bee
ZZZZZZ

> The next week the pupils presented their findings and they discovered: patterns are everywhere in the built environment and in nature; patterns often have a purpose (strength in a wall, safety in camouflage); patterns can be made by sound, not just visually; patterns come in all shapes and sizes and colours; patterns may soothe or deceive our looking. The teacher thought that next week they might look for patterns, and create some, in sound, in music, in words – even in mathematics.

This example – fictitious as it stands but based on several different lessons – makes a number of important points about children's learning and how teachers can promote it.

First, a child has to be 'ready' to learn something before he or she can do so. This phenomenon has been well documented over the years (Bourne 1994: 216–17). The built-in choices that the teacher has allowed here take account of different levels of readiness. Thus Sharon and Tracey's response to the task is rather dependent on the teacher's ideas in the introduction to the lesson; but Rodney has provided a completely different kind of response which is both in a different medium and at a very different cognitive level. Vygotsky (1978) noted that children progress through learning by building one idea upon another – what he labels 'scaffolding'. In this lesson the teacher has laid a foundation that scaffolds to the next level in at least two ways. First, in the report-back lesson they learn from each other; and then she takes back some control in opening up the concept of pattern (e.g. through mathematics).

The structure of the learning here is also interesting because it takes account of preferred learning style (Jarvis 2005: 80–93) and the idea that children may have predispositions to some kinds of learning rather than others, which have to be coaxed into life. They have begun, though, to reflect on their own learning through their discoveries and applications of patterns, so there is a metacognitive element at work here (Kerry and Wilding 2004: 248–53). Yet one can sense in the responses to the task a degree of self-motivation and self-direction which marks this out as effective learning (Nutbrown 2002: 56). Much of the good work has been achieved through the coalescence of several key factors: choice, the use of the child's environment (Ratcliffe and Grace 2003: 144), cross-curricular connections (Bowring-Carr and West-Burnham 1997: 69), and the perceived value of each person's contribution (Stoll *et al.* 2003: 48).

In the rest of the chapter we will go on to look at the way in which a variety of presentational forms can promote children's enthusiasm for learning, and at some real examples of learning that concentrate on personal experience.

First-hand experience

It has long been established that children learn better by doing than by being told (Fisher 1991: 11), and in the spirit of this approach the chapter turns now to look at the genesis of a first-hand learning experience. At Beatrix Potter School in London, we trace out the process by which an idea for such a learning experience came about. The work was featured on the BBC's Breakfast programme over several days and what follows in Case Study 11.2 is an insight into how the events took shape in the mind of the headteacher. The passage is a mind-map and not a chronological account of what happened; and that approach is retained in order to demonstrate that some planning of this kind is serendipitous rather than formally structured.

Case Study 11.2 The evacuation project: headteacher Steph Neale reflects

When does one hit upon a unique idea for an educational theme? The National Curriculum brought a sense of order to teaching, but over the years was often seen as a straitjacket that teachers rarely escaped from. Yet, as a result of a logbook documenting a school's evacuation, teachers leapt out from the straitjacket and created a day of stunning experiential learning that has yet further to develop.

In a chance conversation about our school log, we suddenly realised we had an event that was pivotal in this nation's history: the evacuation of children from cities and towns across the UK in 1939. We had used this log for the Year 5 Second World War topic with the new Wandsworth Museum, through the good offices of Andrew Lynch assisted by a set of people who strongly believed that history is better taught from seeing and experiencing it.

Our initial intention was to draw up a plan, think of resources, and look for sources of visits and so on – a conventional approach. But this did not grab the imagination. Better, could we not try to find some of the original names in the log and locate the people? Okay; how do you locate people from some seventy years ago? In practice, it's fairly straightforward; we used various societies, local knowledge, and press releases. Word-of-mouth also spread news of a sort of reunion.

Children were charged with part of the task. Some eight evacuees appeared with their unique stories, and all holding various photos and original documents. As head, I thought: why not recreate what happened, get the kids dressed, and evacuate them locally? Nice and simple. But nothing is ever that simple. One Y2 pupil asked me, after an assembly about the log, why could we not go and see where our children went. So Andrew discovered the local history society of Shamley Green – to which our evacuees had been sent – and suddenly our idea took on a wholly different direction.

Our aim had always been to capture on the Web the voices of the evacuees, the children's thoughts on how they would feel, and to surround this with activities: a dig for victory garden, building an air raid shelter, singing air raid practice songs. We would use a range of devices to capture the ideas and set up an online resource for all.

Now, suddenly, I thought: we could hire a train, maybe a steam train, ride it as in 1939 and play as the children did on the green whilst being billeted.

Unique hands-on live experience looked good. At Shamley Green teachers and children met Michael Harding and the Shamley Historical Society; artefacts, billeting knowledge, and photos came out and suddenly there were real people who had been there as kids in 1939. It was a moment of sheer pleasure: that one could envisage our children talking to people who left our school and the people they were billeted with.

I discovered that hiring a real and very large steam train was actually easy. Railtrack came on board to fit in the train on the timetables and suddenly we had an evacuation train. We started reading to the children extracts from the 1938 log about the first preparations for evacuation. The children were fascinated by the realisation they were sitting in the same rooms as the children of 1938.

We were also very fortunate to discover Joy Gardiner, who had the original letter to parents from 1938 (as well as her letters home from 1939 onwards as a seven-year-old). From this the children at Key Stage 2 researched the evacuation procedures using the 1938–9 log as a source. They prepared their own letters for parents as though informing them of events. Research highlighted the scale of the undertaking in London alone. Teachers prepared the children using a range of resources from the period. Various companies and the Imperial War Museum all have superb copies of original documents, books, and posters. Teachers explained what happened and, using extracts from the school log, explained how the head had organised events. As we approached the summer break we had children from Year 1 upwards well versed in the period.

Year 1 had thought about their toys in the suitcase and at Year 6 how they would feel, as the oldest, leaving their parents, surrounded by younger children. There are a whole range of accounts and sources on the Web about children and their reactions and feelings during evacuation. Year 5 were charged with discovering these and selecting the most appropriate for each class.

For the parents, we sent home the original letter to them about their roles in the forthcoming evacuation and how they were to prepare the children. We also sent home images on how we might dress the children. We revisited Shamley Green, with the date now booked as 29 September. They had moved forward preparations from their end, and the village green was ours courtesy of Waverley Council. The whole village wanted to join in, and many ex-combatants and families who had housed the evacuees were talking to Michael at the Historical Society.

It was very clear that this event had really struck a chord with the village. They wanted to show the children where the London children had been billeted and where, sadly, one young boy had been killed. We became aware that people wanted children to comprehend how important the past and this event were to many: we now had a whole range of people able to tell their experiences as local children receiving these London children, as service personnel at Shamley Green, and as participants of the period.

Such an opportunity for present children to go where our children of 1939 had been, and to meet the very people who had been there, is unique and offers an experience of real history: the children themselves are making their own history. They began to get an idea about how the war affected real people's lives. Meeting people personally involved and handling objects from the period of time was very important. The preparation and lead-up activities taught in the classroom were equally important, giving context in order to help children to understand things happening on the day.

The atmosphere at Shamley Green and inclusion of historic vehicles and tents added to the children's understanding of 1940s Britain. Children took digital cameras, flip videos, and a set of handhelds. Photos recorded every event and more. Digital cameras are very forgiving, and out of some eight hundred images on the average data-card the children could create a montage of the day with a degree of professionalism. Flip videos allowed children to record conversations with evacuees, veterans who had served in the Second World War, and to collect the thoughts of the re-enactors and period vehicle owners.

The older children plotted on GPS the location of the billets and plan to link them to original photos of the period and photos of the sites today. All will be placed on open access to anyone interested in the resource. The video pieces will go towards a compilation video of the day.

But the learning did not stop there. Now a 'People's Voice' activity will follow. Wandsworth Museum will teach the children oral history skills and then the children will interview the evacuees and the people of Shamley Green over the next year. The ultimate goal is a unique online resource about this period of UK history.

What other experiences added to the impact of the event?

Empathy is something that comes with maturity, but those who were able to do so were definitely thinking of the experiences of the children who had been evacuated. For some of the younger children the experience was powerful; it was hard for them to draw the line and know where the re-enactment ended. But certainly some children were able to get under the skin of the event. The re-evacuation (especially the Blitz experience) has helped to give depth to the children's responses of how it might have felt to have been living then (activities that allowed children to document their feelings after the event have helped teachers to see evidence of this).

A Year 5 teacher thought that her class would get restless on the guided walk around the billets, perhaps finding it was too long; but she was surprised to see in the letters they wrote afterwards that many considered it to be one of the highlights of their day. The fact that staff were relaxed, and that older children were given responsibility for younger children, helped them to feel important and has helped the school community to bond.

Some of the younger children had been scared in the run-up to the event, and they had had a few crying episodes; but were all enthusiastic when it came to the day. As well as being relevant for the children currently studying the Second World War, the experience has unexpectedly acted as a point of reference to many other areas of learning. For example, a Year 1 child asked the teacher if the toys they were looking at (in their Toys in the Past module) were from before or after the Second World War. Again, it has been beneficial for cross-curricular learning and feelings of self-esteem, bonding individuals together within and outside school.

The work has fulfilled many of the themes and aims in our PSHE curriculum. It has also helped people to engage with the community and talk about things in school within their home environments and feel proud of their achievements. Community involvement is probably the most valuable thing to come out of the event for the school, and the extent of this was unexpected. The people who came out to wave the children off made them feel extremely special and part of something important. It was something that the parents could be involved with which was valuable. This project brought the whole community together including ex-parents and pupils (all ages). It was the unexpected things (television, newspapers, people making a fuss, feedback from external parties, teachers dressing up with them) that helped the children to feel proud they were part of something special to many people, and of something unique.

We intend that much more will emerge as we gradually develop the resources we have put together. Year 6 will perform the play *The Evacuees*, songs of the period are being learned by the choir. Creative writing using the experience of the day is showing surprising talent and innovation in a whole range of children. Without any doubt, the impact of the day and the preparation has re-energised the staff and given parents a view of the curriculum they did not expect. Parents have described how focused the children were on getting the day right, their real pleasure in looking up information which had real purpose and meaning to their studies and understanding.

Teachers were motivated and can see how to adapt the principles here to other areas. Obviously they cannot create an evacuation but they realise the value of innovation and excitement, a word that falls a little flat in the National Curriculum.

This case study about the birth of an exciting learning experience is interesting, not least for its spontaneity. There are other curriculum approaches, too, that lend themselves to work which breaks out of the straitjackets that Neale referred to above. To some of these we now turn our attention.

Video presentation and photography

Visual literacy is a cross-curricular skill and a life skill of the highest order. We are all bombarded daily with images: they are not random. They attract our attention, draw on our sympathy, and are intended to persuade our thinking, bend our understanding of events, try to create needs in us (such as the need to purchase), and alter our moods.

Images relate (of course) to global events, but they permeate even the most trivial activities of our lives.

Our ability to absorb images, filter them, edit them, interpret them, evaluate them – all this has to be rapid, even instantaneous.

Yet some people have no visual literacy skill – a skill every bit as real and objective as numerical skill, reading skill, or writing skill. If one picture is indeed worth a thousand words – or even only a hundred – then visual literacy is a skill of paramount importance.

Whether the image is moving or still, the issue is the same. It is about the tool-box that we bring in our minds – the tools with which we deconstruct the images we see, and piece together not just the messages they purport to convey but the underlying themes we are meant to construe from them: even the underlying, subliminal propaganda of imagery.

Equipping children with the skills that relate to visual literacy is almost (one might argue on the basis of sound evidence) more important than most of what else they learn in school. In the days of i-players, mobile phone imagery, computer screens, fantasy computer games, digital cameras, and constant media pressures (such as rolling news), can it be doubted that this is *the* central life skill for the twenty-first century?

Yet it has nothing to do with subject learning. It is not art. It is not even photography. It may include those things, but it transcends them. It embraces all knowledge, and it demands of the viewer a breadth of vision in the interpretation that is incredibly demanding.

From time to time, considerable claims are made for the impact of visual literacy activities. Thus the United Kingdom Literacy Association (Bearne and Grainger 2004) claimed 'an improvement in writing and attitudes to writing by boys. If boys' writing is a concern in a school then the school should consider developing these aspects to support its improvement.' The DfES (2005) demonstrated that by the end of a project involving visual literacy approaches to writing, boys 'were more able to express ideas about the process of writing and effective writing behaviours and indicated that they saw themselves as much more in control of their own writing'. But it is not just boys who need visual literacy skills.

A useful website might be: http://www.teachingexpertise.com/articles/visual-literacy-3961. It is suggested here that using visual literacy skills could affect writing by pupils in the following ways:

- Increased quantity
- Increased quality
- Wider vocabulary
- Greater use of imagery
- Increased fluency
- More adventurous approaches
- Improved attitudes
- Improved motivation.

Kinds of visual stimulus material include the following:

- Looking at and discussing still pictures
- Film and television images
- Hidden images
- Media such as advertising
- Picture dictionaries
- Linking pictures and sound
- Charts and diagrams.

In what follows, the Reflection panel is used to raise your awareness of your own visual literacy as well as that of your pupils.

Reflection

Try some of these visual literacy ideas to test your own awareness.

Perspective

Take a digital camera with a zoom lens. Stand in your school or the school's road. Shoot six pictures, the first one wide angle, then progressively zooming to telephoto, ending with maximum zoom. Now examine the pictures. How does perspective change your perception (or your pupils' perception) of the scene?

Editing (subconsciously?)

In the previous task, why did you choose to look in the direction you chose? What would you have seen in the opposite direction, and how would the view have altered your perception of the location?

Catching the eye

I wrote two texts, both on education. One was presented by the designer with a dark blue cover showing an 'old master' painting in rather sombre hues. The other had a yellow cover with a child's monochrome drawing on it. Which book ran to fourteen impressions?

Manipulating your pictures

Shoot with a digital camera any picture, but preferably one with fairly simple, strong lines (such as a headshot, a picture of a bridge, or a striking building). Download the picture into your computer and manipulate it using a programme such as Photoshop Elements. You can turn the colour shot monochrome; you can play with the different levels of saturation; or you can use the filter options, for example to create a watercolour effect. Which images are most striking and why? What does it tell you about matching 'mode' to subject matter?

Interpreting what you see

Choose a striking portrait and give each pupil a copy. Ask them (without consulting) to write down twenty words that describe the face. Compare the results. To what extent do they overlap and differ? (This is a good task for developing vocabulary, too.)

Bamford (2003) talks about visual syntax, which involves some of the elements we have looked at in the Reflection above. These include:

- *Scale*: images can distort relative size and importance.
- *Motion*: blurring an image can create an enhanced impression of speed.
- *Shape*: 'real' objects can be turned into abstract ideas.
- *Arrangement and juxtaposing*: clashes of position (soft toy holding sharp knife) can jar the sense or challenge our understandings.
- *Manipulation*: manipulating an image also manipulates its meaning.
- *Use of foreground or background*: try shooting two objects (e.g. a 'no parking' cone and a parked car) first with one item in the foreground, then the other. How does the result change the meaning of the image?
- *Tone*: soft tones (gold, sepia) imply tranquillity, nostalgia, comfort; hard tones (red, black) are disturbing and jarring.

Pupils in the twenty-first century need very highly developed visual skills. Whenever they look at an image they have to ask themselves, almost consciously, a number of questions about it. They have to be aware of how they are interpreting the image. They need to know that images are often designed to have social impact, and that means to manipulate our understanding of the topic (simply put, a shot of a dead pheasant may mean cruel sport to some and good eating to others). We, and our pupils, have to ask ourselves about who owns the ideas behind the images we see; and whether we are evaluating them adequately so as not to be subjected to propaganda. Visual learning can extend understanding; but only once we have learned the rules of visual literacy. In the same way we can use and create images to support the messages we want to convey – to persuade, inform, cajole. These processes disguise moral dilemmas – those dilemmas are a part of the learning process and should be teased out and deconstructed.

A couple of years ago I was fortunate enough to have one of my photographs selected for the shortlist of prize contenders in an international competition. The image was duly printed in a book of winning pictures (O'Brien 2007). Photographers were asked to contribute a short insight into imagery, and this was mine: photography is a window into the soul; it illuminates the observer and the observed. Therein lies its ambiguity: how much of an image is what we see? How much of it is what we were intended to see? What do our answers tell us about us? But also, what do they tell us about the creator of the image? Some people are said to walk around with their eyes shut. They don't. They see what the rest of us see, but they lack the visual literacy to interpret its significance. In today's world they are, potentially, victims.

Other media

Having looked in some depth at the issues that underpin visual literacy (though there is, of course, much more that could be said – the topic would deserve a book to itself), we move on in this chapter to examine some other approaches that might be used with pupils or that pupils might use. In so doing, it would be useful to bear in mind the broad principles that this chapter has established so far, in particular about criticality, and about the ability of these media to be used both as means to promote learning and as means to express what has been learned. In such a short chapter these issues can be dealt with using only broad brushstrokes, and the reader is urged to follow up each as its potential seems relevant to his or her work.

Video-conferencing

Increasingly, schools are gaining access to their own or other people's video-conferencing facilities. Video-conferencing works much like a video-phone: during a conversation it is possible for groups to see one another and to see what each is doing. An obvious use of this kind of facility is for groups at a considerable distance to share learning: it is perfectly possible for classes to communicate across countries.

The issue with all technology is: how far is it merely a gimmick, or to what extent can it become a genuine learning tool? Video-conferencing allows the users to transport themselves with some immediacy into the situation of the other party. A class in metropolitan Birmingham can share experience with a group on the Cumbrian fells. A class in Nigeria or Eastern Europe can have very personal contact with classes in Hemel Hempstead or Harrogate.

Thus learning through video-conferencing can provide rich experience that comes close to first-hand experience, whether in cross-curricular or narrower fields. Its success, like so much else in teaching, depends on good planning and preparation. Access to facilities is often time-limited, and teachers need to know how to extract the best usage out of the time available.

Video-conferencing has another important use. It can allow two groups in quite different places to share, and participate in, exemplary lessons. It may allow a class to be taught by someone with a specific skill or interest to which they would not otherwise have access. The National Portrait Gallery offers video-conferencing sessions to schools (http://www.npg.org.uk/learning/schools/primary-schools/videoconferencing.php) – and these provide expert information and discussion quite literally 'to your door'. But the potential for this kind of usage is massive.

Video-conferencing is likely – like most technologies – to become more widely available. As it does so its potential will be limited only by the imagination of the users. As an educational tool it will provide the opportunity for making the world smaller and for opening pupils' horizons. It allows for two-way communication in which learning can take place, and through which young people can communicate their understandings to others.

Drama and production

Most teachers will need little persuasion that drama, in one form or another, has a powerful learning potential. Of course, we are all familiar with the 'school production', and much learning takes place as a result of it (subject matter, and skills like confidence). Similarly, role-play is often used to help pupils get inside the skin of a topic, to deal with the affective issues in a lesson. These processes are commonplace.

What is being argued here is that, at times, a response to a classroom task might be best expressed in drama rather than – for example – in a piece of writing or an artefact. The case for drama in this sense is well put by the Curriculum On-Line website whose (somewhat unwieldy) Web address appears at the end of this chapter. This site claims that:

> Drama requires impersonation, personification and role-play involvement. It is an ideal methodology for the teaching of history, as
> * the involvement of children in role-playing means they will empathise with characters in the past and come to defend their actions against the arguments of others
> * drama aims to re-create human experience. The pupil-actor is personally affected by the experience and this motivates him/her to know and understand more
> * drama militates against a simplistic approach to a topic. All points of view are articulated so that situations are no longer viewed in 'black or white' terms.

Of course, it is not just history that benefits from this cross-curricular approach. Subjects across the whole curriculum can be illuminated by drama. Teachers can download a model drama policy from the Arts on the Move website which can be adapted to individual school needs: http://www.artsonthemove.co.uk/education/primary/primary.php. For the present purpose, the section to emphasise in this document relates to its concern for cross-curricular links:

There are strong links to other subjects including English, history, music, PE, PSHE and Citizenship, geography, art and religious education. Drama methods can be used within these subjects to explore a variety of roles, topics, feelings, situations and facts.

Specific aspects of all subjects can be explored using drama, such as character motivation, scenes and situations, roles, emotions, pivotal moments, debates, decisions and personal choices, and reactions or responses.

The points made about drama and role-play may apply equally to other forms of classroom talk, such as debates, discussions, and presentations. These, too, can be used both as tasks set by the teacher, or as means chosen by pupils as ways to express their knowledge.

Media reporting

One obvious way of communicating, in today's world, is through the media. This may be the radio or television interview, or it may be through newspaper and magazine articles. Learning can often be made more immediate by imagining that the class is 'present' at an event (at Henry VIII's court or in the shelters during the Second World War, for example). Interviewing can also be a means to investigate a topic, on the model of the 'World at One' interviews with politicians. Newspapers and magazines present both visual (see above) and written versions of events in the local area or on the national scene. Using the techniques can have a number of learning outcomes:

- Alerting pupils to bias in reporting
- Helping them with speaking and listening skills
- Teaching them the skills of asking insightful questions
- Promoting confidence on both sides of the microphone (and many others).

A very practical application of these skills is in the School Council, where pupils can use the democratic process of representation to elect their members, make a case, argue a point, and bring about incremental change in what happens in their school. Guidance on School Councils is available on http://www.innovation-unit.co.uk/about-us/publications/new-resources-for-primary-school-councils.html. This source has some good materials presented for young people in cartoon format.

An example of pupils acting as media reporters was included in Kerry (2002: 68–75). The task described there (producing a class newspaper) is timeless, but the major learning point of the exercise was not about the means of production, or the content, or about writing skill. It was about time: the need to work to deadlines, to work within the team, to achieve the end-product within the allotted parameters. That approach mirrors life, and is thus valuable learning across the curriculum in every sphere of learning.

Information and communications technology

The last section in this collection of media activities for pupils relates to the use of ICT. There are plenty of people with expertise in the hardware and software of ICT, but this section is concerned not with these aspects but the principles for the use of ICT, especially to access the Web. Effective ICT use requires teachers to harness the potential in ways that enhance learning, and – just as importantly – not to use the technology in ways that subvert learning. It is this that the principles rehearsed below attempt to ensure.

- ICT gives access to huge quantities of data. Teachers often refer to pupils accessing these data as being engaged in 'research'. Research is a term best left for finding new things and breaking new ground. What the Web does for most people most of the time is to provide a simple means of access to existing data. The Web is an excellent means of data collection.
- Data collection is only a stage – in thinking terms, a fairly low-order operation – in the process of learning. Pupils should be encouraged to avoid bad habits. Data which are merely cut-and-pasted have no life in the minds of the pupils; the information is not theirs, it is someone else's. The stitching together of unabsorbed snippets of data should be discouraged.
- Data collection gives access to a world of thought that involves: sifting, comparing, contrasting, following new leads, checking contradictions, analysing, synthesising, making judgements, and evaluating. These are higher-order thinking tasks. The Web should be used to feed these higher-order operations, not to replace them.
- All Web searches should be set against the clearly stated objectives for that lesson or learning activity, and should involve the higher-order processes identified above.
- Classroom tasks should be so structured that the Web is used as a tool, not as an end in itself – except for the brief period where access skills are being learned.

Beyond the use of the Web for data collection, inspections suggest that:

Almost all children respond to ICT in a positive way and are motivated by the inclusion of ICT-related activities during lessons; they are particularly motivated by the whole-class aspect of ICT in learning and teaching, where, for example, a data projector or an IWB is used, leading to good discussion and high levels of engagement. In a small number of the schools, the children take ownership of ICT initiatives, such as updating the scrolling display in the school foyer, or older children mentoring younger classes in the use of ICT. Children's involvement and interest are promoted where there is good integration of experiences using ICT into real learning situations and where use is made of the local area.

Where there is a whole-school culture of using ICT to enhance the children's learning across the curriculum, there are many examples of the thoughtful use of applications where the children's ICT experiences are planned and are appropriately challenging.

(http://www.etini.gov.uk/information_and_communication_
technology_in_primary_schools.pdf)

Many sources note that the commonest uses of ICT are for word processing; and there is nothing wrong with using it for this purpose. But, once more, such a use reduces the computer simply to the status of a tool. To raise its value above this, it is important to have applications that make demands at higher-order levels of thinking: solving design problems, writing stories, producing leaflets, and so on.

Using a computer as a tool for learning is no different from other approaches to classroom teaching: its effectiveness depends on the quality of the task it is intended the pupils should achieve through its use. The more practical, realistic, and embedded these tasks are in the thinking skills that delineate high-quality learning, the more value the work will have – a thought that leads appropriately into a consideration of problem-solving as a learning tool.

Real problem-solving

An increasingly common mode of working in primary schools is, quite rightly, the attempt to encourage pupils to solve real problems, and problems on their own scale that mirror the real world. In Case Study 11.3 we see one such problem at work. The benefits of such first-hand, experiential learning are self-evident in the text that follows. Taking a more theoretical stance, what research suggests is that the values of problem-solving lie in improving cognitive demand, helping pupils to develop models through which to solve problems, and the application of problem-solving models to real-life situations (Wallace *et al.* 2008).

Case Study 11.3 Themed week on money

The curriculum was suspended for the week before the autumn half-term and replaced by a money 'themed week' (see Chapter 8).

The short-term learning objectives (i.e. one half-day) for the mixed age class of Year 4 and Year 5 were clearly articulated – today, Wednesday, was a 'food sampling day' where, for comparison, the children sampled a series of expensive products and cheaper 'own-store' brands. The tasting was blind. On Thursday, the medium-term objective was to bake scones in preparation for the long-term objective of selling the scones at the Friday local Farmers' Market.

The children had earlier had a 'The Price is Right' Assembly where the whole school had been involved. 'The Price is Right' Assembly was based on the television programme, each child was given a number on entering the hall, and different contestants were called up for different games. The first game was 'Contestants' Row' where four children had to guess the price of an object, for example a mobile phone. After the price was revealed, the child whose guess was the closest got to play that round's pricing game. For each round the children had a series of objects and they had to guess the price of the object; in one game the children were required to match the correct prices to the correct object. The children who were in the audience could help the contestant by shouting out the price which they thought was closest to the actual price.

The 'food sampling day' linked to the 'The Price is Right' Assembly in that children were given the opportunity to sample various products in order to assess the quality of the products on offer compared to the price. The children sampled jelly babies, kiwi fruit, chocolate, pizza, sponge cake, cheese, jelly beans, and lastly scones. One of the pair of products was Asda own brand, Smart Price type of thing, the other was a branded item, such as Galaxy chocolate or a more expensive Asda own product.

A small piece of each of the two foods was tasted – the children were asked to consider which they preferred, and why; which they thought was the cheaper

---

product; whether, once the products had been identified, the more expensive food merited the difference in price between the two products; whether they thought the ingredients in one product might be more healthy than in the other.

But it was not all 'taste and enjoy' – for example, the children had to compute mentally the difference between the two prices and they were not able just to say 'I like (a) better than (b)': valid reasons for making the decision had to be explained. Questions were distributed around the class with the children eager to contribute.

With the tasting nearly at an end, the class teacher explained that the last items to be tasted, some scones, were to act as the bridge between that day's tasting and the following day's activity.

A conventional lesson followed the tasting immediately after break which set the scene for further activity – group work to decide which ingredients to purchase for the practical lesson on Thursday. The teacher outlined the practicalities of the scone baking session the following day, and the children's attendance at the local Farmers' Market to try to sell the resulting produce.

The links between the three activities were explained to the children: in their conventional lesson they had to weigh up the merits of whether to purchase, for example, the expensive flour or the Smart Price flour. They were steered into thinking that one might yield more profit than the other and in the context of 'money week' profit might be the important criterion.

Once the children had tasted the foods, they were split into small groups so that they could decide which flavour scones they would make to sell at the Farmers' Market and what 'standard' ingredients they wanted to purchase. The children decided to buy a mixture of more expensive and cheaper ingredients. They thought carefully about what they had learned and which ones would affect the quality of the final product. The children decided we could buy Smart Price flour, sugar, currants but that we should buy more expensive eggs and cheese because of what they had tasted earlier on in the session.

The children enjoyed making their scones the next day, and when we visited the Farmers' Market on the Friday, all of the produce which had been made by the whole school was sold. We came back to school with a profit of £39.94 overall. Only two children from each class were able to attend the Farmers' Market, so on their return to school they shared with the rest of the class what they had done, and what they had learned. The bread and fairy cakes made by children in other classes sold the most quickly, and we could have made a larger profit had we used all of the ingredients which had been bought, but this was hindered by time limitations. Further discussions of what we achieved and what we learned will be discussed at Enterprise Club and we plan to carry out a similar event at the Nativity on North Hykeham Green in December.

Conclusion

What this chapter has aimed to do has been to open teachers' eyes to the rich and varied methods that they might employ not simply to present learning, but to gather feedback about learning from pupils. In the process we are helping to promote life skills, enterprise skills, and the kinds of skills that will be needed for pupils to become economically self-sustaining citizens. The bonus is that these approaches can lead to learning that is genuinely imaginative and dynamic.

References

Bamford, A. (2003) *The Visual Literacy White Paper* Sydney: Adobe Systems

Bearne, E. and Grainger, T. (2004) 'Research in progress – raising boys' achievements in writing: joint PNS/UKLA pilot research project' *Literacy* 38 (3): 156–8

Bourne, J. (1994) *Thinking Through Primary Practice* London: Routledge / Open University

Bowring-Carr, C. and West-Burnham, J. (1997) *Effective Learning in Schools* London: Pitman

Department for Education and Skills (2005) *Raising Boys' Achievement* London: HMSO

Fisher, R. (1991) *Teaching Juniors* Oxford: Blackwell

Jarvis, M. (2005) *The Psychology of Effective Learning and Teaching* Cheltenham: Nelson-Thornes

Kerry, T. (2002) *Learning Objectives, Task Setting and Differentiation* Cheltenham: Nelson-Thornes

Kerry, T. and Wilding, M. (2004) *Effective Classroom Teacher* London: Pearson

Nutbrown, C. (2002) *Research Studies in Early Childhood Education* Stoke-on-Trent: Trentham Books

O'Brien, B. (2007) *The World's Greatest Black and White Photography No. 1* London: The Spider Awards

Ratcliffe, M. and Grace, M. (2003) *Science Education for Citizenship* Maidenhead: Open University

Stoll, L. Fink, D., and Earl, L. (2003) *It's About Learning and It's About Time* London: Routledge Falmer

Vygotsky, L. (1978) *Mind in Society* Cambridge, Massachusetts: Harvard University Press

Wallace, B., Berry, A., and Cave, D. (2008) *Teaching Problem-solving and Thinking Skills through Science* London: Routledge

Internet sources

http://www.artsonthemove.co.uk/education/primary/primary.php

http://www.curriculumonline.ie/en/Primary_School_Curriculum/Social_Environmental_and_Scientific_Education_SESE_/History/History_Teacher_Guidelines/Approaches_and_methodologies/Drama_and_role-play/

http://www.etini.gov.uk/information_and_communication_technology_in_primary_schools.pdf

http://www.innovation-unit.co.uk/about-us/publications/new-resources-for-primary-school-councils.html

http://www.npg.org.uk/learning/schools/primary-schools/videoconferencing.php

http://www.teachingexpertise.com/articles/visual-literacy-3961

Chapter 12

Planning effective team teaching for cross-curricular learning

Peter Harrod and Trevor Kerry

Introduction

This chapter looks at team teaching as a way of organising pupils' learning. It suggests that team teaching may be used for all or part of a child's learning experience, but that it is especially suited to periods where learning is presented as cross-curricular. The chapter examines some definitions of team teaching; various models which can be applied to it; its advantages as a means of organisation; and its limitations. The chapter also emphasises that team teaching is an advanced teaching skill which demands proper preparation and appropriate staff training. The chapter sets out advice and examples for those who want to try their hand at working in this collaborative way.

Background

A chapter about team teaching is especially appropriate in a book about integrated approaches to curriculum. It is a simple logic: cross-curricular knowledge is broader than subject-based knowledge, so teams of two or more teachers are likely to have wider and more varied perspectives on offer to support the basic philosophy and approach. But it is easy to make unwarranted assumptions about teachers and teaching. Teachers can teach, and therefore they can adapt their teaching style appropriately to any kind of external circumstance and can work in it without training.

The fallacy of this assumption struck home some years ago during a study of a new primary school space (Kerry and Wilding 2004: 259–80). The space was an open plan building, well equipped and carpeted, in what had been a former swimming pool. The newly refurbished room could hold three classes at once, but was occupied by two teachers and two parallel groups. It opened directly into the playground and the school field. The researchers were asked to investigate why this expensive and attractive space was not delivering a learning benefit to the pupils after a year of operation.

This is not the place to rehearse the story of this research. Suffice it to say that we looked at the cognitive levels of learning (see Chapter 2); at pupils' time-on-task; at the classroom organisation and its suitability for the location with special attention paid to the use of group, individual, and whole class work; at behaviour and the kinds of deviance in evidence when pupils were not occupied with their work; and at how pupils of high, middle, and lower levels of ability operated within the lessons. We also listened to and collected evidence from pupils, teachers, the headteacher, and the governors who had raised funds for the rebuilding.

Our conclusions were quite damning in terms of the quality of the learning experience (though the teachers involved were highly competent, experienced, and dedicated professionals). We found that, while behaviour of pupils was good (so the scene was set for effective learning), there was little cognitively extended task demand, work was rarely differentiated other than by outcome, opportunities to cater for the most and least able were lost, and pupil voice was nowhere in evidence. A space that should have been in itself a dynamic learning area was not 'owned' by anyone and therefore it was sterile and unstimulating. Social relations were good all round; but lessons were often unfocused, as far as we could discern, and there were overt signs of boredom from the pupils.

What was patently obvious was that two teachers vying with one another to teach two independently planned lessons (of which one might require children to be active and quite noisy, and one static and quiet) in a single space produced neither rational teaching nor effective learning. If frustration was running high among staff it was worse for the pupils. Our report to the governing body made this clear. A précis of this, but generalised to fit more diverse situations, gives the flavour:

> The move to the advanced skill of team teaching and the more effective use of support personnel would be helpful, but would imply a degree of collaborative forward planning on the part of teachers, so that they consulted with one another in advance on what would be taught when, by whom, and in what circumstances. This would not preclude pupils being allocated to 'tutor groups' for organisational and pastoral purposes. It would allow the teachers to bring their individual strengths to curriculum and lesson planning, and to the delivery of individual areas of learning. It would open up more potential for problem-solving approaches by pupils. This in turn would provide for a better approach to differentiation in lessons, which are currently orientated towards whole-class work; even where pupils are organised into groups they currently tackle identical tasks. Above all, the staff involved in this team teaching need to be trained in the appropriate skills. Consideration should be given to any courses that might be available and to opportunities that they might have to visit team teaching in action in other schools. The benefits of team teaching should be communicated to all stakeholders, not least parents and governors.

Reflection

Have you tried team teaching? If so, what did you find were its strengths and weaknesses? If not, what are the factors that most attract you to it, or put you off?

In this chapter our intention is to analyse the prerequisites, the caveats, and the benefits that relate to team working by teachers. In so doing, we are not advocating that every school or every lesson should be based on this model. We are arguing, however, that the model has strengths that can be exploited for pupils' benefit in all schools and by all teachers in appropriate circumstances. What is clear, from the example above, is that the model cannot work without a proper understanding of its philosophy and practice, and it is to this that we turn our attention.

Team teaching: historical roots and present definition

The origins of 'team teaching' are succinctly reported in Freeman (1969). There seemed little doubt to him that team teaching originated in the USA in the early years of the twentieth century, through projects such as the Dalton Plan. However, UK interest in the concept dates back to the 1950s, inspired by initiatives in the USA culminating in the publication of Trump's (1959) 'Images of the future', in which Trump predicted that the school of the future would include activities of one hundred or more pupils under the supervision of one or more teachers, and would follow many different patterns. Such a scheme has echoes of the 'Monitorial' system in England. Freeman suggests that team teaching had its roots in the availability of 'modern' audiovisual equipment, including teaching machines, CCTV, overhead projectors, and similar devices.

Given the different guises in which team teaching appears, it is hardly surprising that there are several different definitions. Indeed, Taylor (1974: 7) argues that it is not possible to offer a complete or exact description of team teaching, since it must be regarded as having an 'evolving and fluid character'. Her study of team teaching experiments in ten junior schools found that there was considerable variety of aims and arrangements, but that the one common factor was that the staff were teaching together, sharing the same group of children and the responsibility for their learning (1974: 120).

Freeman himself cites Shaplin and Olds's (1964) definition, following a survey of various schemes, as 'instructional organisation in which two or more teachers are given responsibility, working together, for all or a significant part of the instruction of the same group of pupils'. Loeser (2008) offers a similar definition, describing team teaching as the practice of including two or more teachers of equal status in a classroom to provide instruction to one group of students. (Whether the teachers need to be of 'equal status' is of course arguable: asymmetrical relationships may have positive advantages for both parties – see the section on teaching assistants in Chapter 7.) Buckley (2000: 5) refers to a definition by Bair and Woodward (1964), in which team teaching is seen as lying 'in the essential spirit of cooperative planning, constant collaboration, close unity, unrestrained communication, and sincere sharing'.

Warwick (1971: 10), in a study of team teaching in secondary schools, points to two different schools of thought which envisage team teaching either as an economic and relatively democratic way of organising and administering a school or as a philosophy of education which emphasises a reorientation of the curriculum to meet more fully the needs of both teachers and pupils. In the latter case, it takes as its starting point the needs of the children, and questions the notion that the requirements of either teacher or pupil are best served by an arbitrary subject division, with each one working in isolation from the others (1971: 12). In giving an overview of team teaching in elementary schools in Nevada as a situation in which two teachers share approximately thirty students in the same room all day, Anderson (in Northern Nevada Writing Project 1996: 3–9) concludes that it is 'obvious that team teaching can look very different from level to level and class to class'. The tentative conclusion is that the best definition of team teaching is a broad one: two or more teachers coming together for a common purpose to help enhance their teaching and their students' learning. It may, on occasion, be even simpler than that: the 'spontaneous cooperation of two like-minded teachers who decided to put their classes together and plan and record together' (O'Neill and Worrall undated).

Reflection

If learning is organised using a teaching team, how might team teaching best be used to meet the needs of individual children?

It is clear that, whatever the precise origins or even the exact definition, the concept rests on certain assumptions and philosophies that are broadly recognised by writers. We have tried to draw these together in Table 12.1, along with some of the disadvantages of the method in Table 12.2 – for its advantages do not amount to a panacea. The tables are a composite of material culled from our cited sources, but also from our own experiences as teachers and as teacher trainers.

Table 12.1 Principles and assumptions of a team teaching approach

Team teaching (with a fellow teacher/s or teaching assistants) allows (in no particular order of importance):

From a teacher's perspective
Reduction of teacher stress
Teachers to share the time and work of planning
More creative and imaginative approaches through joint planning
Teachers to collaborate on curriculum development projects
Teachers to share and/or contrast teaching philosophies
A movement away from teacher autonomy into shared responsibility for learning
Opportunities for teachers to grow professionally by learning from the practice of others
Experience by teachers of different but complementary teaching styles
Opportunities for teachers to operate in a cooperative learning environment
A model of good practice to less experienced teachers and/or trainees or NQTs
Teachers to be freed up for planning activities without disturbing lessons

From a pupil's perspective
Sharing expertise in a cross-curricular topic-centred approach
A model in which cross-curricular understandings are seen to produce improved outcomes
Matching preferred learning styles with teaching styles more effectively and flexibly
Providing pupils with more effective learning outcomes
Offering a model of good practice to pupils in terms of co-operation, teamwork, positive interaction, and collaborative effort
Learning for pupils which is more closely personalised
Improved opportunities for pupils' social learning
Sharper focus on pedagogic skills
Experience by pupils of different but complementary teaching styles
Introduction of a positive competitive edge to teaching and learning, including sharper learning objectives and success criteria leading to better pupil performance
More varied opportunities to differentiate having shared some basic knowledge
Generating respect for differences among teachers

Table 12.1 Continued

From a management perspective

Reduction in teacher–pupil ratios

More effective pastoral care and behaviour management of pupils

Team members to refine organisation and management skills

More meaningful and reliable formative assessment data

Weaker teachers to be supported

Using Higher Level Teaching Assistants to provide models of good practice to others

Opportunities emerging to show collective support for whole-school policies

Willingness to embrace the symbiotic nature of the teacher–pupil relationship

Emergencies or unforeseen events to be better catered for

The advantages of team working identified in business (e.g. heightened morale and commitment) to rub off in a school situation

---

Table 12.2 Possible disadvantages of team teaching

From a teacher perspective

Interpersonal problems/problems of relationships within the team

Possible incompatibility of teaching styles

Need for sensitivity by management in realising team memberships

Need to have willing participants

Need for an agreed division of labour

The loss of teacher autonomy

Fear of poor performance in front of peers

Logistical factors, such as findings opportunities to share planning time

From the student's perspective

Some students may be confused by conflicting opinions

Some students just want to be 'told the facts'

Preparation for lessons can be more demanding

From a management perspective

Team teaching requires an upfront investment of time in training etc.

Team working may be a complicating factor in interviewing and appointing staff

Resistance from senior management, governors, parents

Team teaching: a practical and research perspective

So far, our consideration of team teaching has – for the sake of simplicity – assumed that it is a single phenomenon; but this is some way from the truth. For example, Goetz (2000) draws out half a dozen models from her own work and the work of Maroney (1995) and of Robinson and Schaible (1995) – the labels are hers:

- *Traditional*: one teacher provides instruction, while the other constructs a concept map on an OHP or computer to support her colleague

- *Collaborative*: several teachers devise the content as a discussion in the presence of the learners, so that the construction itself becomes a learning process
- *Complementary/supportive*: one teacher teaches while the other looks after follow-up activities or provides study skill support
- *Parallel*: the class is divided into two small groups and each teacher teaches identical material, using the situation for more individualised support
- *Differentiated split class*: each teacher teaches the same topic but the class is divided e.g. into more able and less able learners, the content being appropriately differentiated for the groups
- *Monitoring*: one teacher teaches, the other monitors behaviour or checks understanding of individuals.

In England, the respected and well-published educationist Joan Dean (Dean 1970: 6) supported a view that team teaching is a broad church of definitions: the only thing they have in common is that the various forms work with groups of children and/or teachers rather than on the principle of one teacher one class. At around the same era, the National Foundation for Educational Research (NFER) in a report on the subject (Taylor 1974) offered the view that the move to this approach was an Americanism (presumably a pejorative term!) adopted by English teachers merely to 'get on the bandwagon' of innovation; and it took the line that it was related to architectural trends towards open-plan schools. None of these assumptions is entirely necessary, or indeed accurate, as a judgement on the method rather than its context. Our own view is that *an innovation or methodology is justifiable only in so far as it brings learning gains*, and this chapter argues for learning gains through team teaching without committing itself to a view that team approaches should represent the only, or the full-time, diet of children in schools.

The Northern Nevada Writing Project (NNWP 1996) looked into team teaching and found it was the shared moments that were the great positive in team teaching: the working environment became more humane and, importantly, interactions increased. Learning and teaching styles could be matched more easily. Teachers believed that the curriculum had been enhanced through the increased-skill range of the staff, and there was more activity – better hands-on approaches in the classroom and more visits out of it. Benefits were not only to the children but also to staff, who were more prepared to take risks in an atmosphere of collaboration and shared responsibility. That is not to say that all ran smoothly in team contexts: the participants suffered from territorial disputes, failures of communication, the need to sustain initial enthusiasms and commitments to joint activity, and the resentments that are inevitable if the decision to team teach is management-imposed.

In a brief and tantalising study of two secondary school teachers in Taiwan, Jang (2006) compared team and traditional approaches. Two teachers taught four classes for twelve weeks, two in the traditional way and two using team teaching. When results from the classes were compared, those taught using team methods were higher than those taught traditionally. Furthermore, the students tended to prefer the team teaching organisation. However, he notes that team teaching did not win the support of the school administration, which set out actively to impede their planning. This is a salutary case of management making decisions based not on educational but on ideological principles.

Reflection

Why might a senior management team in a school look less than favourably on a move towards team teaching?

In the UK Dewhurst and Tamburrini (1978) had undertaken studies in 71 infant and junior schools. As a result they had identified five models of team teaching which seemed to emerge from practice at the time. These were:

- *The Assignment Model*: teachers work co-operatively, and pupils engage in activities either individually or in small groups. Tasks are either self-chosen or individually assigned by teachers. Each teacher usually takes responsibility for one aspect of the curriculum, although the approach is not subject-dominated.
- *The Rotation Model*: groups (home- or class-based) are timetabled to move in turn from one designated area to another for different curriculum activities, with a balance over a day or a week, etc. Teachers tend to remain in one activity area.
- *The Setting Model*: the basics are taught in sets according to ability in maths and language, while project activities (afternoons) are planned co-operatively by teachers ('skills and frills').
- *The Half-day Model*: similar to the model above, but without 'setting', the basics being taught in mixed ability classes.
- *The Occasional Model*: work on a special project for a limited period, with teachers sharing particular interests and expertise.

Dewhurst saw these organisational methods as serving one or more of three core purposes: they depended on a child-centred philosophy of education with individualisation at its heart; they espoused a knowledge-based philosophy of integration as a means of presenting subject matter; or they were economic, being designed to maximise staff, expertise, and space. These summary points are each of considerable significance.

The reader will have noted that, while we have striven to give up-to-date references for team teaching, some of the material appears relatively dated. This is because, while team teaching was recommended as long ago as the Plowden Report (1967) as an organisational method for learning that was worthy of exploration, the Plowden backlash of the 1980s (*pace* the National Curriculum under a Conservative administration), and the continued dominance of the teaching profession by ultra-traditional Ofsted leaders such as Chris Woodhead under New Labour, effectively spelled its death-knell for a time as a widely adopted mode of working. So perhaps this is a good moment to see team teaching in action in a contemporary classroom in Case Study 12.1.

Case Study 12.1 Team teaching

Although team teaching has not been widespread in the UK since the 1970s, one school that has bucked the trend is the Priory Witham Academy School (Infant and Nursery Section, formerly Moorlands Infant School) in Lincoln. Its whole-school approach has evolved over the last 12 years or so, and has been the subject of a 'mini' case study by the present authors. In common with the case studies reported in Freeman (1969: 82), the participating teachers were sent an interview schedule questionnaire in advance of the interview itself, outlining issues and questions judged to be relevant to the study. These questions were based on earlier studies by Close *et al.* (1974: 116) and NNWP (1996: 96), allowing for some comparative analysis. Teachers were given the opportunity to respond both individually and as a group. The results may be conveniently examined in three broad areas: principles and philosophy; principles into practice; and advantages, limitations, and outcomes.

The main principles underlying the approach were as follows:

* A whole-school approach, led by the headteacher
* Team planning
* Group collaboration and participation
* All teachers involved in the same activity
* Group and/or class rotations
* Assessments and profiling by all teachers to ensure reliability
* Involvement of teaching assistants and, where available, parent helpers
* Practice never remains static; it is continuously evolving.

The approach, while having a common ethos and shared objectives, was variable according to the age-phase and subject matter. In the Early Years Foundation Stage, for example, the whole team approach and cross-curricular nature of the work lent itself naturally to a team teaching culture, and this provided a basis for adoption in modified form in Key Stage 1. As one teacher reported, it is perhaps easier to implement in the early years, as the children are used to moving around the class from one activity to another, and to having access to all areas at all times. There was a general consensus that this stage was perhaps more conducive to team teaching. In Key Stage 1 the approach had evolved over time through afternoon topic-based work. Typically there were three teachers and six assistants in the early years, whereas in Key Stage 1 there were two teachers and four main assistants. In both cases, however, flexibility was the watchword.

Three examples of how the principles worked in practice were a week with an art focus, science-based days, and a book week. During such projects, there would be a whole school rotation, with Reception children working together with Year 2 pupils. Staff would provide leads from their own interests and expertise. It was felt that team teaching is less applicable in mathematics, because of the nature of the subject, and the need for step-by-step learning. By contrast, staff were highly enthusiastic about how it operated in literacy, where good results had been achieved. For example in phonics sessions, consistency of approach resulted from all teachers planning together and being involved in the shared delivery of the sessions. Moreover, the opportunity to be able to observe the children more closely led to more reliable formative assessments, with more focused target-setting. Applying Dewhurst and Tamburrini's (1978) model, the approach would seem to be a mixture of the 'assignment', 'rotation', and 'occasional' models.

Many advantages of the school's approach to team teaching were identified and shared enthusiastically. These included:

- The value to the children of different teaching styles and strategies
- The opportunity for children to approach different teachers and assistants
- Sharing ideas during planning, teaching and evaluation
- Preparing and sharing resources; reducing the workload
- Easier and more reliable assessments, including profiling and target-setting
- Teachers' knowledge of a greater range of children, so that their abilities and levels were more easily identified, and their needs addressed to enhance differentiation and personalised learning
- Behaviour management as a shared responsibility, and different strategies available
- Subject knowledge and staff interests and expertise, for example through subject co-ordinators, shared to the benefit of both children and colleagues
- Teachers' own professional development of skills, knowledge, and understanding enhanced by observing colleagues at work
- Greater safety and security for the children
- The social and emotional skills of the children developed
- The culture of shared enterprise and responsibility presenting a good role-model for the children's own social development.

In addition to the advantages of the approach, some limitations and constraints were identified and discussed, as follows:

- There were some logistical problems involving timetabling, and the match between different individual class timetables.
- It was pointed out that a weak teacher *could* have a negative effect on the approach, but that there were no weak teachers at the school!
- There needs to be mutual respect among teachers and assistants; clashes can occur, but need to be addressed professionally, through discussion leading to resolution. The focus should be on practice, and not personalities.
- There has to be give-and-take; compromise is sometimes inevitable.
- There could be some potential problems with children with special needs, including insecure children who need the security of one identified teacher. This needs to be approached sensitively, with gradual integration into a team teaching environment.
- The approach needs to evolve continuously through trial and error, and the need to train and accommodate new members of staff. There is a need for constant

review, particularly when allocating staff to teams for the forthcoming academic year, bearing in mind personalities, and a balance of strengths and experience.

- New staff need time and support to adapt to the approach. One experienced teacher described how she had moved from another school, and needed a period of adjustment, supported by colleagues. An NQT described how much he had learned from more experienced teachers, for example in developing a range of behaviour management strategies. A trainee following a Graduate Teacher Programme in the school also reported that he had clearly benefited from team teaching, lending credence to O'Neill and Worrall's (undated) finding that students in teacher training are helped and supported through such an apprenticeship approach.

The results of this study are remarkably comparable to those reported in similar studies in the 1960s and 1970s, and discussed elsewhere in this chapter.

Two general conclusions may be drawn from this 'mini' case study. It is certainly clear that team teaching can be, and has been, successful even within the relative straitjacket of the National Curriculum, when there is leadership, conviction, and a collaborative ethos with the willingness to make it work. As Freeman (1969: 88) reported, such a system cannot work without teamwork and dedication. It is equally clear that the present trend towards a more integrated cross-curricular approach to teaching and learning will facilitate and encourage those schools wishing to embrace a team teaching philosophy and pedagogy. Moreover this study, albeit small scale, confirms that team teaching is a dynamic, flexible, and organic process which, while varying in style and purpose from one school to another, is essentially an approach which allows teachers to pool their energies and expertise for the benefit of the children. The Priory Witham Academy School (Nursery and Infant Section) presents a blueprint for this process, and a shining example of good practice.

Pulling together the key factors

The very best of assessments of team teaching, clear-sighted about both its pros and its cons, is by Buckley (2000), albeit conducted with older students. Many of the points made by Buckley are contiguous with those made elsewhere in this chapter and by other writers, but some of the issues to which he draws attention are particularly pertinent. For us, this statement for example:

> Teamwork improves the quality of scholarship and teaching as various experts in the same field or different fields approach the same topic from different angles and areas of expertise: theory and practice, past and present, different gender or ethnic backgrounds. Teacher strengths are combined. Teacher weaknesses are remedied. Teachers complement one another's expertise.
>
> (2000: 11)

It is hard to gainsay this commonsense assessment. It accords with our own experience. In one situation in which we taught, a humanities and social studies curriculum was devised by an English specialist, a geographer, and a specialist in social and religious studies. We brought both male and female perspectives to the issues. We had particular individual interests: film, poetry, the links between arts and science, outdoor activities, survey work, photography. Each of us had a circle of acquaintances whom we could bring in for 'live' specialist inputs. We could free one another up to undertake detailed planning. The impact of the curriculum was 'more than the sum of its parts' and a parallel group, taught in conventional ways, even went so far as to lobby the headteacher to be allowed the same kind of experience.

Buckley also explodes myths. He challenges the view that all children learn at the same rate: one of the inevitable pillars of whole-class traditional teaching. He, rightly, notes that lesson lengths are not efficient just because they are all the same (in the system described in the last paragraph we opted for whole days, half-days, double and single lessons across the working week – these gave maximum flexibility). He challenges the myths of class size; in fact, some activities are best conducted with small groups, some can take place perfectly appropriately with very large ones. He points to the limitations of self-contained classrooms, but is really hinting that the kind of one-teacher-one-classroom mentality is outmoded: we have argued elsewhere that for too long English education has been bedevilled by the 'fine and private place' mentality of classroom organisation. If you are wondering about the allusion, it comes from a seventeenth-century poem and refers to the grave. Buckley challenges the boring diet that many pupils endure, of endless regurgitation (see Chapter 2) – the graveyard of learning.

But he is not concerned solely with teachers: Buckley also looks at team teaching from the pupil perspective:

> The clash of teacher viewpoints, changes of voice and rhythm, and alternation of different styles and personalities are stimulating and exciting. This gets and keeps attention and prevents boredom . . . The teachers model critical thinking for students: they debate, disagree with premises or conclusions, raise new questions, point out consequences. The contrast of viewpoint encourages more class participation and independent thinking.
>
> (2000: 13)

All this is true. It urges us to make one more point: team teaching brings closer the ideal that teachers and learners are in fact all engaged in the process of learning. Reforming the curriculum is important, even long overdue. But simply establishing new content, however that is conceived, is not enough; pedagogy and content have to proceed hand-in-glove. So we come to our conclusion, which is a quotation from O'Neill and Worrall (undated):

> Team teaching is essentially a flexible system, and can be used in whatever ways a team of teachers think is best for themselves and their children. We commend team teaching unreservedly to teachers and everyone else concerned with practice, theory, and policy-making in education.

References

Bair, M. and Woodward, R.G. (1964) *Team Teaching in Action* Boston: Houghton Mifflin

Buckley, F. (2000) *Team Teaching: what, how and why?* Thousand Oaks, California: Sage Publications Inc.

Close, J., Rudd, W.G.A., and Plimmer, F. (1974) *Team Teaching Experiments* Windsor: NFER

Dean, J. (1970) 'Team teaching' *New Era* 53: 6

Dewhurst, J. and Tamburrini, J. (1978) 'Team teaching in primary schools' *Education 3–13* 6 (2): 19–24

Freeman, J. (1969) *Team Teaching in Britain* London: Ward Lock Educational

Goetz, K. (2000) 'Perspectives on team teaching' *Egallery* 1 (4) available on http://www.ucalgary.ca/~egallery (accessed 31 March 2009)

Jang, Syh-Jong (2006) 'Research on the effects of team teaching upon two secondary school teachers' *Educational Research* 48 (2): 177–94

Kerry, T. and Wilding, M. (2004) *Effective Classroom Teacher* London: Pearson

Loeser, J. (2008) 'Team teaching' EBSCOHOST website, Research Starters, Education, Team Teaching

Maroney, S. (1995) 'Team teaching' http://www.wiu.edu/users/mfsam1/TeamTchg.html

Northern Nevada Writing Project (1996) *Team Teaching: the Northern Nevada Writing Project Teacher-Researcher Group* York, Maine: Stenhouse Publishers

O'Neill, M. and Worrall, M. (undated: probably 1972) *Team Teaching in a Primary School* Newcastle University: Institute of Education

Plowden Report (1967) *Children and Their Primary Schools* London: HMSO

Robinson, B. and Schaible, R. (1995) 'Collaborative teaching: reaping the benefits' *College Teaching* 43 (2): 57–60

Shaplin, J.T. and Olds, H.F. (1964) *Team Teaching* New York: Harper and Row

Taylor, M. (1974) *Team Teaching Experiments* Windsor: NFER

Trump, J. L. (1959) *Images of the Future* Santa Monica, California: Rand Corporation

Warwick, D. (1971) *Team Teaching* London: University of London Press

Worrall, P., Mitson, R., and Dorrance, E.B. (1970) *Teaching from Strength: an introduction to team teaching* London: Hamish Hamilton

www.teachingexpertise.com

Postscript

Trevor Kerry

This book might fairly be construed as having been written to promote a particular view about the nature of learning: a cross-curricular view. In the process, hopefully, it is has indicated that it is a view that holds in high esteem the notion of quality in learning.

The emphasis of this text, then, has been on learning rather than teaching. But that does not mean that teaching – and teachers – are unimportant. The skill of the teacher is the glue that holds learning together. Teaching is the quiet facilitation that ensures learning happens and can be articulated.

It's like those weird spectacles at the movies: you can shut one eye and everything is green (learning); shut the other and everything is red (teaching); open both and everything is stunningly three-dimensional. Learning and teaching work together to produce real education.

So it is fitting to end this volume not with reflections on learning: there have been many of those throughout the text. Rather, the Postscript will deal with some thoughts about teaching.

In making the points that are about to be made, the writer is only too aware that some readers may take umbrage. It is a risk that has to be taken. Let me make just this plea: read to the end before you reject the thesis. Then, once the evidence is marshalled, if it falls short – jettison it.

The thesis is this. Teachers, as a group in society, have been in danger of losing their role as community experts and degenerating into being kings or queens of the pub quiz. We, collectively, need to rescue ourselves from this fate.

What do I mean by that? Go back a century (many of your schools will have log books stretching back that far, so you can trace the process out for yourself) and the schoolteacher was one of the few intellectuals in the community. She (it was often a 'she' in the primary sector even then) ranked with the squire, the parson, and the doctor as the academic elite of the community.

Since then there have been many changes. Leave aside issues of salary, gender equality, class, and so on: just hang on to the notion of intellectualism. Ask yourself: would that situation still be true today?

Even in villages, very few teachers could post an honest 'Yes' to that question. So let us delve a little into why not; and then speculate on what might be done about it.

The thesis here is that, in recent decades, there has been a steady and deliberate erosion of the profession of teaching. There have been three main routes through which this erosion has operated, the first two being deliberately constructed.

The first route is via the political control of schools and schooling. This reached its zenith in 1988 with the introduction of the National Curriculum, closely followed by the establishment of a police force to monitor its implementation: Ofsted. It was inevitable that, at the start of initiatives like these, their application should be seen as totalitarian and unquestionable. Colin Richards (2001: 28) sums this up well:

> Despite introducing a national curriculum, the conservative government of 1988 did not provide a rationale for the curriculum or even consider that one was desirable. The only semblance of a rationale was given in what civil servants in 1988 disparagingly called the 'motherhood and apple pie' clauses of section 1 of the Education Reform Act, which entitled every pupil in a state school to a balanced (never defined) curriculum which (a) promoted the spiritual, moral, cultural, mental and physical development (never defined) of the pupils at the school and of society (never clarified); and (b) prepared such pupils for the opportunities, responsibilities and experiences of adult life (but presumably not life in the here and now!).

There followed through the 1990s, according to Richards – and he is right – periods of rethinking in the face of poorly formulated NC requirements, and equivocal research results about whether the National Curriculum was working or not. But, regardless of success or failure, other features of the educational scene militated against teachers' professionalism. Richards lists, for example, measurable targets, preoccupation with inspection, publication of performance tables, increasing assessment loads on pupils in primary schools, the 'standards' game played by schools to release themselves from, or evade, special measures, and the urge to ape so-called benchmark schools that followed the government's requirements strictly to the letter. This is a climate in which teacher professionalism cannot grow or flourish; it must inevitably wither.

Alongside this deeply negative view of the 1990s has to run the obsession of governments of both colours with Ofsted, and in particular with the Chief Inspector. In terms of insights into primary education, it is highly doubtful whether Woodhead, who occupied the post for six years, would have made a credible candidate for his post against any criteria compiled by primary experts of the time. Any fair-minded person can read Woodhead's column in the national press since he left the role and discover that he could hardly be further from espousing the philosophy of a state comprehensive system of education as a universal social good. But the wonderful irony is: even he feels now that Ofsted (without his presence?) is 'irrelevant'. In a *Guardian* article, MacLeod sums it up like this:

> Woodhead, who led Ofsted from 1994 to 2000 before falling out with the education secretary David Blunkett – not exactly a fan of trendy methods himself – told the *Economist* that the inspection regime was 'an exercise driven by the analysis of the data, and as such, I think, contributes very little to a school's understanding of what it's doing.
>
> 'It has become part of the problem in another, perhaps more sinister, way. It has become an agent of state enforcement.'
>
> A change of heart by the old enforcer? Well, no. It's more that Ofsted is no longer following his policies.

So, from 1988 through the 1990s there was a steady erosion in schools of teacher autonomy, and with it a loss of professionalism: this last had no opportunity for exercise. It was like a dog shut in a kennel, and dogs shut in kennels lose condition. Menter *et al.* (1997: 136–8) sum the situation up from a more theoretical perspective, identifying the resulting stress:

> Managers in our study [of primary schools] felt levels of stress, ambiguity and ambivalence that paralleled the reported anxieties of teachers . . . We should note the departure of experienced heads from the profession . . . Primary school work is no longer integrated, unalienated labour . . . it was possible to discern a paradigm shift in the nature of education management towards managerialism . . . We hope that our critical perspective on the new managerialism will *reinforce strategies of resistance* to it, and lend some support to education workers who feel themselves trapped in the ambivalence and ambiguity. (My emphasis)

But there was worse. The second route to the erosion of the teaching profession came through its recruitment and training. Teacher education during the period became firmly teacher training. If schools could be defined for effectiveness by the extent to which they achieved measurable targets, then teacher education was just a matter of giving the instructors the tools to enable pupils to hit those targets. If schools failed to reach prescribed levels of performance, it had nothing to do with social issues, health, nutrition, income, housing, resources, or parental support – it simply indicated that the teachers responsible were inefficient or inadequate. Teaching as a profession was eroded by teaching as a craft. (Ofsted inspectors themselves were trained using exactly these methods.) This is a recipe for deskilling: but then, it was intended to be. Welch and Mahoney (2000) outline the issues well. In the period under review governments wanted to reserve power in education to themselves, and they did this by eroding the influence of Local Authorities and depro-fessionalising teachers. As a strategy, it almost worked.

Then, of course, there was the third important factor in the change of teachers' professionalism: social context. A hundred years ago educated people were at a premium, now they are commonplace. In the space of less than a lifetime access to higher education has risen from 5 per cent of the population to 50 per cent. While at one time the teacher was probably one of a handful of graduates in the community, now many parents of pupils are better qualified than the teacher in many communities. Though there are moves afoot for all teachers to possess masters' degrees, the success of this will depend on a number of factors. Most pressing are these. First, will finance be found to make this happen, and how quickly? Second, will the new degrees have the 'painting by numbers' characteristics that have dogged other government-controlled qualifications? Teachers can no longer expect to form an elite by qualification alone. So where else do they look to regain credibility? It has to be from within the expertise that defines pedagogy – that's what teaching is about.

But just as I began this book on a note of joy (see Preface), so it is possible to end on a note of hope. Many of the negative initiatives noted above have either been but partially successful, or they have failed, or they have been revealed for the deceptions they were. With the advent in 2009 of not just one, but two, influential Reports (Alexander and Rose) on the development of more effective primary education, there have been two results – considered throughout this book – which are cause for great rejoicing. The first is the loosening of the curriculum straitjacket as our authors have described. The second is the rediscovery, in the process, of a degree of teacher autonomy.

This growth in autonomy is a platform for potential growth within, and of, the profession. Just as when Moses led the enslaved Israelites out of Egypt it needed a generation to pass over who had known nothing but enslavement, so for our profession it may need time for teachers whose training was honed in the 1980s and 1990s to become educated to the new professionalism. But even if it takes a time, it is an opportunity that cannot be squandered. Too many people have invested too much time and too much energy in bringing it about for the new freedom to be jettisoned so easily this time round.

So I want to end this book with a vision. The vision is this: teachers need to rediscover their professionalism and be proud of it. To do that they need to be able to develop a philosophy for what they do. Such a philosophy:

- Articulates our own ideas
- Takes on board an awareness of others' ideas
- Teaches rules of logical and coherent thinking
- Is the basis of values
- Encourages us to think about questions of ultimate concern
- Influences what we do and how we act.

Developing a professional philosophy stretches us. We gain a new intellectualism. Not the intellectualism beloved of many academics, of obscurity, obfuscation, and unintelligibility. But an intellectualism based on curiosity, insight, wisdom, and judgement. Teachers will then have regained the ground of being among the elite of the community.

References

MacLeod, D. (2009) 'Woodhead says Ofsted is irrelevant: change of heart or sour grapes?' *Guardian* 22 May 2009

Menter, I., Muschamp, Y., Nicholls, P., Ozga, J., and Pollard, A. (1997) *Work and Identity in the Primary School* Buckingham: Open University Press

Richards, C. (2001) *Changing English Primary Education: retrospect and prospect* Stoke on Trent: Trentham Books

Welch, G. and Mahoney, P. (2000) 'The teaching profession' in J. Docking (2000) *New Labour's Policies for Schools* London: David Fulton: 139–57

Index